Tales from the Trenches

Politics and Practice in
Feminist Service Organizations

Diane Kravetz

UNIVERSITY PRESS OF AMERICA,® INC.
Dallas • Lanham • Boulder • New York • Oxford

Library of Congress Control Number: 2004100980
ISBN 0-7618-2772-2 (clothbound : alk. ppr.)
ISBN 0-7618-2773-0 (paperback : alk. ppr.)

To my parents
Samuel and Dorothy Kravetz

Contents

Preface   vii

Introduction   1

1   The Founding of Five Feminist Service Organizations   27

2   The Defining Principles of Feminist Service Organizations   49

3   Promoting an Equality Based on Difference   68

4   Building a Sisterhood Based on Difference   87

5   The Impact of Funders and Fund-Raising   104

6   Providing Social Services/Pursuing Social Change   117

7   Developing Feminist Organizational Structures   144

Conclusion   183

Bibliography   205

Index   221

About the Author   227

Preface

Tales from the Trenches: Politics and Practice in Feminist Service Organizations celebrates the accomplishments of women who established five feminist service organizations in the 1970s. These organizations included a shelter for battered women, a rape crisis center, a rape-prevention ride service, a residential facility for female offenders, and a statewide organization for chemically dependent women. Based primarily on interviews with 57 founders, staff, volunteers, and/or board members of these organizations, the book examines from the 1970s into the mid-1980s how women translated their understandings of radical feminist ideology into concrete goals, social change strategies, services, and organizational structures. The political visions, experiences, and impact of the members of these five organizations are both informative and inspiring.

The achievements of feminists in delivering alternative services to women at the local level have been central to the health and vitality of the contemporary women's movement. Members of service organizations such as rape crisis centers, shelters for battered women, and women's health clinics have had a dramatic impact on the public's understanding of women's problems and the development of new approaches to address these problems. Their work has benefited women as a group as well as the individual women who have used their services. However, the feminists who first created these organizations in the 1970s have received relatively little notice. Moreover, there is little recognition that the early feminist service organizations were created by radical feminists or that the tenets of radical feminism influenced the goals, services, and structures of diverse types of service organizations, including some that were established within mainstream bureaucracies. In writing this book, I hope to contribute to ensuring that this exciting and successful part of women's history does not go unrecorded and unrecognized.

Tales from the Trenches is based on a study I conducted in the mid-1980s with Linda E. Jones, who was a Ph.D. student at the time and is now a professor at the University of Minnesota. I greatly appreciate the time, energy, and devotion Linda committed to this study throughout the complex data-collection process. The primary purpose of the study was to provide an historical record of the growth and development of five successful feminist service organizations, providing information that would otherwise be unknown except to their members. The study focused on five very different organizations, including two that did not identify themselves publicly as feminist, to illustrate the diverse types of alternative service organizations that women established both outside of and within mainstream bureaucracies in the 1970s, the period when this type of feminist organization first emerged. It examined how the members of these successful organizations incorporated feminist beliefs and strategies into their work and how they implemented a social change agenda through community education and advocacy, organizational structures, and the delivery of direct services. It explored members' views of the internal forces and external circumstances that shaped the development of their organizations.

The perspectives of the members of these organizations are represented through the extensive use of direct quotations. This method provides readers with access to the voices of feminists who were in the forefront of creating this particular form of feminist practice. Their comments vividly communicate the optimism, idealism, determination, and perseverance that fueled early feminist activism, as well as their conflicts and disappointments. The book explores how members dealt with the problems created by antifeminist resistance as well as the dilemmas that characterized many feminist efforts in the early years of the women's movement, including internal problems stemming from ideological splits, homophobia, and their commitment to collective organizational structures. It highlights their hard-fought gains and the struggles that accompanied their progress.

From the perspective of the new millennium, this work has taken on additional significance. The increasingly pervasive backlash against feminism has effectively erased the public's understanding of the conditions of women's lives prior to feminist change efforts. Today, too many women are surprised to learn that the activism of radical feminists provided the roots for many of the attitudes, opportunities, and services they take for granted. The media revels in propagating now widely accepted myths and misrepresentations of radical feminist beliefs and activities. It is my hope that *Tales from the Trenches* can play a part in countering this misinformation and ignorance.

These case studies provide numerous examples of the social attitudes about and practices toward women that prevailed prior to feminist change efforts.

This information enhances understanding of the significance of feminist activism in the past, and it increases sensitivity to the ways in which gender inequality continues to increase women's vulnerability and victimization. Moreover, members' portrayals of their own experience illustrate that feminism does not constitute a system of beliefs that is imposed onto people's lives. Instead, feminism serves as a lens through which members viewed their worlds, integrating feminist beliefs and values with their own individual concerns, priorities, and histories.

Women's detailed and heartfelt accounts illustrate that even in the 1970s, "being feminist" was a dynamic process, responsive to new experiences, changing conditions, and individual differences, and that there were diverse ways in which women incorporated the ideals of the early radical feminists into their work. These accounts demonstrate that radical feminists maintained their zealous commitment to feminist values while, at the same time, they established productive relationships with politically conservative consumers, funders, police and prosecutors, medical personnel, and other service providers. They provide valuable examples of feminists establishing services and structures based on thoughtful applications of core feminist principles to specific circumstances rather than remaining within the confines of conventional assumptions or prescriptive politics. Throughout, the book refutes stereotypes of radical feminists as dogmatic and inflexible. It provides models of early radical feminist activism that are more adaptive, more complex, and more effective than generally acknowledged.

Although historical in focus, members' discussions of the benefits of women helping women, the appropriate roles of men in woman-centered work environments, gender equality and difference, and dealing with homophobia include principles that can apply to current practice. Members' approaches to, for example, member and client empowerment and the incorporation of bureaucratic features address important issues that feminists currently face in feminist organizations and in changing conventional organizations.

Writing this book has been a lengthy and solitary process. The support of colleagues at Swarthmore College, the University of Washington at Seattle, and the University of Wisconsin-Madison has been very important. I am very grateful for Jeanne Marecek's many conversations over the years about feminism, feminist services, the psychology of women, and the trials and tribulations of getting this book published. I appreciate Nancy Hooyman's review of an earlier manuscript. Her thoughtful feedback was extremely helpful, and her very positive view of the contributions of the book to the literature encouraged me to persevere. Jim Mandiberg's input and advice was very valuable, as was Bill Heiss' unwavering concern and support. I am deeply grateful to my husband, Mark, and children, David and Rebecca, who have remained patient and encouraging as this project continually demanded more time than I ever anticipated. With much love, I thank my parents, Samuel and Dorothy Kravetz, for always believing in me and the importance of this book.

Finally, I remain deeply indebted to the women who were willing to candidly reflect upon their commitments, goals, and accomplishments. They spoke passionately and frankly about the positive and reaffirming aspects of their collective efforts and about their times of anguish. They have provided new understandings of early feminist activism and the pioneering efforts of women who created and built feminist service organizations.

Introduction

One of the most impressive features of the contemporary women's movement has been the emergence of myriad feminist service organizations. These include women's centers, abortion-referral services, rape crisis centers, shelters for battered women, feminist therapy collectives, and women's health centers. Activists in these organizations have had a dramatic impact on the public's understandings of women's problems and on the development of new approaches to addressing them. By transforming the policies and practices of conventional health, mental health, and social services, feminist service organizations have been a central force in promoting many of the social changes we take for granted today. The work of these organizations has benefited women as a group as well as the individual women who have used their services.

Tales from the Trenches: Politics and Practice in Feminist Service Organizations examines the political visions and experiences of women who created five feminist service organizations in the 1970s, the period of history when this type of feminist organization emerged. The book traces into the mid-1980s how women translated their understanding of feminist ideology into concrete goals, social-change strategies, services, and organizational structures. It is based primarily on analysis of in-depth interviews with 57 women who were founders, staff, volunteers, and/or board members. Quotations from these interviews are included throughout this book. To maintain confidentiality, only the speaker's organization is consistently identified, either in the text or at the end of the quotation, using the abbreviations in the list below. The following organizations are examined in detail:

- Advocates for Battered Women (ABW), a shelter program for battered women and their children, established in 1977

1

- The Rape Crisis Center (RCC), an organization that assisted victims of sexual assault (women, men, and children), established in 1973
- Women's Transit Authority (WTA), a nighttime ride service for women, established in 1973 to increase women's safety and to prevent rape
- ARC House (ARC), a residential facility that served primarily as an alternative to prison or jail, established in 1976
- Women Reaching Women (WRW), a statewide volunteer organization that assisted chemically dependent women, established in 1978

All of these organizations were based in Madison, Wisconsin. With the exception of Women's Transit Authority, however, their services extended beyond Madison. The Rape Crisis Center and Advocates for Battered Women served the small towns and rural areas of Dane County. ARC House and Women Reaching Women served communities throughout the state.

Advocates for Battered Women, the Rape Crisis Center, and Women's Transit Authority were explicitly feminist nonprofits situated outside of conventional organizations. Their founders and early workers had few models on which to base their services and structures. By the mid-1980s, however, feminist organizations throughout the country offered services for victims of rape, incest, and battering, and community education efforts to inform citizens about and to prevent woman abuse were increasing.

In contrast, ARC House was a freestanding nonprofit organization primarily funded by the State Division of Corrections. Women Reaching Women was a project within a parent organization, the Wisconsin Association on Alcohol and Other Drug Abuse (WAAODA). Embedded in conservative, male-dominated bureaucracies, ARC House and Women Reaching Women did not identify themselves publicly as feminist organizations. By the mid-1980s, scant attention had been paid to women's issues in the fields of substance abuse and criminal justice, and few services were designed to meet the unique needs of female offenders and chemically dependent women.

In all five organizations, feminist critiques of society and feminist analyses of needed social changes provided the foundation for their work. Their incorporation of feminist thought ensured that the relationships between women's personal problems and their social and political circumstances remained central in the design and implementation of organizational goals, structures, and services. The work of each of these organizations was an integral part of the larger feminist agenda.

Members of these five organizations worked for social change by influencing social policy and legislative reform and by altering the policies and practices of law enforcement officials, health care providers, mental health practitioners, and social service workers. They educated the public through the distribution of written materials; media presentations; public speaking programs presented to school, civic, and church groups; and public service announcements, press releases, and publicity campaigns. They provided a range of direct services to consumers and advocated on their behalf.

Advocates for Battered Women provided shelter and protection for battered women and their children for up to 30 days and educated the community about woman abuse so the community would respond to and take responsibility for ending such abuse. Members offered support, crisis intervention, and counseling to the women who used the shelter and helped them obtain medical services, housing, jobs, and financial aid. They provided legal information and assistance to residents and nonresidents, including helping battered women obtain domestic violence restraining orders without engaging the services of a lawyer. Advocates for Battered Women maintained a 24-hour crisis line; provided walk-in, short-term counseling for nonresidents; provided child care services and children's groups; and held a weekly support group for community women. They emphasized changing community attitudes and the institutional barriers that perpetuate violence against women and children, the training of professionals who worked with battered women, and outreach to ensure that battered women knew what services were available.

ARC House was a community-based residential facility for adult female offenders. It served as an alternative to jail or prison and, to a lesser extent, as a transitional living facility for women leaving incarceration; and it was a state-certified alcohol and other drug abuse (AODA) residential treatment facility. Through an intensive program averaging six months, staff members concentrated on alleviating the emotional, social, and economic factors that contribute to women's illegal behavior. Their overall goal was to help women become emotionally and economically independent and to obtain employment, education, and independent living arrangements. Through direct services and referrals to other community agencies, ARC House addressed chemical dependency, past physical and sexual abuse, dependent and abusive relationships, health problems, employment and money-management needs, alternative leisure time use, child abuse and parenting education, and child custody and other mother/child reunification issues. Some women were joined by their children. Staff advocated for the needs of female offenders in the community and in prison.

The Rape Crisis Center provided services to female and male victims of sexual assault, including child sexual assault victims; and assisted their families and friends. They provided crisis intervention with police, family, and hospital personnel; legal advocacy within the criminal justice system; short-term counseling; and an evening telephone crisis line. Members accompanied victims through medical examinations, police interviews, and court procedures and provided nonlegal advocacy with landlords, family, friends, school personnel, and employers. Also, they offered a support group for adult women who had experienced childhood incest. Their community education efforts were directed toward promoting public understanding of the problem of sexual assault and increasing women's awareness of self-defense measures. They worked for changes in the laws regarding rape and rape trials and with law enforcement and health agencies to change their responses to victims of sexual assault.

As a rape-prevention ride service, the Women's Transit Authority set as its goals to help prevent sexual assaults that occur outside at night by providing safe nighttime transportation for women; to increase women's mobility, which is inhibited due to fear of sexual assault and women's generally lower socioeconomic status; and to increase public awareness of the need for safe and affordable transportation for women at night and the more general problem of widespread violence against women and the importance of its prevention. Members provided free transportation to women and to women and their children from 7 p.m. to 2 a.m. within a four-mile radius of the center of the city. They also created pockets outside their general boundaries to serve low-income areas of the city. Of highest priority were women in danger, women who had been assaulted, Rape Crisis Center advocates needing transportation to meet with clients, and battered women needing transportation to the shelter. Other ride services in the country were university-based and traveled a designated route. Women's Transit Authority was unique in that it served women in the city at no cost, on and off campus, and provided door-to-door service.

Women Reaching Women was a statewide project designed to increase the numbers of chemically dependent women in treatment by informing women of available services and assisting them in gaining access to service delivery systems; advocate for the needs of women in treatment; and provide the support necessary for women to be successful in their recovery. Separate chapters of Women Reaching Women were established in counties throughout the state. Chapter members conducted public awareness campaigns; facilitated support groups for women who had completed treatment, were significant others of AODA abusers, or were children of AODA abusers; and established First Friends projects in which volunteers from Alcoholics Anonymous, Alanon, and Alateen provided newcomers with information about their programs and accompanied them to their first meeting. They also tried to find ways to provide child care for women in treatment and aftercare.

The pioneering efforts of the members of these five organizations were influenced by and reflected developments in the contemporary women's movement, a movement that emerged in the mid-1960s. Feminist service organizations were among the movement organizations that framed their goals and structures largely in terms of the ideology of radical feminists in the women's liberation branch of the movement.

THE EMERGENCE OF FEMINIST SERVICE ORGANIZATIONS

We had a tremendous belief in the rightness of what we were doing and the wrongness of what we saw going on in society and how that had to be changed, and a strong commitment to seeing that that was done. (ABW)

Discussions of the early years of the women's movement point to the development of two branches in the mid-1960s: one focused on women's rights and the other on women's liberation. Although their political perspectives overlapped, the two branches emphasized different goals and strategies (Carden, 1974; Freeman, 1975; Hole and Levine, 1971).

The women's rights branch of the movement consisted of large, national organizations with formal memberships, elected officers, and local chapters. Examples include the National Organization for Women (NOW), the Women's Equity Action League, and the National Women's Political Caucus. The National Organization for Women, founded in 1966, was the first women's rights organization, and it remains the largest. These bureaucratic organizations focused on improving the status of women through reforms in legislation and governmental policies. Their goals were to eliminate discrimination based on sex in education, employment, and electoral politics and to promote equal rights and opportunities for women.

Activists in the women's rights branch were mainly women who had achieved some degree of success in paid employment and were leaders in voluntary and civic organizations. Many were members of state-level commissions on the status of women (Carabillo, Meuli, and Csida, 1993). They applied the skills they had learned in the workplace and as leaders in political, labor, religious, and other community organizations. Because of their experiences in these organizations, these women were comfortable with and functioned well within conventional organizational structures with clearly defined hierarchies of authority and responsibility. To achieve their goals, they pursued incremental change and exerted traditional forms of influence. They prepared reports for policy makers, developed insider contacts in executive agencies and legislatures, lobbied elected representatives, and launched national media campaigns.

The early accomplishments of women's rights organizations in the legislative arena were remarkable (Davis, 1991; Kessler-Harris, 2001; Rosen, 2000). Their victories provided the leverage that enabled women to gain access to and demand fair treatment in higher education and in the workforce. For example,

Title VII of the 1964 Civil Rights Act prohibited sex discrimination in hiring, firing, promotions, and working conditions. Under pressure from NOW and other women's rights organizations, in 1967 President Lyndon Johnson signed Executive Order 11375, which strengthened Title VII. This order directed employers who received federal contracts to provide equal employment opportunities for women and to develop affirmative action programs to redress the effects of past discrimination. In 1972, under pressure from women's rights organizations, Congress gave the Equal Employment Opportunities Commission (EEOC) the power to sue employers on behalf of victims of sex discrimination. In addition to investigating individual complaints, the EEOC pursued a number of significant class-action lawsuits during the 1970s and 1980s, including successful litigation against AT&T, General Electric, and General Motors. In 1980, sexual harassment in the workplace was included as a violation under Title VII of the Civil Rights Act of 1964. Other legislation included the 1974 Equal Credit Opportunity Act, which allowed married women to obtain credit in their own names, and Title IX of the 1972 Education Amendments Act, which prohibited sex discrimination in education by institutions that received federal funding. One result of Title IX was a substantial increase in support for women's sports in most universities and colleges, which led to a dramatic upsurge in girls' and women's participation in athletics and the development of women's competitive team sports.

From 1975 to 1982, NOW and other women's rights organizations also devoted their energies to passage of the Equal Rights Amendment (ERA), which read: "Equality of rights under the law shall not be denied or abridged by the United States or by any state on account of sex." The ERA passed Congress in 1972 (49 years after it was first introduced in Congress) and was ratified by 30 states in 1972 and 1973. With increasing antifeminist opposition, however, the ERA was three states short of the number required for ratification when the deadline expired in June 1982. To defeat the ERA, opponents had promulgated numerous myths about the ERA, including claiming that it would force women into military combat, legitimate homosexual marriage, require coed public restrooms, deny a woman's right not to be employed outside the home, and place children in state-run child care facilities. Many of the goals that feminists had in promoting the ERA were eventually accomplished by means of other legislation. Still, the virulent opposition to the simple proposition that women should have the same citizenship rights as men was a harbinger of the stronger resistance to change that would confront feminism in the years to come (Buechler, 1990; Conover and Gray, 1983; Faludi, 1991; Mansbridge, 1986).

In contrast to the women's rights branch of the movement, the women's liberation branch consisted of numerous small, decentralized, nonhierarchical grassroots groups. They were often referred to as the women's liberation movement. Their goals were to radically alter cultural beliefs about women, to eliminate the oppression of women, and to transform personal relationships and social institutions to reflect feminist values (Cassell, 1977; Echols, 1989). Many of the women involved in this movement were left-wing activists who had been involved in the civil rights, antiwar, and student movements of the 1960s and had transferred their community-based political activism to issues of particular concern to women (Evans, 1979). Compared with women's rights activists, they tended to be younger women with less professional and workplace experience.

Women in this branch of the movement generally labeled themselves as radical feminists. Their analyses centered on the ways in which women's problems stem from male domination over women in personal relationships, in family life, and in the workforce, and the privileging of male perspectives and needs throughout society. Based on their understandings of the effects of male supremacy on women's lives, radical feminists envisioned an egalitarian society based on cooperation; mutual respect; and the equitable distribution of resources, power, and responsibility between the sexes. In their small groups, they used nonhierarchical, consensus-based processes so that the means through which they achieved their goals would be consistent with the goals themselves.

Much of the early work of radical feminists was conducted in consciousness-raising (CR) groups and focused on political analysis and the development of feminist ideology (Allen, 1970; Dreifus, 1973; Sarachild, 1970; Susan, 1970). In CR groups, they discussed their own everyday experiences as women to develop a shared understanding of the common experiences of women as a group: "Feminist method is consciousness raising: the collective critical reconstitution of the meaning of women's social experience, as women live through it . . . [In their small groups, women came to understand] the collective reality of women's condition from within the perspective of that experience, not from outside it" (MacKinnon, 1982, pp. 543, 536). Through consciousness raising, radical feminists came to understand that "the personal is political" (Hanisch, 1970), that is, that women's personal issues and problems were inextricably connected to their social, economic, and political circumstances. Changed consciousness became a fundamental component of feminist approaches to social change.

In addition to their own work in small groups, radical feminists held demonstrations and protests; gave speeches; organized other women's CR groups; and disseminated their views through pamphlets, newsletters and magazines, and journals, including *Voice of the Women's Liberation Movement*; *Notes from the First Year*; *Off Our Backs*; *Sojourner: The Women's Forum*; and

Quest: A Feminist Quarterly. The thinking of radical feminists was introduced to the general public through collections of essays, including *Liberation Now! Writings from the Women's Liberation Movement* (Babcox and Belkin, 1971); *Radical Feminism* (Koedt, Levine, and Rapone, 1973); *Sisterhood Is Powerful: An Anthology of Writings from the Women's Liberation Movement* (Morgan, 1970); *Woman in Sexist Society: Studies in Power and Powerlessness* (Gornick and Moran, 1971); *Women's Liberation: Blueprint for the Future* (Stambler, 1970); and *Voices from Women's Liberation* (Tanner, 1970). Books such as Shulamith Firestone's *The Dialectic of Sex*, Germaine Greer's *The Female Eunuch*, and Kate Millett's *Sexual Politics*, all published in 1970, advanced strong challenges to male dominance and female subordination and proposed radical changes in social organizations and male-female relations. The proliferation of CR groups during this period and public awareness of feminist thought can be largely attributed to their efforts.

By the mid-1970s, the distinctions between the memberships and strategies of the two branches of the women's movement had blurred (Eisenstein, 1981a; Ferree and Hess, 1985; Ryan, 1992). Women of diverse backgrounds were exploring the meaning of gender in their personal lives and organizing around every aspect of women's experience. There was no part of female experience that did not require rethinking, and there was no aspect of society that did not require change. Every sector of society was subject to feminist analyses and political pressure. The women's movement had created broad-based social concern with a wide array of women's issues, had encouraged women to recognize their own oppression, and had provided a means for women to join with others to make meaningful changes in their lives.

During this time, the personal growth and support aspects of CR groups began to appeal to women who did not identify themselves as "radical." CR groups, now also called support groups, became widely identified as a way for a broad range of women to examine issues of social conditioning in their own lives (Eastman, 1973; Perl and Abarbanell, 1976; Pogrebin, 1973). In these groups, women developed a sense of closeness to each other and to other women, and they began to perceive themselves as members of a larger group composed of women. By altering women's perceptions of themselves and of society at large, CR groups continued to serve as mechanisms for personal and social change. Participation in CR groups led women to pursue change in themselves, their families, their workplaces, and their communities.

With increasing feminist consciousness among women, a multitude of feminist organizations emerged representing a wide range of political ideologies, goals, and change strategies. These included national women's political and professional organizations (e.g., the Coalition of Labor Union Women, the National Association of Black Professional Women, the Older Women's

League, and Working Women: A National Association of Office Workers) and a multitude of women's caucuses within academia, business, government, labor, and the professions. Feminist academics organized women's studies courses and programs across the country. As increasingly diverse women became engaged in feminist activities, the women's movement as a whole began the long process of becoming more inclusive and more respectful of differences among women.

By the mid-1970s, the early radical feminist groups had largely disappeared, partially because one of their major goals, consciousness-raising and political education, had been achieved (Davis, 1991). Also, many women's liberation groups were unable to survive internal and intergroup conflicts over goals and strategies (Echols, 1989; Ryan, 1992). Moreover, as the women's movement gained more legitimacy, the media shifted their attention to the less militant representatives of feminism, limiting the influence of radical feminists by removing them from the national spotlight (Davis, 1991).

Still, the energies and aspirations of women who identified with the work of the early radical feminists did not decline. The early radical feminists revealed how cultural ideology and social structures combined to oppress women. The next step for women was to analyze the effects of male domination in specific arenas and to develop a range of strategies to address the diverse ways in which female oppression takes form. Feminists applied radical feminist political philosophies and methods to their specific areas of interest through myriad specialized activities and organizations.

The values and goals of radical feminism were evident in the evolution of woman-centered art, music, literature, and theater; in the founding of feminist coffeehouses, bookstores, publishing houses, music companies, theater groups, and art galleries; and in the development of feminist service organizations. All of these groups were dedicated to women's taking direct control of their lives by creating alternatives to male-dominated institutions. In feminist service organizations, efforts centered on developing alternatives to conventional health, mental health, and social services. Existing services were viewed as oppressive and unresponsive to women's needs. Members of these organizations also worked to alter the practices of conventional service agencies and to educate the public about the relationships between gender inequality and women's individual problems and victimization.

Across the country, feminists developed women's centers to assist women in dealing with issues related to education and employment; health care; sexual orientation; separation, divorce, and widowhood; rape and rape prevention; family violence; and difficulties in personal relationships. These centers offered advocacy, support groups, counseling, 24-hour hotlines, community education, and referral services; they provided access to feminist literature and information about community activities (Campbell, Levine, and Page, 1980; Galper and Washburne, 1976). Feminist practitioners also provided services as members of feminist therapy collectives (Elias, 1975; Feminist Counseling Collective, 1975; Women and Mental Health Project, 1976).

Beginning in the early 1970s, the lack of adequate laws, policies, and services led to the development of rape crisis centers. Typical services of rape crisis centers included staffing 24-hour hotlines, accompanying victims to hospitals and police stations, and providing advocates for women throughout court proceedings. Their rape-prevention efforts included community education and women's self-defense courses. Feminist activists in the antirape movement challenged laws, police behaviors, courtroom tactics, hospital procedures, and psychiatric interpretations that revictimized rape victims by blaming them for the violence. Feminists worked to replace women's sense of shame with a sense of outrage, to develop new counseling methods for helping rape victims, and to educate the public about the political nature of rape and rape-prevention approaches (Connell and Wilson, 1974; Gager and Schurr, 1976; Gornick, Burt, and Pittman, 1985; Walker and Brodsky, 1976).

The political analyses of male privilege and female subordination that were developed with respect to rape provided the foundation for understanding other forms of male violence against women and the need for institutional change in the treatment of battered women (Delacoste and Newman, 1981; Dobash and Dobash, 1979). Feminist efforts in the antirape movement facilitated the development of battered women's programs and shelters: "Such work handed ideological tools, collective work structures, and political resources to the battered women's movement. Without this precedent, the new movement might have faced far greater resistance and hostility from bureaucracies, legislatures, and the general public" (Schechter, 1982, p. 43). Formerly battered women, both feminists and nonfeminists, joined with other activists to open shelters and crisis lines to provide support, safety, and legal advocacy for battered women; to promote public education; and to change the treatment of battered women by police, prosecuting attorneys, physicians and nurses, and social workers and counselors (Martin, 1976; McNeely and Jones, 1980; Pahl, 1985a, 1985b; Schechter, 1982; Vaughan, 1979).

This period also marked the emergence of the women's health movement, a movement that combined the grassroots efforts of the community health movement and the women's movement. Feminist activists in this movement provided alternatives to the traditional system where male physicians, administrators, and legislators controlled women's health and health care. Women's health centers provided abortion services, pregnancy screening and counseling, birth control, and health education. Many health activists were involved in rape crisis centers. It was understood that women's control over their bodies was central to their control over their lives (Boston Women's Health Book Collective, 1973; Dreifus, 1977; Marieskind, 1980; Marieskind and Ehrenreich, 1975; Ruzek, 1978; Simmons, Kay, and Regan, 1984).

Beginning in the late 1960s, feminists across the political spectrum raised public consciousness as to the large numbers of women who had chosen to have abortions and the high risks associated with illegal abortions, including sterility and death. In addition to demonstrations, marches, and lobbying by national organizations such as the National Association for the Repeal of Abortion Laws (NARAL) and Planned Parenthood, feminists in small groups worked underground to help women obtain safe abortions. The most dramatic example of this was Jane, a collective in Chicago that arranged for 11,000 illegal abortions between 1969 and 1973 (Rosen, 2000). Jane began as a secret counseling and referral service for women in need of abortions, which were then illegal in Illinois. By 1971, the members of Jane were providing safe and humane abortions themselves, primarily for poor women, at low cost or no cost (Kaplan, 1995; Schlesinger and Bart, 1982). After years of feminist activism, the 1973 Supreme Court decision in *Roe v. Wade* rendered unconstitutional state laws that denied women abortions; women and their doctors were entitled to make all medical decisions during the first six months of a pregnancy.

Antiabortion groups soon mobilized to restrict women's access to abortion and to reverse *Roe v. Wade*. As with the opposition to the ERA, antiabortion efforts became a major force in mobilizing the antifeminist New Right (Buechler, 1990; Conover and Gray, 1983; Luker, 1984). In 1977, Congress passed the Hyde Amendment, which restricts the use of federal Medicaid funds to pay for abortions, effectively denying women on public assistance the right to choose an abortion. States established mandatory waiting periods, parental consent laws, and bans on abortion unless the woman's life is in danger. Activists in the women's health movement continued to provide referral services to help women locate providers willing to do abortions, services to help women negotiate complicated regulations, and services that offered loans and grants to women unable to pay for abortions (Staggenborg, 1991).

The antirape, battered women's, and women's health movements provided the context for feminist change efforts in specific fields of practice. Here, change was promoted primarily by feminist academics and practitioners who worked in these fields and directed their efforts toward changing conventional attitudes and practices. With respect to the problems addressed by the organizations discussed in this book, in the 1970s and early 1980s, there were numerous feminist analyses of women's issues in the criminal justice system (Bowker, 1981; Chesney-Lind, 1977; Crites, 1976; Klein and Kress, 1976; Smart, 1976). Similarly, feminists were examining the impact of sexism in the

AODA system (Burtle, 1979; Corrigan, 1980; Eddy and Ford, 1980; Gomberg, 1974, 1979; Sandmaier, 1980a). Some alternative services for chemically dependent women were developed in the 1970s (Flynn, 1981; Sandmaier, 1980b; Weathers, 1980). Founded by Jean Kirkpatrick in 1975, Women for Sobriety was a national organization designed to serve as an alternative to Alcoholics Anonymous (Kirkpatrick, 1986). Few programs existed to assist female offenders (Pendergrass, 1975; Slack, 1975).

In the 1970s, public policy and law at all levels of government had become increasingly and significantly less oppressive for women, and there was considerably less public support for discriminatory policies and practices (Klein, 1984). Many federal agencies targeted women's issues as deserving of special attention and provided seed money as an impetus for establishing services for women at the state and local levels (Sapiro, 1986). Service work was assisted greatly by funding from Volunteers in Service to America (VISTA); the federal Law Enforcement Assistance Administration (LEAA); and the Comprehensive Employment Training Act (CETA), a Department of Labor job training program (O'Sullivan, 1978; Schechter, 1982; Tierney, 1982).

The election of Ronald Reagan as president of the United States in 1980, however, marked the beginning of a concerted effort to reverse this trend. Feminist service organizations were jeopardized as Reagan shifted responsibility for social services back to the states and cut federal funding (Hyde, 1995). They struggled to survive in a sociopolitical environment increasingly pervaded by the antifeminist efforts of the New Right (Conover and Gray, 1983; Dehart-Mathews and Mathews, 1989; Eisenstein, 1981b; Faludi, 1991; Taylor, 1989). Over time, many of these organizations came to resemble conventional services (Tierney, 1982). Many did not survive the cuts in federal funding and the backlash against feminism (Sealander and Smith, 1986). Others, like the five organizations discussed in this book, continued to have a strong feminist orientation.

THE POLITICAL IS PERSONAL

For the members of these organizations, being identified with the women's movement in the 1970s and early 1980s was a source of devotion and resilience but also a source of strain. Three aspects of "being feminist" pervade women's accounts from that period and provide a foundation for an understanding of their experiences. First, members were well aware of the importance of the women's movement for their own successes and the benefits of their being located within a city that had a strong feminist presence. However, it was also true that, as feminists, they encountered opposition not only in conservative bastions but also in "progressive" communities such as Madison, Wisconsin. Second, feminism as a personal belief system was an important source of members' dedication. However, the deeply personal nature of their activities meant that disagreements over policies and programs could quickly become arguments over personal beliefs and could degenerate into personal attacks. Third, feminist principles provided a common ground around which members could rally, but the widely diverse meanings of feminism also caused internal strife.

Identification with the Women's Movement

The women's movement provided inspiration and support for the members of these organizations. A tremendous sense of energy and excitement derived from women's new consciousness about themselves, connections with other women, and shared political activism. Their organizations benefited from being in a community where many feminist organizations and activities flourished.

> A positive force is having a candidate for district attorney be able to take a stand on women's issues and end up winning the election. That's part of the community we live in. It's more supportive of a shelter than a lot of places would be. (ABW)
>
> ARC House got a lot of support from the women's community. You can't have a program as radical as ARC House without it. (ARC)
>
> There's a strong women's community in Madison. Rape Crisis would look a lot different if it were in some other town. Madison, being the kind of political place it is, has made what we do here possible. (RCC)

Being associated with the women's movement provided the social and political support necessary for the emergence and growth of these organizations. At the same time, stereotypes of and biases against feminists and hostile criticism of the women's movement were sources of stress.

> At that point, the women's liberation movement was really strong, and you couldn't talk about anything around that. You had to be cautious. Being associated with any kind of women's group back in the mid- to late 70s had negative connotations. (WRW)

Groups consisting solely of women that were formed in response to and as a part of the women's movement were understood to be feminist, and their very existence was considered to be radical, a flagrant challenge to the status quo. Members were aware that their early efforts were inherently radical. For example, one early member of Advocates for Battered Women remarked: "In the beginning, we were intent on getting a shelter and providing services. That was radical in itself at that stage." An early member of ARC House expressed the same sentiment: "Providing alternatives to prison for women was a very radical thing to do at the time."

As a form of separatism, feminist activities that were by women, for women, and on behalf of women challenged assumptions of male authority and female dependence on men and disrupted conventional male-female relationships (Freedman, 1979; Frye, 1978). Members of these organizations were challenging dominant cultural values that defined women as innately and inevitably different from and inferior to men, as destined to be dependent, nurturant, and domestic. In direct opposition to these cultural values, they were asserting their power. Moreover, they were asserting their power by working in conjunction with other women rather than relying on the expertise, power, and protection of men. The existence of these organizations jeopardized the complacency of those who were unwilling to question the benefits they derived from gender inequality and to acknowledge the pervasiveness of male violence toward women.

Some feminist groups were militant and confrontational; others pursued limited agendas with considerable restraint. Regardless of the stance such groups adopted, many people viewed them with suspicion and scorn simply because they were *women helping women* (Hole and Levine, 1971). Antagonism toward the organized efforts of women's groups is best exemplified by responses to Women Reaching Women, the organization that most carefully and deliberately framed its work in conventional terms.

Immediately, there were negative feelings about our title, Women Reaching Women. Just the mere fact that we were organized was a negative thing for a lot of people . . . As soon as you're a women's program, you're labeled radical and feminist. The label is going to kill you in the end . . . A lot of the volunteers wanted to make sure that they weren't associating with some kind of radical feminist organization. It was important to them that they didn't get viewed as angry, bra-burning feminists.

Some women are frightened because of the name, just the name. Women will say to me, "Women Reaching Women, what does that mean?" They know they need treatment. They heard something about us. It sounded safe, but yet, it's all women. What are people going to think about them if they're associated with this project? A lot of it comes out of fear of what the media has portrayed of the women's movement.

Many of the feminists who received media attention embodied traits disdained in females; they were forceful, self-reliant, and confident. By their words and actions, they demonstrated that feminists as a group trusted themselves and other women to hold prerequisite wisdom; challenged the importance of men emotionally, economically, and sexually; and refused to accept and conform to women's "appropriate" place in society. Not surprisingly, then, it was commonly asserted that all feminists were lesbians, the underlying assumption being that "normal" women would not reject male authority and question male benevolence.

At one level, associating feminism with lesbianism acknowledged feminists' rejection of male privilege and male control and the primacy of their emotional, social, and political bonds with other women, and the fact that many feminist activists were lesbians (Bunch, 1975; Eisenstein, 1983; Freedman, 1979; Taylor and Rupp, 1993). On another level, however, the country's obsession with the sexual preferences of feminists reflected a dominant cultural strategy to discount woman-centered activism and discourage new recruits into the movement (Abbott and Love, 1971; Hole and Levine, 1971; Koedt, 1973; Weitz, 1984). Members were keenly aware of the ways in which homophobia in their community made their work more difficult.

> Many women, along with all the other garbage they hear from their partner, hear, "The shelter for battered women is run by a bunch of lesbians." It's, of course, based on no information, but it's one more threat that he throws at her. (ABW)
>
> There was a time when there was a big rumor about how ARC House was staffed by a bunch of lesbians. I'll be damned if I'm going to pretend that there's something wrong with women loving women, and I'll be damned if I'm going to sit around being scared about what people think . . . The lesbian thing wouldn't be important except that we're dealing statewide with people who can decide to release clients to us or not. (ARC)
>
> Some of the volunteers didn't even want to affiliate with Women Reaching Women because they were afraid that people in their community were going to think that they were lesbians. A lot of people connect the word "feminist" with lesbian and connect the word "lesbian" with the most god-awful thing they can think of. They're so threatened by that. They don't have any understanding. So, if you start out by saying feminist is what Women Reaching Women is, then you immediately push them away. (WRW)

The dilemma that members faced was having to deal realistically with the ways in which homophobia was used to discredit their work and, at the same time, not becoming complicit in the process. Denying that they were dominated by lesbians would reinforce prejudice by giving credence to the view that being dominated by lesbians was a troublesome problem that needed to be addressed. Generally, education and acknowledging the diversity of their members were viewed as the most effective strategies. In some cases, ignoring such attacks was the best option.

We tried to cope with it by simply ignoring it, refusing to deal with some of the hateful comments that we got. It was clearly based on bigotry, and if you respond to that kind of bigotry, you give it a validity that it doesn't deserve. So our choice was not to respond to it, because we didn't consider it to be a valid criticism. That's worked. (WTA)

Members of every organization reported that ridicule and hateful accusations diminished significantly over time as the value of their work and their contributions to the community became increasingly apparent.

Feminism as a Personal Belief System

In each of these organizations, members' efforts were fueled by idealism and commitment. As in other feminist organizations, the highly personal nature of their involvement defined the importance of these organizations for most of their members (Freeman and MacMillan, 1976; Hartsock, 1976; MacDonald, 1976; Schlesinger and Bart, 1982).

Feminism gives a reason for people to stick in there. The work is extremely difficult. They have to have some ideological reason for being there, or they burn out very quickly. It gives a sense of unity. With a lot of feminist projects, the feminist ideology itself is powerful enough to keep them going. (ARC)

The fact that Transit's a feminist organization has been real helpful in attracting committed volunteers, people who don't want to just sit back and discuss their feminist ideas, but who want to do something concrete, produce a product that they can see and be proud of. (WTA)

It was an accident that I got introduced to Women Reaching Women. I had a personal situation within my own family. Then, the more and more I got into it, the more and more I felt tied to it. It's like part of me now. I had my awareness heightened. I haunted libraries initially, to prove that what I was hearing wasn't right. I couldn't believe it. Now I'm a believer. (WRW)

Working in a feminist organization was an avenue for women to act on their personal politics. However, the deeply personal meaning of their work created emotionally charged work environments (Morgen, 1995; Taylor, 1995). Shared understandings were personally validating; victories were exhilarating and deeply satisfying. Correspondingly, differences among members could lead to bitter conflicts, disillusionment, and debilitating levels of emotional distress (Freeman, 1973; Mansbridge, 1973, 1982, 1983; Morgen, 1994; Riger, 1984; Ristock, 1990; Ryan, 1989).

Feminist awareness that *the personal is political* transformed individual problems into political concerns, and women derived strength from recognizing that their personal problems were, in fact, reflective of larger social forces. This core principle, that *the personal is political,* also meant that every aspect of women's lives could be interpreted as signaling their political beliefs: "A lot of assumptions are made. The terms people use, the way people dress, a person's sexual preference, might all have to do with whether or not you're perceived as being radical or more traditional." (ABW) Within the movement, feminists were inundated with expectations as to what constituted "feminist" attitudes, ways of behaving and relating, and lifestyles. Within these organizations, members held high expectations for themselves and for one another.

> We felt that, unless we gave our souls, we weren't feminist enough. If we were, we had to be willing to put in those extra hours because this is more than a job. It's fighting for the cause. (WTA)
> We try to hire people who have their hearts in the right place. That makes it a trying job because, by definition, we're asking for a job that you don't put away when you leave the office. (WTA)

When expectations were met, positive and productive personal relationships developed. For example, when expectations of mutual support and emotional bonding were realized, the ideological forecast of sisterhood was achieved.

> I have a closeness to my colleagues that I never believed would ever be possible in a work setting. That's because, as feminists, we take responsibility for the well-being of our co-workers, taking care of each other in a job that could emotionally destroy us. That's because we are feminists. We know we're sisters, and we have to take care of each other. Our strengths are the sisterhood that we share, the mutual support and respect. (RCC)

However, "being feminist" did not insure that members would share specific beliefs, agree upon priorities and tactics, or like and support one another. When expectations were not met, distrust and disapproval often followed. Rejection of a woman's ideas could constitute rejection of her deeply held personal values and beliefs and thus, ultimately, be perceived as rejection of the woman herself.

> I saw a lot of cruel things being done, people that were in tears, and that's not sisterhood to me. I try to think about why that is. I don't know if it's because people are so emotionally involved in what they believe in that anybody who doesn't agree or has a different way of looking at it is a threat, an enemy. I don't know if it's indigenous to feminist organizations. I've talked to people who seem to think it is. (ABW)

Interaction in highly personalized workplaces could be difficult, anxiety-producing, and painful. Yet, in these organizations, personal issues and political work were not, and could not be, separate. Members' goals and values were the raw materials in the production of feminist organizations; the survival of their organizations depended on the personal and political commitments of the women who worked within them. Paying attention to the personal was crucial. Moreover, members' personal investments and high expectations of themselves and other feminists contributed to their persistence in the face of what otherwise might have been insurmountable deterrents.

Diverse Meanings of Feminism among Feminists

For the members of these organizations, feminism provided a politicized lens through which they interpreted personal relationships, political strategies, and work options. They were unified by their common goals: to challenge gender inequality, expose gender-role stereotypes and bias, and interrupt violence against women. At the same time, members recognized that feminism represents many different philosophical and political frameworks and there are multiple interpretations of what constitutes feminist practices and strategies within each of these frameworks (Hirsch and Keller, 1990; Jaggar and Rothenberg, 1993; Stetson, 1997). Even with apparent agreement on specific beliefs, individuals held different views on which specific policies and practices were consistent with agreed-upon values and goals.

Differences in values, lifestyles, and priorities created multiple voices vying for influence and validation. The more that members viewed their organizations as publicly representing and advancing feminism, the more time and energy devoted to, and the more exhilaration and anguish derived from, deliberations over what constituted feminist goals, services, and structures. The existence of diverse and conflicting understandings of feminism was acknowledged most frequently by members of the three explicitly feminist organizations. However, identifying with the early radical feminists, members in every one of these five organizations positioned themselves in terms of "being radical." For example, Rape Crisis Center members consistently described themselves as "radical feminists" and their organization as a "radical feminist agency." In ARC House and Women Reaching Women, members were very aware that their words and actions were not as "radical" as those of other feminist groups. They attributed their stance to the conservative nature of their sponsoring agencies and of their consumers.

> We're strongly feminist but not as visibly feminist in terms of how we say it, because we found it was such a turn-off with Corrections and with the clients

themselves. We talk about the same things but not in quite as radical a language, for survival reasons. We're promoting the same kind of things but not using the same trigger terminology that some of the other feminist projects have more leeway to do. I see it as a luxury that some feminist organizations can pretty much take any stance they want to. We would have been destroyed if we would have taken that attitude because of the system we're in. (ARC)

Women Reaching Women helped initiate programs in the community that didn't look like we were terribly radical, like showing films. Only later did we start putting together women's groups. That was a little too radical. They didn't want to be seen as meeting alone with women. Their husbands, a lot of people, were very threatened by that, so we didn't do that in the beginning. We had nice, non-threatening programs for the volunteers to do. Those worked pretty well, and people enjoyed them. It helped others to view us as a non-threatening organization, that we didn't have radical views that we were trying to impose on people. (WRW)

Often, the term "radical" is reserved for those feminists who are working for changes in societal structures, as compared with those working toward equality for women in existing systems. In these interviews, however, members of all five organizations expressed the critical importance of structural change in the society at large. Being "radical" referred to members' being explicit about their feminist beliefs and publicly confronting patriarchal policies and practices. Being "not radical" referred to choosing to be less vocal about one's feminist beliefs and having a willingness to adopt more conventional strategies, while still sharing many of the beliefs and goals of those who were "radical."

In every organization, members asserted that they dealt with the diverse meanings of feminism by having a shared commitment to the goals of their organizations and to their organizations' survival.

You can rally around a philosophy or a political analysis of what's going on. Even if you all don't agree on all the points, you look for those points of commonality, and you can rally together around them. We had an underlying sense of purpose, and we resolved a lot of things by coming back to that. (ARC)

We're all moving toward the same goals. At times, political differences have made the organization tense, but there's always been a feeling of movement. I've seen it as a feeling of growth, like we are able to deal with these things and move on. Despite the differing opinions and personal conflicts, there is this spirit of always working things through. We will work it through. (RCC)

Overall, members of these five organizations drew strength and confidence from being part of the women's movement, and they contended with the negative effects of antifeminist bias on organizational life. They reaped the rewards of working toward goals and applying values that were personally meaningful, and they suffered the tensions associated with having deep personal investments in their work. To build and maintain a distinctly feminist service organization, members needed to identify a range of values and beliefs that broadly constituted feminism and, within this broad framework, to negotiate the meanings of feminism as they applied to specific circumstances. Their endurance and success provide affirmation of members' ability to identify over time a sufficiently common vision to permit shared goals and unified efforts.

THE STUDY

Tales from the Trenches: Politics and Practice in Feminist Service Organizations is the product of a comparative case study that was conducted to provide an historical record and acknowledge the accomplishments of five successful feminist service organizations, providing information that would otherwise be unknown except to their members. The study included five very different organizations, including two that did not identify themselves publicly as feminist, to illustrate the diverse types of alternative service organizations that women established both outside of and within mainstream bureaucracies in the 1970s, the period when this type of feminist organization first emerged. The study traced the chronological development of these organizations and described their missions, services, and impact.

In addition, the study was designed to provide new insights and information about the realities and complexities of feminist practice in feminist service organizations. The study examined the dynamic interplay of ideology and experience by documenting how women incorporated feminist beliefs and strategies into their work. While exploring members' views of the internal forces and external circumstances that shaped the development of their organizations, it focused on the processes through which goals, social change strategies, services, and organizational structures were developed and changed over time.

A related goal was to promote new understandings of the work experiences of the pioneering feminists who developed these organizations. The study emphasized members' investments and intentions, successes and strains, disappointments and conflicts. It explored how members dealt with the dilemmas that characterized many feminist efforts in the early years of the women's movement, including internal problems stemming from ideological splits, homophobia, and their commitment to collective organizational structures, and the problems created by antifeminist resistance.

Much of the literature on feminist service organizations was published in the 1970s and early 1980s and consisted largely of descriptive information about specific problems and the services developed to address them (e.g., Gottlieb, 1980; Masi, 1981). *Women and Male Violence: The Visions and Struggles of the Battered Women's Movement* (Schechter, 1982) provided the most comprehensive analysis of the goals and methods of such organizations. The more current research on feminist service organizations consists largely of case studies of one type of organization (e.g., Martin, DiNitto, Byington, and Maxwell, 1992; Perlmutter, 1994; Simonds, 1996; Srinivasan and Davis, 1991) or analyzes these organizations in the context of larger social movements, for example, the pro-choice movement (Staggenborg, 1991), the women's health movement (Hyde, 1992), and the antirape movement (Matthews, 1994). Ferree and Martin's (1995) edited book, *Feminist Organizations: Harvest of the New Women's Movement*, considers theoretical issues in a wide range of different types of feminist organizations. Among these are feminist health clinics (Morgen, 1995), an abortion clinic (Simonds, 1995), a coalition of service organizations in the battered women's movement (Arnold, 1995), and rape crisis centers (Matthews, 1995).

In comparison with this literature, *Tales from the Trenches* is unique in its in-depth comparative analysis of five organizations in one community that were founded under different circumstances, addressed different problems, helped different populations of women, and worked within different organizational contexts. It is also unique in that it focuses on the experiences of feminists who established feminist services within conservative, mainstream bureaucracies in the 1970s to assist chemically dependent women and female offenders. There exists little recognition in the literature that feminist services were being delivered within mainstream bureaucracies in the 1970s and early 1980s. There is only minimal literature on early feminist services for chemically dependent women; little has been written on feminist services for female offenders in the 1970s and early 1980s. Finally, this book is unique in the extent to which it presents the visions and experiences of the members of these organizations in their own terms and in their own voices.

Several data collection methods were used from June 1983 through July 1985. Written responses by the organizations' staff members to a 27-page questionnaire provided descriptive information on current staff, volunteers, and board members; chronological descriptive information on organizational goals; the selection and responsibilities of board members; staff qualifications, selection, and responsibilities; volunteer recruitment, training, and responsibilities; funding sources; services offered; and physical facilities. Written documents (copies of by-laws, grant proposals, annual reports, job descriptions, policy statements, brochures, newsletters) also provided information on organizational goals, services, funding, and structures. In addition, social work graduate students conducted interviews with 57 members and 30 community contacts. The interviews were tape-recorded and transcribed verbatim.

To provide an external perspective, 24 women and six men who had close contact with these organizations as part of their formal roles in their own departments and agencies were interviewed. For each organization, those interviewed included people directly involved in its funding and people in law enforcement, health care, and social services who worked closely with its members. Most (67%) of those interviewed had worked with an organization for 4 to 7 years. Some (13%) had worked with an organization for 8 to 12 years; 20% had been involved for less than 4 years. The interviews focused on these individuals' views of the organization's goals and services, including initial impressions of strengths and weaknesses; the factors involved in funding decisions and referrals; and the organization's effectiveness, impact, and future. Most of these interviews were 40 to 60 minutes long. Community members' views are presented mainly in chapters 6 and 7 (see sections on "An External Perspective").

Tales from the Trenches is primarily based on analysis of in-depth interviews with 57 women who were founders, staff, volunteers, and/or board members. Interviewing women has been a primary method for feminist researchers invested in understanding female experience based on women's portrayals of their own realities (Gluck and Patai, 1991; Maynard, 1994; Oakley, 1981; Reinharz, 1992). The interviews explored how and why the organizations were established; the development of goals, social change strategies, services, and structures over time; and the issues and dilemmas that members confronted as they worked to incorporate feminist beliefs and strategies into their services and structures. They ranged from one to three hours in length.

Specifically, the interviews with founders and early workers obtained descriptive information about the people who were most instrumental in founding these organizations. They explored (1) the factors that provided the impetus for starting the organization, (2) the issues and activities that were part of the initial discussions and planning efforts, (3) the major goals of the founders, (4) any major differences or conflicts among the founders, (5) what occurred and who was involved between the initial discussions and planning through the time when services were first provided, (6) the nature of the initial services, and (7) the major accomplishments and difficulties encountered over this period.

The interviews with current and former volunteers, paid staff, and board members focused on (1) the incorporation of feminist principles into the goals, programs and services, and structure of the organization; (2) the ways in which feminist principles had been functional, dysfunctional, or both; (3) the major transitional periods or turning points; (4) the impact of external forces; (5) political differences among members and how they were addressed; and (6) the major successes, failures, strengths, and weaknesses of the organization. Other issues discussed throughout these interviews included lesbian/straight differences, the participation of women of color, the participation of men, decision-making processes, dealing with conflict, and the impact of funding sources. In addition, based on the roles women held within their organizations, some interviews obtained more detailed information on issues related to the experiences of board members, staff, or volunteers; obtaining and maintaining funding; and changes in goals and services over time.

Of the current and former staff, board members, and volunteers, 87% were actively involved in their organizations at the time of their interviews, and 56% had been members of their organizations for three or more years. Over one-third of these women had been active in their organizations for five or more years. Many of these women held different positions over time. Volunteers became paid staff, board members, or both; board members became service providers; and in some instances, women delivered services and were board members at the same time. Moreover, there were generally close ties among current staff, board members, and many volunteers, and relationships continued among past and current members. Thus, women's accounts were based on their own experiences, often in more than one role; the experiences of others based on direct knowledge; and third-person accounts. Inevitably, the women interviewed selected those aspects of their experiences that they recalled and were willing to discuss at a particular time, with a particular interviewer, and within a relatively short time. Their views of specific events and interactions were shaped by their own experiences and by the passage of time.

Similarly, my analyses were influenced by my personal investments and experiences. I came to the University of Wisconsin-Madison as an assistant professor in the School of Social Work in the fall of 1970. In Madison, throughout the period covered in this book, community activists joined with university staff, students, and faculty in a wide range of projects on and off campus. On campus, I was an active member of the Association of Faculty Women (AFW). Our efforts included agitating for equitable funding for women's athletics and increased hiring and retention of women faculty and staff. I was most deeply involved with a coalition of AFW faculty, students, and community women committed to women's studies. Political pressure finally led to the appointment of a chancellor's committee on women's studies, of which I was a member. The women's studies program was established in the fall of 1975. I was the chairperson of the women's studies program from 1976 to 1979 and associate chairperson from 1982 to 1986. Given my own level of feminist activism over the period of this study, I was familiar with many of the issues that members of these organizations raised in their interviews. Also, since the early 1970s, my research and teaching have focused on women's issues in social work and on women and mental health. I highly valued the social change efforts and service contributions of the women who worked in feminist service organizations. Their organizations provided much-needed models of appropriate and effective services for women and, more generally, of feminist practice, and I did not want their work to go unrecorded and unrecognized.

I view this project as a form of collaboration with the founders and members of these five organizations. They provided the commitment, the energy, and the vision. They took the risks, and they are the ones who profoundly changed the conditions of women's lives in their community and in communities throughout the state of Wisconsin. As I wrote this book, my tasks were (1) to document the histories of these organizations, based on the information collected; (2) to locate their work in time and place so that readers can better understand the political and social circumstances that shaped their work; (3) to frame their issues and concerns in terms of the relevant literature; and (4) to report the patterns that can be gleaned only from having the privilege of hearing the voices of many different women working in different contexts toward similar goals. My goal has been to present the views and experiences of women in their own terms, acknowledging that, ultimately, this book reflects my reconstruction and interpretation of their experience (Acker, Barry, and Esseveld, 1991; Glucksmann, 1994; Gorelick, 1996; Kelly, Burton, and Regan, 1994).

Issues of validity in qualitative research are generally discussed in terms of establishing the "trustworthiness" of the study. Although generalizability is not a goal of qualitative studies, validity can be partially tested by the extent to which the reported data and accompanying analyses "ring true" to members of similar organizations and are consistent with findings of similar studies. The perspectives reflected in these interviews are not unlike those reported in other studies of feminist organizations. The extensive use of quotations assists readers in judging for themselves the fit between women's words and my interpretations. Other means of establishing trustworthiness in this study included *data triangulation,* that is, using multiple sources of data; searching for *negative cases and disconfirming evidence*; and *member checks,* wherein some members have had the opportunity to provide feedback (Altheide and Johnson, 1994; Denzin, 1978; Lincoln and Guba, 1985; Mathison, 1988; Rubin and Rubin, 1995).

Data analysis began with my completing a lengthy, descriptive summary of the historical development of each organization. The summaries were based on information from the written questionnaire, agency documents, and the interviews. Drawing broadly on the constant comparative method (Glaser and Strauss, 1967; Strauss and Corbin, 1990), I then immersed myself in the texts of the transcribed interviews to establish categories for organizing the data. My goal was, to the extent possible, to derive my understanding of what was said based on the data, not on preconceived notions. Using an inductive approach, I categorized participants' responses throughout their interviews and combined categories into themes and subthemes as patterns emerged. Categories and themes were first considered within organizations and then comparisons were drawn across organizations.

Within each organization, I identified major themes, areas of consensus, and issues around which members held divergent views. I continually assessed the convergence among the accounts of different women, the written questionnaires, and the documents, paying close attention to the dates when documents were written, how close the interviewees were to the events described, and the expressed levels of confidence with which the material was presented. When major differences in views occurred within or across organizations, I looked for the factors that appeared to be related to these differences.

The writing process itself was the final stage of analysis. Developing themes, discussing them in terms of the related literature, contextualizing them in terms of developments in the women's movement at large, and discussing the factors that might account for similarities among and differences between organizations led to changes in my thinking. In many instances, writing flowed easily from the themes developed. In others, the process of writing revealed inconsistencies, gaps, and questions that required my return to the sources of the data for clarification, elaboration, and substantiation. This process continued until consistent patterns were evident and exceptions to these patterns had been identified. As described by Deborah Padgett: "This state of grace is known as *saturation*, a term meaning the 'cooking' process is drawing to an end" (1998, p. 79).

Many of the views these women expressed were consistent with those represented in other studies of feminist activism in the 1970s into the mid-1980s. However, their reported experiences shed new light on, for example, the positive impact of funding requirements; how differences among lesbians and nonlesbians were handled; how members' views of women and men informed organizational services and policies; how women who identified with early radical feminism utilized both radical and reform strategies; and how members created new understandings of what constituted a "feminist" organization. Members provided new insights into the commonalities and differences among freestanding feminist organizations and feminist organizations embedded in conservative bureaucracies, and how dual missions of social service provision and social change were maintained. These five organizations stand as evidence of the effective exercise of political power by feminists at the local level, and their successes tell an important story about the nature of feminist efforts.

Chapter One

The Founding of
Five Feminist Service Organizations

It was a wonderful time. People saw problems and got together to work on them.
It seems fairly simple, but no one else was doing it. There was a real need, so
we did it. It was the early 70s. Anything was possible. (RCC)

In tracing the history of *Quest: A Feminist Quarterly*, Charlotte Bunch recalled, "In its early stages, the women's liberation movement was fueled by
our sense of discovery, our sense of sisterhood and unity among women"
(1981, p. xv). The founding and development of the Rape Crisis Center,
Women's Transit Authority, Advocates for Battered Women, ARC House, and
Women Reaching Women were supported by this same set of factors: discovery, sisterhood, and unity among women. The women involved in these
organizations viewed their work as a form of political activism: "That was the
most significant thing," said one founder of the Rape Crisis Center, "the belief that we could change things."

The founders and early workers in Advocates for Battered Women, the
Rape Crisis Center, and Women's Transit Authority viewed their work as part
of the diverse efforts of feminists to radically change the power differences
between women and men, differences that were supported and maintained by
male violence against women. Eliminating the problems of rape and battering
required no less than a radical transformation of society; helping women who
were victims of male violence was one essential aspect of a much broader
agenda. These workers brought to their efforts anger, a prideful intolerance of
the status quo, and a political predisposition against compromise. They pro-
claimed their intention to radically change women's lives by the sheer force
of women's joining together. Sustained and nurtured by feminist energy in
their small groups and by a supportive and reaffirming network of feminists
in the community, they explicitly asserted the political nature of their work

27

and sought funding that would allow them to remain outside of the established social service system.

In contrast, ARC House and Women Reaching Women were affiliated with conventional, male-dominated, and highly conservative systems. Feminist professionals established Women Reaching Women within an existing statewide alcohol and drug abuse organization. ARC House was established as a freestanding nonprofit organization funded primarily through the criminal justice system. It was founded by women whose impulses to create a new organization were supported by their evolving feminist consciousness. From the beginning, pragmatism and compromise were dominant strategies in these two organizations. The ties between their work and feminism were not explicit in their written materials or public discussions.

For all of the problems these activists targeted, women were underserved and ill-served; appropriate treatments and services were nonexistent. Rape and other forms of woman abuse were viewed as private problems of individual women that required individual, not social, solutions. Women victims were blamed for the abuse, and their pains were ignored or pathologized. Within the fields of criminal justice and substance abuse, treatments and services were male-centered. The unique problems and needs of female offenders and chemically dependent women were unrecognized or dismissed as unimportant.

The founders and early workers in these organizations were white, and the great majority were college educated. The founders of Women Reaching Women were in their late 30s and early 40s. In the other organizations, most founders were in their mid- to late 20s, unmarried, and with no children. Given the composition of the women's movement in the 1970s and the time and energy required to establish these organizations, this demographic picture is not surprising. In all cases, the founders were establishing organizations for which no established models existed. Their goals, services, and structures emerged over time, largely out of their own experience. All benefited from the availability of federal funds targeted for innovative services. This was a time when government was viewed as a legitimate and essential source of assistance for the poor and the oppressed.

COMBATING VIOLENCE AGAINST WOMEN

In 1972, following a series of violent rapes in Madison and an overall increase in the number of reported rapes in the county, groups of women began to meet to discuss how they might respond. By early 1973, a community meeting on rape had resulted in the formation of the Women's Coalition on

Rape Prevention. The coalition publicized the problems of rape victims, met with various law enforcement officers and the district attorney to express their concerns about the behaviors and attitudes of police officers involved with rape victims; and publicly pressured city officials to respond. Fairly quickly, the group divided, with one segment focusing on helping the victims of rape and the other developing a ride service to prevent rape. The first group became the Rape Crisis Center; the second, the Women's Transit Authority. The Women's Coalition on Rape Prevention had decided to provide concrete alternatives for women.

The Rape Crisis Center

Most of the early activists in the Rape Crisis Center were in their mid- to late 20s. Some were undergraduate or graduate students; others were employed. Although some knew each other well, others met through their organizing efforts. They belonged to a loosely knit network of women, many of whom were active in other women's groups, cooperatives, New Left political organizations, or a combination of these. Among the core organizers was a member of the City Council who was employed part-time and returning to school for a Ph.D. in counseling, a high school graduate who was a bookkeeper in a car wash, several social work and law students, and a woman who worked as a clerk for the state. Helping women who had been assaulted was their primary motivation.

> There were several problems. One was the brutal treatment women got in the courts if they decided to prosecute. Often she was attacked, her character assaulted by the attorneys. The other problem was in the reporting of the rape. At times, the police did not handle that in a sensitive way, and the emergency rooms didn't know what to do. Often, the woman was alone and without support.

As one of the first rape crisis centers in the country, the organization was breaking new ground; members had relatively little information or guidance about how to proceed.

> I don't think any of us knew what it was going to be like. I certainly never anticipated what the work would turn out to be or how intense it would get at times.
> We got a book called *How to Start a Rape Crisis Center* [Rape Crisis Center of Washington, D.C., 1971], but it was just the basics. It became clearer every time we met how much more we needed to know.
> We got some good people to do some training. We role-played a lot. We did a lot of self-training and discovered how many people had rape experiences but

hadn't identified them as rape. All of us who didn't think we had been rape victims realized how many rape or near-rape situations we had lived through. We began to get an awful sense of how socially acceptable it was.

Their initial funding consisted of private contributions, the largest share donated by the founder of the Midwest Medical Center, Madison's first abortion clinic. The Rape Crisis Center opened its hotline in July 1973 with 20 volunteers, mostly students from the University of Wisconsin-Madison. With two rooms at the YWCA, volunteers provided free and confidential counseling, information, referrals, and emotional support every night from 7 P.M. to 7 A.M.

> The first folks who called in weren't kids but adult women who had never had a place to talk. That's when it became clear that we were meeting an immediate need for people who were holding it back for 20, 30, 40 years, just waiting for somebody to say, "Here's a place you can call."

The members' primary objective was to provide nonjudgmental support and to assist rape victims in whatever ways they could, based on what the women themselves wanted. "We wanted them to know that we were on their side and to understand it was not something women brought on themselves." They counseled women over the phone, mostly through active listening, and encouraged women to come in and talk with someone at the Rape Crisis Center or seek counseling, to "support themselves in some way." In some emergency situations, they would arrange to go out to meet with a woman.

A second goal was to educate and influence others who had contact with rape victims. They wanted to change the treatment rape victims received and to increase reporting by having the police respond in more helpful ways.

> We started working with the personnel in the emergency rooms and the police department and the sheriff's department, trying to make them aware of what we felt a woman needed. We gave them information that they could give her on what she could do if she wanted to prosecute. We tried to get them to let women know that we were available. Most of them agreed to do that . . . There were some problems with the police in that they were afraid that we were antipolice. It was hard to overcome that kind of distrust. When they saw that we handled things in a reasonable way and didn't come storming in there making all kinds of accusations, they began to trust us more.
>
> Our definition of sexual assault was much broader than the law at that time and much broader than what most people would have used as the definition. Any woman who felt that she had an experience that she wanted to define as sexual assault was entitled to services. The law said that a woman had to resist to the utmost. A lot of the clients we had didn't fit that definition of rape and were being discounted and disbelieved. We wanted to make people in the sys-

tem listen to what women's experiences were, not what the law was. That was based on feminist principles, that a woman's personal experience was important and valid and should be listened to and taken into account.

Their third objective was to combat rape by educating people about rape. They worked to raise the consciousness of women in the community and to demystify feminism.

This was the first time that these women had any exposure to feminism, and they didn't know it was feminism. It was something that they could relate to, something they could understand. When you would speak to a group of women in the community, you would give some powerful feminist rap, cloaked a little bit. Then, they'd come up to you afterward and say, "Can we give you some money? What can we do?" Or, "I was raped and I didn't even know it." There would be so many people believing then that if you were raped by somebody you knew, then it wasn't rape. An hour or two was never enough. All of a sudden, so many of those women realized that we were not women to be threatened by. If anything, we were exactly the women that they wanted to have there with them if they were in trouble.

The organization's political statement read:

We, the women of the Rape Crisis Center, are angry. We are angry at society's unwillingness to acknowledge the violence of rape. We are angry at society's unwillingness to acknowledge the frequency of rape. We are angry at the dehumanizing response rape victims get from law enforcement agencies, families, friends, juries, and the community at large. We are angry at a society that encourages and forces us to be victim-like and then castigates us for filling that role. Out of our anger and concern, we have formed the Rape Crisis Center. We are committed to the belief that, contrary to our socialization, we women can be assertive and self-sufficient and can handle responsibilities and risks; it is imperative that women help other women demonstrate this.

We are a political group with political, i.e., personal and social change goals. We believe that rape and the frequency with which it occurs are integrally related to the attitudes held by men toward women and to the attitudes held by women toward their role in society. Rape is not an aberration; it is the logical violent extension of these attitudes. Without a vital change in these attitudes and expectations, rape will never be eradicated and will continue to be the most frequently occurring violent crime in the United States.

In 1974, a VISTA volunteer helped the Rape Crisis Center coordinate its activities; and in 1975, the city agreed to cover the organization's operating expenses. Through the Wisconsin Council on Criminal Justice, it received LEAA funding in 1974 to establish the Dane County Project on Rape as a task force of the Rape Crisis Center. The grant provided funding for paid staff to offer follow-up advocacy for victims of sexual assault who chose to make a police report. The decision to accept LEAA funds was a difficult one.

> There was a big hassle. The Wisconsin Council on Criminal Justice came to the Rape Crisis Center and said, "Do you want this LEAA money to start an advocacy service?" In those days, LEAA had the same connotation that the Playboy Foundation money has. There was a big discussion and a lot of hoopla about whether to take that or not. They did, and we've maintained a pretty independent posture.

When the Project on Rape began, its goals were to increase the sensitivity of the criminal justice system to victims' needs and to increase public knowledge about the problem of sexual assault. The four paid staff would provide advocacy for women who chose to report and some longer-term counseling. Rape Crisis Center volunteers would continue to operate outside of the criminal justice system, independent of any restrictions that funding sources might place on them.

The Project on Rape was deliberately housed separately from the Rape Crisis Center. Since the Project on Rape was developed to assist women who chose to report, there was concern that rape victims might expect Project staff to insist that they contact the police. Having different names and being in separate offices ensured that women who were uncertain about calling the Project on Rape could call the Rape Crisis Center, confident that they could remain anonymous, that confidentiality would be maintained, and that they would not be asked to report to the police. (To simplify discussions of this organization, throughout the book, I refer to their paid staff as members of the Rape Crisis Center, not the Project on Rape.)

Women's Transit Authority

The founders of the Women's Transit Authority were a small, tightly knit group of students in their early 20s who were active in a number of other feminist groups. Their goals were to establish a volunteer-run rape-prevention ride service provided for women by women.

> The whole focus on rape prevention came about because women didn't have equal access to the resources of the city at night. There was a lot of anger around that. It wasn't safe to walk the streets at night, so they didn't have access to the libraries, to the university, to recreational resources. The solution they came up with was, "Some of us have cars, so let's share those resources with other women who don't and give each other rides."

The goals were to provide safe transportation to affirm that we could take care of ourselves. It was a way to focus our anger and energy, to do something, to coalesce and make something happen. It was, "Hey, we could do this. We could work out of the Women's Center." That was pretty much the beginning discussion.

Beginning in the spring of 1973, Women's Transit Authority operated out of the Women's Center located near the University of Wisconsin-Madison campus. Their riders were students and other women who lived near the university. Driving their own cars, they followed set routes with publicized locations, taking women to any location around the university and the downtown Madison area, which is adjacent to the campus. Since they didn't have two-way radios, throughout the night, drivers would find a pay phone and call into the office to find out if anyone had called for a ride. After a few months, the volunteers had to stop. The drivers weren't insured to carry passengers, and their requests for donations to cover the cost of gas caused problems with local cab companies.

That summer, the university offered to provide Women's Transit Authority with cars, gas, radios, office space, and insurance. Women's Transit Authority was strongly supported by two female administrators in the dean of students' office and a female detective with the university police department, and by two key male administrators, the dean of students and the chief of police. They believed that Women's Transit would be an important part of the university's rape-prevention efforts. Women's Transit Authority accepted the university's offer, although, as with the Rape Crisis Center's decision whether to accept LEAA funds, this decision was preceded by considerable debate.

Some felt that once we accepted the cars and the radios and the office from the university, that we would be co-opted and wouldn't be able to maintain our integrity. Other people thought, "Well, what else is available?" It was spring, and we wanted to keep something going. When the university offered us cars and space, it seemed like the only game in town.

Even more than the women who established the Rape Crisis Center, these young women were inexperienced in running an organization and delivering a service. The funding from the university facilitated their survival by providing resources and by holding them accountable.

One of the requirements from the university was that the service be regular. We suddenly had to be a lot more serious about what we were doing. We couldn't afford to run a slipshod organization and lose the privileges we had with those cars. It also provided a certain safety factor. We were driving vehicles that were in good shape instead of sometimes driving vehicles that were a mess.

Through publicity and face-to-face recruitment, the founders expanded their group to about 30 women. Most volunteers worked as drivers. The dispatchers staffed the phones; the coordinators worked to ensure that the shifts were full, that the service ran smoothly, and that there were enough volunteers to keep the service open as many nights as possible.

As with the Rape Crisis Center, Women's Transit Authority's written materials asserted the feminist goals and values of the organization. Their bylaws read as follows:

> Women's Transit Authority (WTA) is a volunteer-run rape prevention ride service provided for women by women. WTA's mission is to help prevent sexual assaults which occur outside at night by providing safe, affordable transportation for women at night. The goals of the service are to provide safe transportation; increase women's mobility which is inhibited due to fear of sexual assault and women's generally lower socioeconomic status; and to increase public awareness of the need for safe, affordable transportation for women at night.
>
> Women's Transit Authority is a feminist organization and holds the principle that women working together will increase the strength of women in the community. Women's Transit Authority provides an opportunity for women to increase their strength by providing women with safe, independent transportation to reduce physical and mental vulnerability to sexual assault, and by consciously and actively defining and organizing against the constant atmosphere that condones violence against women.
>
> Women's Transit Authority works toward the day when this service will no longer be necessary. For this to happen, everyone in society must learn that sexual assault is neither inevitable nor acceptable. Both men and women must reject the violent cultural norms that encourage sexual assaults.

From 1973 to 1975, Women's Transit Authority was a volunteer-run organization, and the addition of two half-time work-study students in 1976 and 1977 did not dramatically alter its functioning. With funding from the city of Madison in 1978, however, Women's Transit Authority was able to hire three half-time coordinators and rent space for a daytime office at the YMCA near campus. Its nighttime office remained on university property, at the Campus Assistance Center. This was a major turning point in the organization's development.

> The organization ran much smoother. The training became more standardized. There was someone who was responsible, who could handle emergencies, make sure the shifts were covered, and represent the organization in the community. The staff were there to aggressively lobby the university to provide us with more vehicles and better radio equipment, to pursue other sources of funds to improve the service, and to recruit outside of the university for volunteers and for donors.

The volunteers were less frustrated, burned out a little less quickly, because the paid coordinators were recruiting new volunteers all the time. There were fewer holes in the schedule, so women didn't have to work quite as often. There was less worry about "Would Transit exist tomorrow?"

The university continued to provide cars, radios, gas, and insurance, but city funding enabled the organization to "cut our apron strings. We became a real private, nonprofit that had other sources of funding besides the university." Also, with its close affiliation with the university, many women assumed that Women's Transit Authority served only campus women. City funding more clearly identified it as a citywide service.

Advocates for Battered Women

Like the Women's Coalition on Rape Prevention, which was organized following a community meeting on rape, Advocates for Battered Women was formed by people who attended a workshop on battered women. On March 8, 1976, International Women's Day, the director of the Milwaukee Task Force on Battered Women gave a talk in Madison describing that organization's project. Following her workshop, a small group began meeting to explore what they could do for battered women in the Madison area.

I knew very little about battered women. When I was in the workshop, I was really saddened and really angered by the situations I was hearing about. I was at a point in my life where I wanted to be doing something with women about women, and it felt like the right thing to do.

People got the sense of, "Here's a real important problem, and nobody's addressing it. It's not being addressed in the police department. It's not being addressed in the Department of Social Services. There's a lot of people out there who need some kind of assistance, who need support." They wanted to create something that would offer alternatives and support for these women.

The initial planning group consisted of four women and one man in their mid-20s to early 30s. Two were students, one in law, the other in social work. Of the others, two were social workers and one worked in a food cooperative. One of the social workers was in a Ph.D. program in counseling. All of the founders were interested in establishing a shelter for battered women and increasing public awareness about the problem and the need for services for battered women. As with the founders of the Rape Crisis Center and Women's Transit Authority, prior to offering services, group members did not engage in political debates; they focused on the tasks that were required to reach shared goals. The male member of this group primarily assisted in obtaining funding, including collecting data to document the need for services. There was consensus within the group that he would remain active only until the shelter opened.

The group decided to name the organization Advocates for Battered Women, recognizing that the proactive stance embodied in the term "advocates" might cause difficulties with potential funders. They focused their efforts on gathering information from existing shelters, exploring possible sources of funding, identifying what was being done in local agencies, collecting data on battered women from police and human service agency records, and increasing public awareness of the problems of battered women. Like the founders of Rape Crisis and Women's Transit, they had relatively little information about the problem, knew of a few cities in the Midwest and in England (Pizzey, 1974) where similar services had been established, and had to educate themselves at the same time that they were educating others.

Over their first year, a slightly expanded group devoted their time to trying to obtain funding for paid staff and to community education. While exploring different funding avenues, they wrote articles for the local newspapers; arranged to be interviewed on radio and TV; conducted in-service trainings for the police, local hospitals, and mental health and social service agencies; participated in the formation of the Wisconsin Coalition Against Woman Abuse, a statewide coalition of groups working with battered women; spoke to local church, business, and women's groups; and educated themselves through reading, discussion, and attending training sessions conducted by other groups. In January 1977, the University Methodist Church donated a small office. The group had increased to about 15 people, which enabled them to staff a crisis hotline, but on a very limited basis. They continued to use this office and to work out of their own homes until the shelter could be funded.

After a number of unsuccessful attempts to get funding, Family Services, where the male member of the group was employed, agreed to sponsor Advocates for a United Way Innovative Grant. The grant, approved in March 1977, established Advocates for Battered Women; it included funding for two part-time co-coordinators. The volunteers, who had worked so intensely for the past year at fund-raising and making their presence known throughout the community, decided to "step back and take a rest," having accomplished their primary goal of obtaining funding for paid staff. That summer, the coordinators trained a small group of volunteers to staff the crisis line and pursued additional funding more effectively.

> We were all new to creating an organization, uncertain about how to use volunteers, how to prioritize things in order to get where we wanted to be. Getting some people who were paid made a big difference. It's hard to run an organization on volunteers.

CETA funding in the fall provided one additional part-time position. With three part-time staff, Advocates intensified its fund-raising efforts for a shelter, continued its community education efforts, increased its discussions with law enforcement and social service agencies that had contact with battered women, and made plans for the shelter.

That was an insane year. It seemed as if there was always community education going on, whether it was being on radio or TV programs, writing letters to the editor, trying to solicit newspaper coverage. There was some consciousness-raising and liaison work that was being done with other organizations, like the police department and some of the hospitals . . . There was a tremendous amount of time and energy that went into fund-raising because we were trying to hit all fronts. There was a tremendous amount of politicking that went along with that, sitting at endless county board and city council and board of public welfare committee meetings . . . These women were calling us in crisis, and we had no safe haven to offer them. That created a tremendous amount of pressure on us to raise enough money to get the shelter opened. It was a matter of going back to people who had said no and trying to convince them that this had to be done. It was really hard on people to talk to women on the phone who were in crisis and not be able to offer them a place to go.

By January 1978, Advocates for Battered Women had CETA funding for nine positions, eight full-time and one part-time, and United Way funding for the shelter. The organization rented an old, large, three-story frame house that could shelter eight women and children. Office space remained in a separate building.

Before the shelter opened, there was a lot of energy going into planning for that, collecting donations of furniture, clothing, bedding; doing the research on what kinds of health and safety codes we were going to have to meet; cleaning and remodeling that facility. It was an early, women's kind of mentality. Halfway houses for male offenders, they didn't go out and scrounge up old furniture people were throwing away. They got somebody to buy them new furniture. We didn't even have that expectation. Part of that was because we were a grassroots organization. Also, none of us had ever opened a shelter before. We really didn't know what was entailed.

When the shelter opened in April 1978, Advocates for Battered Women provided shelter, support, and advocacy for battered women and their children; maintained a 24-hour crisis line; facilitated a weekly support group for residents of the shelter and nonresidents; offered training to other agencies; and continued its public education activities. Like the Rape Crisis Center and

Women's Transit Authority, Advocates for Battered Women explicitly linked its work to feminism. The organization's mission statement read as follows:

> Advocates for Battered Women is a grassroots feminist organization in Dane County committed to ending violence in the lives of battered women. The purpose of our work is twofold: to provide services to battered women and their children, to change societal attitudes and institutional barriers that perpetuate violence against women.
>
> A.B.W. believes that woman abuse is a form of oppression used to maintain the inferior status of women. We believe that society condones this behavior by perpetuating violence through the promotion of powerlessness, particularly through the mechanisms of sexism, racism and classism. We are committed to creating a society in which woman abuse, as part of the larger problems of oppression and violence, will no longer exist.

Also as with the Rape Crisis Center and Women's Transit Authority, members' efforts were based on personal dedication, not on an understanding of what would be required.

> A big problem, that I don't think any of us perceived then because we were so enthusiastic and committed, was that we didn't have any experience at doing most of the things we were trying to do, either putting together an organization and running a service for battered women or trying to raise money . . . The whole ideological component of what we were doing was pretty strong. The problem was that we didn't know how to translate that into what we were doing. We were real naive about what we were getting ourselves into. The benefit of the naivete was to have this strong belief and just go ahead and do it.

CREATING FEMINIST SERVICE
ORGANIZATIONS IN MALE-DOMINATED DOMAINS

By the mid-1970s, the helping professions in which women were well represented as workers and as clients, such as social work and counseling, were beginning to be influenced by the efforts of feminist activists. There was increasing openness to evidence indicating that women were poorly served by traditional health, mental health, and social services. Practitioners were becoming more familiar with the rapidly expanding literature on women's issues in their own fields and more willing to examine the effects of sexism on their own beliefs and practices. The efforts of feminist practitioners and educators within the fields of health, mental health, and social work benefited from the activism of feminists outside of the professions, including feminist consumers who advocated on their own behalf and on behalf of other women.

In contrast, the criminal justice and the AODA systems were dominated by male administrators, practitioners, and clients. Workers in these fields, both male and female, often failed to acknowledge, much less address, the unique needs and concerns of their female clients. The small numbers of women workers and clients in these fields limited the avenues for change from within. Similarly, the problems of female offenders and substance abusers were given less attention in feminist writings, courses, and political activities. Nonetheless, the lack of services for women and the availability of federal funds allowed some inroads by feminists within these fields.

ARC House

ARC House was founded by four members of a women's group that was part of the Madison chapter of Ananda Marga, an international social service meditation society that focused on spirituality, community service, and social change. The philosophy of Ananda Marga emphasized the significance of social conditions for individual well-being, the importance of self-realization, respect for the unique value of every person, and that service to humanity is an essential part of personal growth.

> The philosophy of Ananda Marga has two components to it. One aspect is the view of the individual, which is essentially that every human life, in whatever form it takes, is equal and of value; and that no matter what your life experience has been, no matter who you are, you have within you the same greatness as any other human being. The other aspect has to do with the view of the society, that change in the society is something that has to happen. In order for there to be a lack of oppression of women or of minorities or any classes, there's a transformation that has to happen overall in the whole society.
>
> One of the sayings of Ananda Marga is "self-realization and service to humanity." That was what originally attracted me to Ananda Marga, that it wasn't just a meditation organization. It had the worldly component to it. It had the idea that you do something with this energy. There is a sense of mission to it all.

Within Ananda Marga, there was increasing awareness of women's issues and a growing sense among women that they should be talking more with one another and doing more as a group. For these four women, their involvement in Ananda Marga provided the sense of mission that led to the founding of ARC House. Their women's group provided the consciousness-raising and support that led to their pursuing a project on behalf of women. In April 1975, they began the process of identifying a community service project that would enable them to help women and would provide personally fulfilling employment for themselves and others in their organization.

They felt that there was something particular that they could offer because of their view of the human being and the philosophic base from which they were coming. Having a common philosophy that had both a feminist orientation and a spiritual orientation was really important.

They started talking to people to find out what kinds of things were needed, which gives you a sense of what an educational process this was. It wasn't that they had a great feminist political analysis of women in the criminal justice system and wanted to do something about it. It wasn't that way at all. It was a real education. I would be surprised if any one of those women were to tell you that she was, at that time, identifying herself as a feminist. In fact, I would say they all became much more conscious of women's issues through the process.

These women were in their early to middle 20s and employed. One had some college education, two had college degrees, and one was completing a master's in education. All four women contributed equally in deciding what project to develop and in preparing the grant. All four intended to work in the project if it were funded, although one took another job before ARC House opened.

Through their discussions with a woman who worked at the Wisconsin Council on Criminal Justice, they discovered that few services existed for female offenders and that they could submit a grant to the Wisconsin Council on Criminal Justice for LEAA funding targeted for innovative programming, with matching funds from the State Division of Corrections. By July, they had submitted a grant to conform with what the Council on Criminal Justice had identified as the primary need. They proposed to establish the Ananda Marga Resource Center, a halfway house for women that would serve as an alternative to incarceration. The facility would also serve, but to a lesser extent, female parolees.

In writing the grant, they didn't have to come up with a whole lot of details about the program. They wanted to create a therapeutic community and looked at various models for that and how to bring in some of the things that they felt were important, knowing that the women were not going to come in there with particularly compatible values in terms of meditation or an interest in spirituality. They wanted to be clear that they were not going to be insisting on any of that, but through who they were, they'd bring in some of their values. A lot of the planning was how to get the tasks done, how to raise the money, how to buy the house, how to write a grant. I don't think they got into a huge amount of philosophy.

Their progress was fast-paced: "When I look at it now, I don't know how they did it that fast, never having had any experience with any of it before." They submitted the grant in July 1975, three months after they first started discussing doing a project for women. The four-year grant was approved in October, to begin January 1976. A house was purchased by Ananda Marga and leased to what became known as ARC House. ARC House opened in January 1976, in a facility that could house up to eight women.

ARC House began as a project of the Madison chapter of Ananda Marga, and the initial staff were all members of Ananda Marga: three women from the women's group, a male member of the Madison chapter who had moved east and returned to be part of this project, and a female member who was recruited from another Midwest chapter. Only one of the original five staff members had professional training and experience in social service work.

Within the first six months, ARC House began to regularly receive referrals from community agencies, local attorneys, and probation and parole officers. Its goals included helping women find employment and become adjusted to living in the community. However, the primary focus was on providing personal growth and support, consistent with the philosophy of Ananda Marga.

> The women themselves had to change their self-image, their sense of who they were. They had to deal with their own past history before they were going to be ready to go out and get a job and hold it. It was different than what anyone had done in the field of corrections in the whole state of Wisconsin. It was focusing on individual transformation rather than community adjustment.

Especially in the early years, the group's idealism was closely tied to its commitment to Ananda Marga, and Ananda Marga provided the network of support that sustained the organization. But the staff did not broadcast their ties with Ananda Marga; doing so would jeopardize their funding and their credibility in the community. For the same reasons, they did not publicly discuss feminist values and goals: "We very seldom mentioned feminism, or the women's movement, or a women's perspective. We were very cautious."

As with the Rape Crisis Center, Women's Transit Authority, and Advocates for Battered Women, the early workers in ARC House had vision and commitment but little experience.

> We were winging it. There had never been such an alternative, so developing the program took a lot of energy. We had a lot of ideas of what it would be like and how far out it would be to provide the program for women. Then, we found how difficult it was.
>
> They were naive, politically unaware people, but the positive side was that they were very idealistic. They came in and pushed through something that was

new and different in Corrections. But they had to be naive to do it.

They took on clients very slowly; members needed to develop their program and earn the respect of probation officers "because they were all skeptical." By the end of the first year, they had taken part in trainings on therapeutic communities and were working with consultants who had experience in intensive therapy.

Women Reaching Women

The impetus for Women Reaching Women came from the activism of Wisconsin women within the AODA field. Several years before the founding of Women Reaching Women, the Wisconsin Women's Alliance on Alcohol and Other Drug Abuse was established. Consisting primarily of professional women, the Wisconsin Women's Alliance was organized to promote better services for women throughout the state. It was out of this network that the idea and support for Women Reaching Women emerged.

The other organization involved in the creation of Women Reaching Women was the Wisconsin Association on Alcohol and Other Drug Abuse (WAAODA), a statewide nonprofit membership association. The members of WAAODA included people from business and industry; professionals in the fields of AODA, allied health, and human services; and other concerned citizens. The association provided public education and advocacy on behalf of the victims of alcoholism and other forms of drug abuse and on behalf of those who worked in the field. It also provided technical assistance to people in the AODA field, local communities, schools, law enforcement agencies, the beverage alcohol industry, and various health and human services.

In 1978, one of the founders and a continuing member of the Women's Alliance was the president of WAAODA. In addition, as a constituent member of WAAODA, the Women's Alliance had a representative on the WAAODA board. The presence of these two activists from the Wisconsin Women's Alliance was critical. When federal funds became available to establish pilot projects to encourage volunteerism in their field, they saw an opportunity to address the needs of women and to increase the funding of WAAODA.

> The president of WAAODA had done a lot to get data and discovered that, of all the people getting treatment in Wisconsin for alcohol abuse, only 14% were women. It was thought at the time, and has since been confirmed, that 50% of the alcoholics and drug abusers in Wisconsin are women. That became a motivating factor. From the very beginning, Women Reaching Women concentrated on getting women into treatment . . . This was a way to get resources to keep WAAODA going and to get more volunteers. I would give a lot of credit to the

president of WAAODA. Also, give the executive director of WAAODA some credit. He was a pretty sensitive male and very willing to tackle issues of particular groups that had special needs.

The president and the executive director of WAAODA wrote the grant, with the active assistance of the Alliance's representative on the board and with suggestions from the Alliance's steering committee. The three who worked most directly on writing the grant were professionals in their late 30s and early 40s. The two women were active in women's AODA groups within the state and nationally.

The Women Reaching Women Project began in 1978 as one of 28 Volunteer Resource Development Projects of the National Institute of Alcohol Abuse and Alcoholism. Its purpose was to make appropriate services for chemically dependent women more available and accessible through a statewide volunteer project designed to increase the public's awareness of the problem of women and alcohol and drug abuse, inform women of available services, and assist women in gaining access to services. "It was a special project that was dedicated to issues that had been overlooked for years and years and years."

The project director of Women Reaching Women hired a project assistant, put together a small advisory group of women involved with women and chemical abuse problems, and began to establish a network of volunteers. Together, they recruited and trained volunteers, and they contacted community agencies to identify what volunteer services were needed and which agencies would be willing to work with their volunteers. They developed the process as they went along, providing some leadership and then relying on local communities to organize themselves.

In practically every county, there are volunteer groups called Councils on Alcohol and Drug Abuse. They started making phone calls to all those people and to the people who were the AODA coordinators on the county boards to let them know we had this money and the kinds of things we wanted to do, and to ask who were the appropriate contact people in their communities. After they got lists of contact people, they started setting up meetings around the state, talking to people about putting a program into their community. They were turning over a lot of decision making to the local communities. They didn't have that much experience when they first started.

Women Reaching Women encountered a considerable amount of resistance in its beginning stages, within WAAODA and among AODA community leaders.

A lot of women were not getting help, but within the AODA community, there were many people that did not believe that this was an issue. "Why such a harangue that women aren't getting into treatment?" "Why should so much money be spent on women's problems when we've got the greater problem, alcoholism, to deal with?" There was a question of whether or not WAAODA even wanted the money. They were almost willing to turn it back. "We'd rather not do it. WAAODA is going to get a bad name." . . . There was a tremendous amount of resistance and antagonism by alcohol and drug abuse community leaders. I can't say that there were more than two or three women leaders in alcohol and drug abuse. The rest were all men. They had to sell a women's program to males who were first off resistant to the idea. To be community organizing for women's issues was really difficult.

Members handled these problems through persistence and by moderating their approach.

A lot of it was having the ability to convince people that it was worthwhile and not turning people off; by tempering our philosophy so that it would be something that they could accept. It was really a sell job, packaging it so that they would buy it, maybe even compromising some of our own feelings on it, not coming off as being radical at all. We had to softshoe it and be very persistent, constantly following through with people and being able to put up with a lot of abuse.

They sent out letters to community groups describing their goals and services, and they mounted a statewide public relations campaign through radio and television announcements. Also, they and their volunteers did a lot of public speaking. They determined what kinds of volunteer services local AODA agencies could use and then made themselves available. In their first year, they organized seven chapters of Women Reaching Women. The chapters did "everything they could think of to make it easier, to take away the barriers and to make women aware so that they got the help they needed, or to prevent the problem in the first place."

FIVE FEMINIST SERVICE ORGANIZATIONS: COMMON AND DIVERSE PATTERNS OF CREATION

In all five organizations, the founders sought to transform the conditions of women's lives by offering new services to address unmet needs, by altering established services, and by raising the consciousness of the community. Three originated as women's movement organizations. In the other two, members integrated feminist consciousness with their ongoing commitments in other arenas. ARC House merged feminism with the goals of Ananda Marga to develop alternative approaches to helping female offenders. Women

Reaching Women applied feminism to create new approaches to assist women with chemical abuse problems. That men assumed major roles in the beginning stages of two of these organizations, Advocates and ARC House, was unusual. These organizations illustrate that feminist ideology influenced the founding of feminist service organizations in diverse ways.

As described in other accounts of feminist service organizations established in the 1970s, the creation of these organizations was greatly facilitated by the generous levels of funding available from LEAA and CETA, as well as other funds targeted for innovative projects. These funds enabled members to proceed with their work more effectively and to document more specifically the need for their services, thereby enhancing their ability to successfully obtain funding from more conservative sources.

The coordinated efforts of radical feminist activists and supportive bureaucrats has received relatively little attention in the literature. Yet, in several instances, funders' reaching out to these organizations was of critical importance for their successful development. Staff within the Wisconsin Council on Criminal Justice, the University of Wisconsin–Madison, Family Services, and other funders assisted these organizations in identifying sources of funding, in meshing their goals with funding priorities, and in developing proposals. Members' experiences affirm the critical importance of the presence of "femocrats," a term coined by members of the Australian women's movement to describe feminists who held central roles in federal and state bureaucracies (Eisenstein, 1991, 1995). In the 1960s and 1970s, feminists in federal agencies worked closely with national feminist organizations to influence U.S. public policy (Freeman, 1975; Davis, 1991; Kessler-Harris, 2001; Rupp and Taylor, 1987). It is evident that, as early as the 1970s, feminists in traditional bureaucracies were also using their expertise and influence to promote local feminist projects, including those explicitly identified with the radical feminist movement.

There were few philosophical debates and divisions among the founders and early workers. This is somewhat surprising since the founders of the explicitly feminist organizations did not know each other well prior to their efforts in establishing their organizations. They had little reason to trust one another or expect smooth interpersonal relationships. Throughout discussions of these early years, members commented on founders' naivete, inexperience, excitement, and fortitude. Perhaps these factors masked differences or rendered differences insignificant during the initial efforts. It may be that differences in political beliefs became significant only after the initial services were delivered, consumer demands increased, the constraints of funding became apparent, and priorities needed to be set. The impact of different political philosophies became more apparent as their work became more concrete and more complex. Also, their initial reliance on volunteers led to a relatively fluid membership; those with significantly different agendas would either not join or not remain long, with relatively little impact on the organization. As services developed and organizational structures were created, turnover would become increasingly problematic.

Members of these organizations began with little experience in and few established models for developing their types of service. To what can we attribute their success? One major factor is obviously their high levels of dedication. The funders, law enforcement personnel, and service providers who were involved with these organizations in their early years described the founders and early workers as "dynamic," "capable," "very determined," "articulate," "highly motivated," "very dedicated," "energetic," "very idealistic," and "highly committed." It appears that the founders' intense commitment and tenacity more than compensated for what they lacked in terms of experience.

In these early years, feminists asserted the validity of women's defining issues out of their own experience and the experiences of other women. Consciousness-raising in small discussion groups and through feminist literature was purported to provide a sound foundation for feminist goals and strategies. Members' effectiveness in defining women's issues and designing approaches that meaningfully addressed these issues provides strong evidence in support of feminist claims regarding the significance of female experience as a source of knowledge.

Finally, the need for these services was great, and little else was being done to provide them. Rape victims were revictimized by the police and in the courts, and workers in social service agencies, law enforcement, and medical services witnessed female victimization and failed to act. Conventional service providers did not acknowledge or address the unique problems and needs of women clients. The successful creation of these organizations is testimony to the abysmal lack of adequate laws, policies, and services with respect to women's concerns and confirmation of the remarkable influence of the women's movement in just one decade.

ORGANIZATIONAL GROWTH BY THE MID-1980s

By the mid-1980s, each organization had expanded significantly. Their staffs were somewhat older than their founders, most being in their late 20s and 30s. Volunteers were generally in their early 20s to early 30s; many were students at the university. Some, but not many, women of color had served as staff, volunteers, and board members. Among the organizations with more than one staff member, all had some staff with advanced degrees, some with BAs, and some who had not attended college. Overall, only 40% of the staff had advanced degrees. Most, but not all, of the other staff had graduated from college. All of these organizations achieved credibility and high levels of effectiveness without becoming dominated by professionals.

Beginning in 1982, through the block grant process, Women Reaching Women was funded by the State of Wisconsin Bureau of Alcohol and Other Drug Abuse. The project director was the organization's only full-time paid position. Four of their 25 chapter coordinators were funded part-time through local AODA agencies or councils. Some county chapters were housed within mental health centers or county human services departments. Some operated out of women's centers, others out of women's homes. Those chapters with local sponsoring agencies were provided with office and meeting space, telephones, postage, and photocopying facilities. The other chapters relied on their own local fund-raising activities (garage sales, bake sales, individual donations) and the ability of their members to provide gasoline, refreshments, and supplies.

The other four organizations had successfully increased their funding and diversified their sources of funding. ARC House and the Rape Crisis Center were funded primarily through purchase of service contracts. Almost 80% of ARC House's funding was from the State Division of Corrections; it also received contracts from the City of Madison's Human Services Commission and the Dane County Board of Public Welfare. The Rape Crisis Center received over 80% of its funding from the city's Human Services Commission, the Dane County Board of Public Welfare, and the Dane County Community Mental Health Board; about 17% of its funding was from private fund-raising.

Just over 30% of Advocates for Battered Women's budget was provided by state funds earmarked for domestic violence programs. Contracts with the city and county provided about 40% of its funding, and United Way provided about 23%. Only about 5% of Advocates for Battered Women's total budget came from private sources. Women's Transit Authority was funded by a grant from the city (30%), various sources within the University of Wisconsin-Madison (40%), and through private fund-raising (30%). Both ARC House and Advocates for Battered Women had expanded their facilities, largely by securing Community Development Block Grant funding.

By the mid-1980s, the Rape Crisis Center had expanded from four full-time staff to eight full-time and two three-quarter-time staff and had approximately 45 volunteers. Women's Transit Authority increased from three half-time to three full-time paid coordinators who worked with approximately 130 to 150 volunteer dispatchers and drivers, providing over 80 rides per night.

The project director of Women Reaching Women worked with 25 county chapters. Some chapters consisted of only a few volunteers; others had as many as 40. Overall, approximately 300 women served as volunteers; most were nonprofessionals.

Advocates for Battered Women began with nine staff positions, eight full-time and one part-time, and provided shelter to eight women and children. In 1982, it purchased two adjacent three-story houses. The shelter housed 16 women and children and provided space for the approximately 40 volunteers who staffed the crisis line and worked with the residents. The second building contained offices for the 11 paid staff (nine full-time and two 80% time), a large meeting room, and a basement playroom for children's groups.

ARC House began as a halfway house for female criminal offenders, only the second such facility in the state of Wisconsin. In 1979, it became a state-licensed community-based residential treatment facility for female offenders. That same year, ARC House added a drug and alcohol abuse component to its program and expanded its facility so that some women could bring their children with them. Initially housing up to eight women, by the end of 1979, it housed up to 10 women and three children. In 1985, ARC House became a state-certified AODA residential treatment facility. By this time, its staff had increased from five to seven full-time positions.

As they looked back, in every organization members were amazed at what they and their predecessors had accomplished, given how little experience they had in the beginning stages and how few resources were initially available.

> The thing that still hits me the strongest is what our beliefs were then. We believed that this could happen. In 1971, we believed that sisterhood was powerful. Now, we know it was. What we believed, we now know is fact. (RCC)

As pioneers, members of these five organizations had to create their own models for translating feminist ideals and ideology into workable services and structures. Their impulses to create new organizations flowed from their evolving feminist consciousness and their desire to create social change on behalf of women in their community. Feminism provided the framework within which they defined their goals, structured their activities, and evaluated the worth of their work. They moved forward with dedication and a strong sense of community, and from their sense of community, they derived their sense of power and the confidence to proceed.

Chapter Two

The Defining Principles of Feminist Service Organizations

It takes a tremendous amount of courage to be able to implement ideology. (ARC)

Members of these five organizations were well aware of the multiple and sometimes conflicting perspectives regarding the attitudes and behaviors that constituted "being feminist." Nonetheless, as I reviewed women's references to "feminism" and "being feminist" throughout their interviews, it became evident that they held similar views regarding the principles that defined their organizations as feminist. These core principles included (1) women helping women; (2) understanding gender inequality as a source of women's problems; (3) promoting both individual and social change for women; (4) empowering consumers through consciousness-raising, self-help, and sisterhood; and (5) empowering members through service work and egalitarian work structures. These five principles shaped members' understanding of problems, the services they developed to address problems, and the methods they used to deliver services. They influenced decisions about the roles and responsibilities of staff, volunteers, and board members; funding; and decision-making processes.

The features within each of these principles are among those discussed in the literature on feminist organizations (Ferree and Martin, 1995; Martin, 1990; Riger, 1994). In these five organizations, however, these particular features were highlighted and clustered in specific ways to constitute five overarching principles. Further, in each organization, these principles were interpreted and applied differently, based on the goals and politics of its members, the nature of its services, and the political and organizational context within which it developed. This chapter provides an overview of these principles. The following chapters discuss the issues and dilemmas related to members' incorporation of these principles.

WOMEN HELPING WOMEN

It's a feminist organization because it is premised on the whole idea of women helping other women. (WTA)

Among feminists in the 1970s and early 1980s, the phrase *women helping women* embodied hopes for and celebration of female autonomy and control. *Women helping women* signaled feminism's emphasis on women's helping one another as a means of counteracting their social powerlessness and vulnerability. The meaning of *women helping women* was not simply that organizations were developed by women to benefit women. Participants saw themselves as providing important models of what women could accomplish, thus challenging gender stereotypes that defined women as passive, weak, and frivolous. These organizations symbolized women's taking power and the belief that women can and should help one another to create social change on behalf of women as a group.

Women helping women was critically important in each of these organizations, but it carried different meanings. In some organizations, the crucial points were that women were delivering services to women and that women were the dominant force. For others, it was essential that *only* women delivered services and that *only* women had decision-making power.

In Advocates for Battered Women, only women worked with battered women, and only women held administrative positions. Male volunteers and work-study students assisted children in the shelter; a men's collective provided childcare for community women attending Advocates' support groups; men helped with property maintenance; and men served on the board of directors.

It's validating knowing that a group of women can get paid to do important work. In terms of the women who use our services, and also for people outside the organization that we work with, it's models for, "Hey, we're doing this, and it's working fine." In terms of changing society, it's women showing that it can be done.

There was usually one male counselor in ARC House, and men served on the board. Still, *women helping women* was a central theme.

Having the primary models on the staff be women and having the leadership of the organization be women is feminist. Although there have been men on the board and the staff, they've never been in leadership roles. They've been important and supportive participants, but they have not been president of the board or director of the project.

Similarly, although some men served on the organization's advisory committees and as speakers, Women Reaching Women's primary focus was on *women helping women*.

> The organization is feminist because it's women working together and supporting one another. If we weren't encouraged to believe in ourselves and believe that we as women have power, I don't know that we could follow through with all the things we need to do. We come up with a lot of opposition.

Women's Transit Authority and the Rape Crisis Center maintained a stance most consistent with a radical feminist perspective. Women's Transit Authority stressed not that women were helping women, but that *only* women were helping women. The organization's primary purpose was to provide women with the opportunity to work together against sexual assault. A few men had helped with office work, male graphic artists had prepared advertisements, and a male CPA had set up its bookkeeping system and had handled its annual audit on an unpaid basis for many years. However, its services centered on its being *women* working to prevent rape.

> Its main point is that it's by women and for women. It gives women a sense of strength to know that it's all of us doing this for each other, and that strength makes women feel stronger.
> So often, we're told to look to men for help, especially if we're in danger. I have male roommates, and they don't always lock the door. That partly comes from them thinking, "But I'm in the house. I'll protect you." It doesn't make me feel any better. I don't want to have to depend on them being around for me to feel safe.

The Rape Crisis Center stressed that it was working with women on behalf of women and, moreover, that the Rape Crisis Center was "a woman-identified organization, both in philosophy and in behavior, women's concerns first and foremost." The term "woman-identified" was first introduced in a position paper, "The Woman Identified Woman," written by the Radicalesbians in 1970 to explain the political significance of lesbianism and the common concerns of feminists and lesbians (Radicalesbians, 1973). Over time, the term was increasingly used to describe feminists, lesbian and nonlesbian, who were deeply invested in caring relationships with other women and in resisting male domination in their personal and political lives (Rich, 1980; Wandersee, 1988).

> The women who are taking initiative to use their power within the organization, those women are lesbian or bisexual or woman-identified, meaning that men are

not a primary focal point. They derive most of their support from other women, even though they may be married or have a boyfriend.

Their identity comes from being women and being with one another, rather than from an identity given to us by men.

In every organization, this principle signified the political investment of feminists. *Women helping women* represented the decision of feminists to create organizations in which their being women helping other women symbolized feminist goals and at the same time served as a means of achieving these goals.

UNDERSTANDING GENDER INEQUALITY AS A SOURCE OF WOMEN'S PROBLEMS

It's difficult for women who are troubled by drugs and alcohol to come forward. The social stigma is far greater for a woman than for a man. As long as we keep making women into either madonnas or whores, they're not going to get the help that they need. If they're whores, they deserve to have their kids taken away. If they're madonnas, who needs treatment? It's a problem. (WRW)

For many years, the tenet *the personal is political* provided the foundation for feminists' understanding of women's problems. Through discussions in small groups, women identified their common experiences as victims of rape, incest, battering, gender bias, and discrimination. They realized that the problems they had viewed as personal and private were actually shared and political. In these groups, feminists developed understandings about how the disparities in power between women and men served to limit women's economic and social freedom and promoted and protected the victimization of women by men. It is now well documented that women's personal issues and problems are inextricably connected to larger social, political, and economic structures and cultural beliefs (Amott and Matthaei, 1991; Kirk and Okazawa-Rey, 2001; Pleck, 1987; Sapiro, 1999; Spain and Bianchi, 1996).

Three of these organizations were part of early feminist efforts to address the relationships between women's subordinate social status and their being victims of physical and sexual abuse. In Advocates for Battered Women, the Rape Crisis Center, and Women's Transit Authority, gender inequality was defined as *the* core problem. From a feminist perspective, male domination is the root cause of woman abuse, and all women are at risk.

If women had an equal footing in the world, you wouldn't have wife abuse. Not only are we here to provide emergency shelter, which these women need, but beyond that, we want to make a statement about the status of women in society. (ABW)

We believe that sexual assault grows out of and is perpetuated by patriarchal society. Women have no power in this society, and thus are commonly used as vehicles for other people's violence. Society isn't responding to the violence against women in a more effective way because we are women. That's evident in the sentences that rapists get and how victims are treated by the police. Society doesn't think sexual assault is so bad because women don't have the power in our society. (RCC)

Recognizing that women need a safe environment is feminist, because it's realizing that women are more vulnerable in our society. (WTA)

In contrast, patriarchy is not viewed as the root of women's substance abuse or criminal behavior, and not all women are at risk for these problems by virtue of being female. In ARC House and Women Reaching Women, negative cultural views of women were understood to have a profound influence on, but not to cause, the problems they addressed. For example, female offenders and substance abusers are likely to have low self-esteem and feelings of dependency, characteristics that are promoted and reinforced by traditional female socialization, female victimization, and gender inequality (Abbott, 1995; Chesney-Lind and Shelden, 1992). In these two organizations, members discussed how sexism shaped the nature of the problems experienced by the women who used their services.

Women offenders are typical in terms of feminization of poverty, being victimized, having a lot of self-concept issues. If there is a women's issue, they've experienced it, multiple, multiple, multiple. (ARC)

Over 80% of them are incest victims. You see the worst exaggeration of everything that affects women. Feminism addresses directly the problems that they have. For the women offenders, it's key to their whole problem. (ARC)

Women Reaching Women is focused on one problem, but it's a cultural problem. One of the reasons that women weren't getting into treatment is because for so long people didn't even think that women would ever have problems like this. It doesn't go with the image of women to have chemical problems. It's all mixed in with how society views women and their role. (WRW)

Women are trained in many, many ways to be dependent, so it makes sense that women would gravitate toward substance abuse. If a woman buys into our culture and becomes dependent on someone to come along and rescue her, to take care of her, and that does not work out for her, many times that woman will gravitate toward substance abuse because she begins to see it as a dependency that she can control. (WRW)

In these organizations, understanding the dynamics of female oppression provided the foundation for assessing needs, establishing goals, and determining the nature of their programs and services.

PROMOTING BOTH INDIVIDUAL
AND SOCIAL CHANGE FOR WOMEN

The goals are not just to provide social services. The goals are social change. They are specifically to improve women's status vis a vis men, to rid their lives of sexist violence. I don't think you can end domestic violence without ending sexism. (ABW)

All five organizations developed an agenda for personal and social change by tackling women's problems on three levels. At one level, they assisted individual women by helping them deal with the tangible effects of gender inequality. Their goals were to increase women's individual power by reducing their economic and social dependency, feelings of hopelessness and helplessness, and victimization. At another level, they sought to change the policies and practices that directly affected the consumers of their services and other women in the community. They focused on changing the attitudes of and information available to professionals, on altering conventional methods of dealing with and treating women, and on advocating for increased and more appropriate services. In this way, they worked to alter the conditions that reinforced the status quo. At the broadest level, their purpose was to increase women's power by changing community attitudes and public policy.

As explicitly political symbols of women's taking power over their own lives, Advocates for Battered Women, the Rape Crisis Center, and Women's Transit Authority consistently asserted their dual missions of promoting personal as well as social change. Their goals included changing social attitudes about and behaviors toward rape victims and battered women and altering the social circumstances that promoted female victimization. Achievement of these goals would benefit all women.

In Advocates, the number one goal is to provide safety for the women and children. With that safety, we provide information to help them make some changes in their lives. Another goal is community education. The third goal is social change. There is a great emphasis placed on making sure that we're doing something in the area of social change, to make sure that violence against women becomes a community issue and not just an issue for staff people in Advocates for Battered Women.

Rape Crisis's goals are to provide direct services to victims of sexual assault and to those close to them and to change the conditions in our society that allow sexual assault to continue . . . We do a lot of community education about what sexual assault is and the function it serves in our culture. We try to teach other service providers our philosophy about sexual assault and about how to treat victims of sexual assault . . . Other goals are to teach women skills to protect themselves against sexual assault, to see that assailants are prosecuted, and to see that laws are made to keep men from assaulting again.

The goals of Transit are first to act as a rape-prevention ride service by providing nighttime transportation to women so that they won't have to stand on a street corner waiting for a bus that won't come for an hour, so that they won't have to hitchhike after dark, so that they won't have to accept rides from male acquaintances with whom they feel uncomfortable. We're protecting women and preventing sexual assaults. We also have the goal of educating women about rape prevention . . . Another part is that Transit has always lobbied for better services for women, like for better bus service.

ARC House and Women Reaching Women began with more individual-oriented agendas and progressed slowly to push for change in the systems that directly affected their consumers. Their goals centered on meeting the needs of particular groups of women.

The goal is for ARC House to make changes at a lot of levels. It's to make a change within the system by providing alternatives to women. It's to facilitate change within the community in how they address the needs of women offenders. We've been doing a lot of education around the special needs of women offenders. And it's to produce change in individual women. Going in and out of the criminal justice system, there was nothing to facilitate change for them in their lifestyles.

One of the primary goals of Women Reaching Women is to do direct outreach to women who are affected by alcohol or drug abuse, to get them into treatment or to provide an environment where they can grow as women and move beyond the problem. But without feminist principles, I don't see this project as being worth a whole lot. Without feminist principles, you can attempt to get more women into treatment, but you're putting them into a treatment system that is not set up to help them become healthy. Without doing something about the treatment system as it now exists, you're trying to help more women get into a dysfunctional system. I don't see how that helps women.

Empowering women is the process and product of feminist service organizations. In addition to their symbolic and political importance, feminist organizations provide opportunities for women to exert power and realize their ability to have a significant influence over their own lives and the lives of other women. They provide a tangible means of achieving the feminist goal of empowerment for the women served as well as for their members. Women empowered themselves as they created new services and organizational structures. They empowered women in their communities through their work with individual women, through their work with other service agencies, by advocating for changes in state laws and policies, and through their public-education efforts.

Feminist analyses of the concept of empowerment have observed that the term "empowerment" is now often defined solely in terms of a sense of personal agency, as a psychological state of mind (Bookman and Morgen, 1988; Kitzinger, 1991). Women are considered to be empowered when they *feel* more powerful, self-confident, and effective. This view assumes that if women *feel* more powerful, they will be more powerful. The problem with this perspective is that, when power is viewed solely as a state of mind, the psychological states of individual women become the sole targets of change. This approach assumes that problems lie within individual women, that individual women are responsible for the solutions, and that individual solutions are possible. By ignoring the structural and cultural aspects of women's problems, such an approach implicitly blames women for their own powerlessness and victimization.

Psychologizing the concept of empowerment fails to take into account that women's individual change efforts are restricted by the powerlessness of women as a group and by structural constraints based on class, sexual orientation, and race. Empowering women from a feminist perspective focuses on helping women gain more control over their own lives by improving their personal sense of efficacy *and* their abilities to work individually and collectively to influence the social, political, and economic conditions of their lives as women (Bookman and Morgen, 1988; Bricker-Jenkins and Hooyman, 1986; GlenMaye, 1998; Gutierrez, 1991; Hawxhurst and Morrow, 1984).

Along with their statements about the importance of empowering women, members commented on the processes and social interactions through which empowerment is best attained. For feminists, goals and the means chosen to reach them are of equal importance, and both must be consistent with feminist values (Bricker-Jenkins and Hooyman, 1986; Riddle, 1978). Thus, empowerment as a goal is attainable only through what are defined and constructed as empowering social relationships: "Stressing the links between the personal and the political led women to conclude that . . . changed consciousness and changed definition of the self could only occur in conjunction with a restructuring of the social relationships in which each person was involved" (Hartsock, 1974, p. 14).

In feminist service organizations, two types of social relationships are of concern: the relationships between members and consumers and the relationships among members. Empowering members and the women who used their services could not be realized through conventional hierarchical and authoritarian forms of influence and control. Creating empowering experiences within the organization was essential for achieving the larger goal of empowering women outside of the organization.

EMPOWERING CONSUMERS THROUGH
CONSCIOUSNESS-RAISING, SELF-HELP, AND SISTERHOOD

> The purpose is to provide services that empower individuals to get through this experience and to learn that they are a good resource for themselves, as opposed to us providing the services and having them dependent on us and feeling like the only way they got through this is because this person helped them. The way they got through this is because they have strengths and they have skills. (RCC)

Empowering consumers through consciousness-raising, self-help, and sisterhood was emphasized most in Advocates for Battered Women and the Rape Crisis Center. This principle was also stressed in Women Reaching Women but in a less politicized way. ARC House worked to empower women through consciousness-raising and sisterhood, but the nature of its work limited its reliance on self-help. Women's Transit Authority primarily represented the principle of self-help.

Consciousness-Raising and Self-Help as Sources of Empowerment

As discussed in the introduction of this book, consciousness-raising is a key element of feminist practice. It assumes that it is empowering for women to understand the ways in which discriminatory employment practices, sex-biased community attitudes, and restrictive family roles create barriers and limit their options for change. Empowered by this knowledge, women can begin taking charge of their own lives, reducing their powerlessness by choosing among behaviors and family and work roles based on their own values, priorities, and needs. In Advocates for Battered Women, ARC House, the Rape Crisis Center, and Women Reaching Women, members helped women assess the relationships between social roles, structural realities, the problems they were confronting, and the changes they were considering.

In Advocates for Battered Women, ARC House, and the Rape Crisis Center, for example, members helped consumers understand the connections between woman abuse and female powerlessness. They hoped that women would come to understand that they were not responsible for their abuse. For their own psychological well-being and appropriate decision making, consumers needed to reject social myths that justified rape, battering, sexual harassment, and incest by blaming women for provoking or participating in the abuse.

> Our counseling is seen as political, to have women understand it was not something they brought on themselves, to help them get angry at the damage that was done to them instead of personalizing it. (RCC)

Our goal is to let her know that she's not responsible for the abuse. We emphasize that "You are not sick. This is happening to millions of women all over the world and changes can be made." (ABW)

We want women to realize the ways in which they've been victimized. We want them to take responsibility and feel powerful in their lives and be assertive, but not to blame themselves for things that are women's issues. (ARC)

Awareness of societal expectations and constraints helped women not to blame themselves for problems associated with being a woman in a sexist society, and to use that knowledge to consider new choices and to assume responsibility for making healthy and self-affirming decisions.

Although most members did not use the term "self-help," many of their comments reflected this principle. In Advocates for Battered Women, the Rape Crisis Center, Women's Transit Authority, and Women Reaching Women, members referred frequently to their providing means for consumers to identify and pursue their own solutions to their problems. They believed that self-help empowers women by helping them to recognize and utilize their own strengths. Relying on self-help assumes that women are capable of making their own decisions and that helping women is best accomplished by assisting them in becoming more powerful rather than maintaining their dependence on others. Self-help demonstrates the belief that women are capable of being autonomous and should be in control of their own lives. At the same time, from a feminist perspective, self-help must be understood in the context of consciousness-raising. Just as women need to become more powerful, they also need to remain aware that society places severe restrictions on their ability to control the decisions that affect their lives. As Susan Schechter explained: "Without material resources—housing, jobs, and sufficient incomes—empowerment as a universal goal is unreachable. If women are not aware of this, there is a danger that self-help can turn into self-blame, as women fault themselves for being unable to control their lives" (1982, p. 253).

The concept of women's self-help embodies another feminist principle that emerged out of the early CR groups, "the authority of personal experience" (Eisenstein, 1983). This principle asserts that "one's own experience, rather than the abstract formulation of some 'expert,' shall be the primary source of new ideas" (Carden, 1974, p. 86). Emphasizing the authority of personal experience reinforces women's efforts to reject prevailing cultural beliefs and socially sanctioned authorities and, instead, to discover and trust their own understanding of their experience as women. Consistent with this principle, members reported that they did not take on the role of expert; they did not assume that they knew the best or most appropriate outcomes for the women who used their services.

Also, their emphasis on self-help required members to maintain nonelitist relationships with consumers. Feminism's rejection of personal and political systems of domination translated into commitments to reduce power differences among women. Members worked to maximize each consumer's ability to take power for herself; members stressed the importance of their remaining nonjudgmental and supportive.

In Women's Transit Authority, self-help was a major purpose of its services. Throughout their interviews, members emphasized that they did not and would not make judgments about why women used their services. They saw themselves as empowering women by providing choices and helping women be less vulnerable, thereby "allowing women to have the independence that they have a right to."

> We're here to serve all women. We don't make value judgments about who deserves our service. We don't say, "This is an acceptable need. We'll take a person to a class, but we won't take them to a bar." We let the consumers decide whether or not they need the mobility, whether or not it's an appropriate use of the service. That is an example of the feminist philosophy of giving women the power to choose for themselves.

Advocates for Battered Women and the Rape Crisis Center also explicitly referred to empowering consumers through self-help. They provided women with information and resources, but they did not assume a decision-making role. In their interviews, members emphasized being nonjudgmental and supportive regardless of the decisions consumers made, and they acknowledged how difficult this stance could be.

The goals of Advocates for Battered Women were to make sure that women realized that they were not responsible for the violence. Otherwise, members would advocate for and provide support to battered women in ways determined by the women themselves.

> Basically, we follow their lead about what they think they need and what they want to do and how we can help them. Women who use our services feel validated, that they have rights and they can make their own decisions, and that people are there to support them.
>
> There are an incredible amount of frustrations working with certain battered women, battered women that you see six and seven times, who continue to go back. Yet, there's always an emphasis that you need to keep any frustration that you feel out of your work. That's a strong feminist principle, that every woman knows what's best for herself, and she should make changes in her own time and in her own way.

Similarly, the Rape Crisis Center sought not to influence consumers in any particular direction, other than to assure them that they were not responsible for the assault; that rape is a crime of violence, not a sex crime; and that women could and should make decisions on their own.

We believe that the act of sexual assault takes choice and power away from women, so our function is not to tell women what to do, but to try and give them back some of that power by not taking a stance on what they choose and being available to fight for whatever it is that they choose to do. It's basically a philosophy of giving back the control that was taken away from them as much as possible.

Sometimes I want rapists put away for a hundred years or more, and then I have to say, "Wait a minute. I'm supposed to be an unbiased source of information. I'm supposed to advocate for whatever it is this person wants. If she wants him prosecuted, then that's what I want. If she wants the case dropped, then that's what I want." I can't afford to get invested in hanging rapists, therapizing rapists, letting them all go, because I have to change gears every day. I'm supposed to be an amplification of her viewpoint. If she wants to not do anything with law enforcement, just get therapy, then that's what I want.

In Advocates for Battered Women, the Rape Crisis Center, and Women's Transit Authority, members frequently referred to "empowering" the women who used their services. In contrast, specific references to "empowering" women were rare in Women Reaching Women and ARC House interviews, perhaps due to the meanings of this concept at that time. Although "empowerment" is now a popular term, in the 1970s and 1980s, it was used primarily by those whose work was specifically designed to alter oppressive political, social, and economic conditions. Empowerment referred to helping oppressed groups organize to become more proactive and effective in dealing with the personal and social consequences of discrimination and prejudice, thus gaining more control over their own lives (Solomon, 1976).

The feminists who worked in the Rape Crisis Center, Women's Transit Authority, and Advocates for Battered Women were among the activists who used the concept of empowerment to capture the political nature of their work. Their goals included challenging the belief systems and social policies that maintained male domination of women. In contrast, the work of ARC House and Women Reaching Women did not emphasize broad-based social, political, and economic change. Consequently, the women who were interested in working in these two organizations were less likely to be part of the community of activists that first spoke in terms of empowerment.

A second and related factor is that empowerment was first used to address individual problems that stemmed from being oppressed. Male violence against women was viewed as an expression and consequence of the unequal power of women and men; and rape victims and battered women were not held responsible for their victimization. However, female offenders and chemically dependent women generally were viewed as having individual problems due to factors such as disease, psychological distress, moral defects, and dysfunctional families, and their problematic behaviors were addressed through treatment, confinement, or a combination of the two. At the time of these interviews, the language of empowerment had not yet been widely applied to arenas in which psychological and behavioral changes were the primary focus.

Nonetheless, ARC House and Women Reaching Women shared the goal of empowering women without analyzing their work in these particular terms. Desired increases in self-esteem and self-efficacy were not based on adjustment or conformity to established social roles for women. Members of these organizations empowered women by helping them understand how the social, political, and economic circumstances of women as a group had shaped their lives, contributed to their problems, and would constrain their options for change and by helping them explore both traditional and nontraditional alternatives. With awareness that women's lack of social power can generate passivity and dependence, they encouraged women to be more autonomous in their personal lives and as clients.

In Women Reaching Women, female empowerment included helping women feel more self-confident and able to "take charge" of their lives on their own terms, based on their own understanding of their needs and goals. Their support groups were designed to help women find their own ways to get well and to stay well, and feminist values were viewed as consistent with these goals.

> Women Reaching Women is a feminist organization because it's encouraging women to become persons in their own right, to take charge of their lives and to make some changes.
>
> We encourage women to trust their guts. It's helping women believe in themselves. Women have been told for so long that the only things they're good at are cleaning the toilet and fixing meals and burping the kids. It's so hard to come out and believe in yourself.
>
> Our basic goals are getting women well, not "well" in the traditional cultural context, but "well" by that woman's definition. It's promoting healthy lifestyles for women within her definition, not within what society has laid out for her.
>
> Feminism to me is advocating for what women need and want. If it's to be a single parent, we help them on that road. If it's to be a traditional housewife, we help them with that. That to me is what feminism is, helping women find their own self-actualization.

Women Reaching Women emphasized that the women who used its services were expected to set their own goals and to choose among their options on their own terms, with newly found self-confidence and self-esteem.

Much like Women Reaching Women, ARC House focused on improving women's self-concepts and independence through changing their views of themselves, including changing their views of themselves as women. ARC House wanted to help women attain more power in their work and personal relationships, to become more emotionally and economically independent. The goal of empowering women is implicit in these goals. However, ARC House could not rely on self-help as a means to reach these goals.

Empowering women through self-help was consistent with the voluntary nature of women's participation in the services offered by Advocates for Battered Women, the Rape Crisis Center, Women's Transit Authority, and Women Reaching Women. In these four organizations, no external constraints were imposed on members' shifting decision-making responsibility to the women who used their services. However, serving as an alternative to jail or prison and as a halfway house for women leaving incarceration, ARC House was dealing with women whose autonomy was severely limited by the terms of their placement in ARC House. Given the constraints imposed on them by being a part of the criminal justice system and based on their own decisions to create more structured services, fully nonauthoritarian relationships between staff and clients were not possible. However, ARC House staff worked to make their relationships with clients as nonelitist and supportive as possible.

> In Corrections, there's a lot of we-they between the law enforcement people and the clients. We try to break through the we-they dynamic and develop more of an equal peer.
>
> A whole other attitude that's feminist is our dealing with them on a level of support and caring. We do a lot of building up, a lot of caring, a lot of touching and laughing and crying together.
>
> I'm a facilitator rather than an authority who knows the right way to do something and assumes that I have the answer. I see myself as having certain skills and resources and a certain flexibility that I can then apply and give my client more choices.

Members of ARC House helped women identify their own needs and choose among the various ways in which they could successfully fulfill the broad objectives set by Corrections.

Sisterhood as a Source of Empowerment

Members of these five organizations believed that, given their shared experiences as women, they were similar to the women who used their services. Women's descriptions of their attitudes toward consumers encompassed feminist concepts of sisterhood, that is, "the genuine attempt to understand and to establish common bonds with other women" (Carden, 1974, p. 86). Although few women used the term "sisterhood," this concept was evident in the four organizations that provided counseling, support, and advocacy. In ARC House, Advocates for Battered Women, the Rape Crisis Center, and Women Reaching Women, members asserted that they worked to establish nonelitist relationships with the women who used their services based on notions of shared problems and shared experience, that is, based on sisterhood. Their beliefs in shared female experience mitigated the perceived status differences between members and consumers, thereby reinforcing feminist principles of equality.

It's important to look at all the things that create each of us being the battered women that we are. I'm not physically battered, but I buy into situations that batter me in other ways, by giving up my power and my strength. (ABW)

Lots of the discussions revolved around things like we could all be clients. We wanted to minimize those distinctions where possible. The women who came to us were our next-door neighbors and friends. We were trying to provide services in a way that was respectful of clients, that they were us and we were them. (RCC)

We have a strong belief in sharing our issues as women, letting them know that we've had difficulties in similar areas . . . There's a lot of similarities in terms of the bigger issues. Economic issues affect all women. Battery affects all women . . . It's like you see yourself. So many of the dynamics of their lives are so similar to all of our lives. So many of their struggles are so similar. (ARC)

One of the basic chapter goals is that we want to help women to stay healthy and stay well. The way we do that is strictly through peer relationships with the women. It's not a one-upmanship, one-down position at all. It's women helping other women on an equal level, and it's very supportive in its atmosphere. (WRW)

While they touted member-consumer commonalities, members also asserted the limits of presumptions of shared experience. Consumers were considered to be experts on their own lives. Moreover, with time, members recognized that assumptions of shared experience masked significant differences among women and that they needed to move beyond their own direct experience to address differences based on age, class, race, and sexual preference.

EMPOWERING MEMBERS THROUGH SERVICE WORK AND EGALITARIAN WORK STRUCTURES

In terms of philosophy, Women's Transit has always operated pretty collectively, with a lot of sharing of power, which is an important feminist principle. I don't think the volunteers would want to come in and just drive or staff if they didn't feel that they had some sharing of power in the organization. It encourages that sense of ownership. She feels part of a larger whole.

In feminist service organizations, goals and services are designed to shift control and power to women, empowering the women who work in the organization as well as the women they serve. Through their participation in service work, women attain new understandings of female oppression and can act to challenge misogynist public policies, to transform community attitudes in a profeminist direction, and to empower other women. Also, organizational life was constructed so that members would be empowered by having meaningful control over their lives as workers (Hartsock, 1976; MacDonald, 1976; Riger, 1984). In the three explicitly feminist organizations, member empowerment was directly addressed.

> Advocates is structured so that decisions are made collectively. That comes out of wanting to equally empower all women, to not use power in a coercive way.
>
> The women-only nature of Women's Transit comes from a feminist understanding of the empowerment that comes from working in women-only groups. At the end of the night, I knew that there were 50 or 60 women who had freedom to travel the city. That was rewarding. It made me feel more powerful. I was helping to make the city safe because I was joining with other women.
>
> At Rape Crisis, we're all responsible. We can't sit back and let somebody else figure it out. It's stressful, but it's also empowering. One of the best things about this job for me, a job working under feminist principles, is that you know you're important. You're responsible, that's for sure.

Although members of Women Reaching Women did not use the term "empowerment" to describe their work, they did state that participating in their groups enhanced volunteers' strength, self-confidence, and leadership skills, all qualities that contribute to female empowerment. Also, chapter members had considerable power over their activities.

> I have seen women come into this project, I was one of them, the real quiet ones. They think that, well, maybe they can fill out the monthly postcards. Pretty soon they're taking gigantic steps. They're taking risks. The project lets volunteers take small risks one step at a time, to start to realize that they have potential, that as women, they have power.
>
> Most of the decisions are done through a group process. We don't have a hierarchy type of thing. We usually work fairly well together. Women with drug and alcohol problems have issues of dependency and issues of inadequacies. This gives them an opportunity to be part of what they haven't had. They can be part of the decision-making process.

Similarly, ARC House staff linked the importance of their participation in decision making to feminism.

In terms of staff and what we believe in, our process is primarily consensus decision making, and I consider that to be a feminist model. Everybody's contributing in forming the program. If a decision is made, it's almost always that we've hassled it out together. We try to give one another equal power as much as possible.

The preceding principles and the underlying tenets that they represent defined the core dimensions of these service organizations. Members shared the conviction that change must occur at both the personal and societal levels to meaningfully improve the conditions of women's lives and held female empowerment to be a central goal for both members and consumers. They believed strongly in the importance of *women helping women,* and they advanced feminist goals by working with women for women according to feminist principles.

FROM PRINCIPLES TO PRACTICE

Major failures? I don't think that we've failed in any way. We've made mistakes, but those mistakes were made because we took a risk. We took a risk that no one else wanted to. We're always learning from our mistakes, and we'll take the risk to do it. (ARC)

Throughout the development of their organizations, these activists were weaving intricate patterns of creation, implementation, and evaluation. They moved forward on multiple, often seemingly contradictory, always interconnecting paths. In their relationships with other community organizations, they worked in opposition in the same moments that they enjoined cooperation. With the women they served, they assured assistance in the same moments that they derived the nature of that assistance. With one another, they made decisions and accepted responsibilities in the same moments that they learned about managing the internal workings of an organization. Within each of these challenges, members needed to make continuing judgments as to how they might incorporate feminist principles and practices.

Tactical questions were numerous. To what extent would short-range decisions make the attainment of long-range goals more likely or less likely? Which possible applications of feminist ideology were unrealistic or unmanageable, and which were very difficult but attainable? What were the unforeseeable and unintended consequences of compromising a strongly held value? Especially in Advocates for Battered Women, the Rape Crisis Center, and Women's Transit Authority, fears of undermining feminist values contributed to a reluctance to compromise.

Sometimes when people are attached to an ideology, they fear that if they give an inch, if they put their toe in the water, somebody's going to shove them into the lake, whether they want to be there or not. (ABW)

Members most feared being co-opted, that is, becoming indistinguishable from conventional organizations, delivering services but not in the context of an overall political vision. The threat of co-optation increased as these organizations attracted public funding and successfully coordinated their efforts with conventional social services. Successful community ties legitimized their efforts, increased their influence in the community, and provided the resources and support necessary for their survival. However, working in close association with established systems could reduce their ability to pursue feminist goals, weaken their ties to the feminist community, and ultimately lead to their becoming indistinguishable from mainstream services (Ahrens, 1980; Morgen, 1986; Sullivan, 1982). Their challenge was to create a feminist space for the benefit of feminist and nonfeminist women with funding and assistance from the very patriarchal systems that they were trying to dislodge. In fact, none of these organizations saw themselves as having been co-opted, but all were aware of the extent to which cooperation necessitated compromise and that compromise could lead to co-optation.

Since Advocates is doing more and more work with the welfare system and the legal system, there's a concern that we don't get too close to people within those systems, that we be cautious not to become co-opted, and that the more you work with those systems, the more likely it is that you might become co-opted. We don't want to be seen as adversarial to the system, but at the same time, we need to have a healthy skepticism for what they're saying they're going to do for battered women. (ABW)

It's a compromise between insisting on certain things and being proactive versus looking at what they're demanding and meeting those demands, and getting some kind of balance between those two things. I don't think you can do one or the other. If you go totally with what you want to do, you can survive for a few years maybe, but you won't survive long-term. Whereas if you buy totally into what they're wanting, you might as well give up anyway, because you're just buying into what already is. (ARC)

After all these years, Rape Crisis has not been co-opted. We are not part of the district attorney's office or an emergency room or a mental health center. It's made it very difficult sometimes to survive because we haven't done that, but that is one way that we have put our beliefs into operation. (RCC)

When Transit first started, it was difficult to cope with the constraints and demands that the university and government placed on the organization, to try and meet their demands for accountability and still maintain our principles. But Transit has found their demands, although at times difficult, something that they

were able to cope with. They haven't had to co-opt themselves to make someone else happy. (WTA)

If we compromised any of our values along the way, it was because we felt
that, in the long run, it was going to be better. The outcome is that we did have
a positive impact on how the field itself views the problem. By taking the slow
road, we did a good job changing people's minds. (WRW)

Through extensive, prolonged, and often difficult deliberations, members
balanced their ideals with the exigencies of consumer needs, funding requirements, and organizational effectiveness. Organizational goals, services,
and structures developed as members dealt with predictable and unanticipated
problems and worked to incorporate their emerging and diverse notions of
feminism. As detailed in the following chapters, their approaches to feminist
practice emerged over time, with these five core principles guiding their decision making.

Chapter Three

Promoting an Equality Based on Difference

> That's the part of the feminist thing I like. We're not following the rules and regs of men. We're doing it our way. It's a new way, different, and we find it better. (RCC)

In establishing their goals and services, members emphasized the importance of their being *women helping women*. Their organizations were developed at a time when this three-word phrase embodied a central message of the women's movement: that women can and should join with one another to create meaningful social change for women, and that important social change occurs not only by the outcomes of women's change efforts, but also by virtue of the fact that women have demonstrated that they can and will challenge the status quo and empower themselves. *Women helping women* captured the symbolic and pragmatic significance of feminist organizations.

The phrase *women helping women* did not have a consistent meaning among feminists, however. Feminists pursued significantly different strategies for "helping women," and their approaches tended to reflect significantly different views about "women" and the importance of female-male differences. In the 1970s and 1980s, these differences were commonly framed in terms of liberal feminism versus radical feminism (Donovan, 2000; Jaggar and Rothenberg, 1984, 1993; Tong, 1998).

Liberal feminism provided the foundation for the work of the large national women's rights organizations whose goals focused on promoting equality for women and men and on eliminating sexism for the benefit of both women and men. *Helping women* involved reforming established social institutions by promoting laws and policies that mandated equal treatment of women and men. Liberal feminism's emphasis on equal access and equal opportunities for women and men minimized the significance of gender differences, fore-

68

casting that equal treatment of women and men would lead to their social equality. From this perspective, defining women as different from men reinforces women's powerlessness. Minimizing the importance of gender differences challenges demeaning views of women, thus supporting goals of social equality.

In contrast, radical feminism called for the restructuring of social institutions as a precondition for gender equality. Cultural assumptions of male superiority were understood to provide the bases for female subordination in the workplace, in the community, and within the family. *Helping women* centered on transforming, not reforming, patriarchal social, economic, and political structures by incorporating the unique investments, values, and needs of women. Celebrating the positive aspects of female experience and underscoring the oppressive impact of male domination on women's lives, radical feminism accentuated sexual differences. It emphasized the unique qualities of women as a group, often extolling the superior nature of women's values, ethics, and ways of relating (Donovan, 2000; Eisenstein, 1983).

From the perspective of radical feminism, the goal of social equality is viewed with considerable skepticism. If qualities conventionally associated with women are devalued in society at large, then becoming "equal" will require that women adopt the more socially valued characteristics, that is, women will need to become more "male." Further, calls for equal opportunities generally assume that women will be gaining equal access to existing groups and organizations. Thus, women would be gaining opportunities to succeed in structures that were designed by men and that operate in accord with values and approaches conventionally associated with men. Liberal feminism's "narrow focus on formal equality with men not only ignored the fundamental problem—women's subordination within the home—it assumed that equality in an unjust society was worth fighting for" (Echols, 1989, pp. 15-16, 139).

Liberal and radical feminism were generally discussed in terms of two opposite approaches. However, both approaches have strengths and weaknesses. Minimizing differences between men and women emphasizes the positive pursuit of gender equality but understates the impact on women of existing power and status differences and the social devaluation of women's traditional values and roles. Alternatively, highlighting female-male differences discourages attempts to improve women's status in traditionally male arenas and reinforces women's position as "other" in society at large (Minow, 1990; Scott, 1990).

Notably, women in these five organizations did not adopt a dichotomous view; they discussed the significance of female equality *and* the inevitable realities of difference. Emphasizing gender differences, they challenged the status quo by radically altering understandings of the nature of women's problems and by creating woman-controlled alternatives for ameliorating these problems. Emphasizing equality and difference, they demanded equal attention and resources to meet women's unique needs.

WORKING TOWARD EQUALITY BASED ON UNDERSTANDINGS OF DIFFERENCE

Women's projects have to work twice as hard as the male projects. There seems to be a lot more scrutiny, and you have to do a lot more work for credibility. I'm really tired of the additional effort that constantly has to go into it. It's the old thing, I've finally realized. Women have to work twice as hard to get to the same level as men. (ARC)

Through their work, members helped women reject the misogynous views that pervaded society at large and develop new understandings of themselves as women living in a sexist society. By helping women discover the importance of taking control over their own lives, members sought to contribute to the more equal distribution of power among women and men. Also, they demanded equality to counter the sexism that women confronted in mainstream services. At the same time, members stressed the ways in which women's problems differed from men's, and they developed new services to address women's unique needs and concerns.

For Advocates for Battered Women, the Rape Crisis Center, and Women's Transit Authority, equal treatment, narrowly defined, was not an issue; there were no comparable groups of men with whom they needed to achieve equality. However, societal ignorance and antipathy toward the problems of women defined the impetus for their efforts. In this broader sense, members of these organizations *were* demanding equality: equal attention to the special problems that women experienced; equal access to community support, funding, and other resources; and equal opportunities to develop services that would effectively address women's different needs.

Working within male-dominated fields, issues of equality were a primary focus in ARC House and Women Reaching Women. For women in the criminal justice system and chemically dependent women, equality meant that their needs would be viewed as equally important as men's and that they would be seen as equally deserving of services. At the same time, members articulated the unique concerns of their consumers as compared with male offenders and substance abusers and developed services to address these unique concerns.

ARC House consistently asserted that women deserved equal opportunities to have their different needs met.

We're dealing with overcoming the paternalism toward women offenders, the attitude that these are fallen angels that need to be protected and that a man is going to come along and take care of them. They need the same vocational training as the men. They need the drug and alcohol programs that the men have. They need corrections industries in the prison. There's such a discrepancy in the way women and men are treated in the system. There is so little in Corrections for women . . . We've spent a lot of time fighting within Corrections to make women's needs known and seen as legitimate as, even if different from, men's, and to get resources for women offenders so they at least have equal programming and also so special needs are addressed. We are the only facility in the state that takes children, for instance, to address some of those special needs which are totally overlooked by Corrections.

With so few women offenders [4%] in the entire system, it's very easy for them to not be visible. It's very easy to interpret the needs of the women through knowledge of what it's taken to work with the men. Most of the people in the system are only acquainted with the needs of men. In addition, most of the decision makers are men, so issues of who is a criminal tend to be defined in male terms. The way the laws are set up is very male-dominated. By that I mean, well, typical, a prostitute gets picked up, but the john doesn't. That's the most obvious.

Most of the men have probably fathered children, but how many of them are trying to feed those kids? Not very many. When a male halfway house is dealing with their clients, they're only dealing with their clients. A female halfway house is dealing with their clients, and right away you've got this woman who's saying, "I've got hungry kids at home. Who's taking care of them? How am I going to take care of them when I leave here? I got into this mess because I didn't know how to feed them properly, so I shoplifted or dealt drugs or prostituted." Also, who is she dependent upon? Did she break the law because she wanted to please her man? Was she getting him drugs? Is he a pimp? Over 90% of the women are dealing with issues around abuse and incest. People don't look at those issues.

It takes twice as much energy to work with a woman, and it's usually because she has so many issues that the criminal justice system considers extraneous. When you're working with a man, he is just as likely to prefer to ignore those issues, if he's got those issues at all. Not as many of the men have to deal with issues of abuse and incest. The women are also less used to thinking in terms of being a working member of society in the sense of working outside the home. People working with the men don't have to convince them that they ought to get a job. The men usually have been conditioned to that kind of thinking already. The women have all kinds of internal resistances to that, "I'm not really going to be a woman if I'm earning my own keep," or they've got this dream of Prince Charming coming along.

Initially, Women Reaching Women focused on increasing public awareness of women's substance abuse problems and informing women about available services. Their central concern was that, while women who abused alcohol and drugs comprised approximately 50% of the abusing population, only 14% to 19% were in treatment. They justified their efforts in terms of equal treatment, not in terms of women's different needs. They wanted women and men to be more equally represented as clients within the AODA treatment system.

> We wanted to open people's eyes to the problems that women were having, that we're not "special," we're part of the mainstream. We have the same kinds of problems everybody else does, and we should be treated in the same manner. Our philosophy was "put women back into the mainstream," not "put us on pedestals or treat us any differently."

Over time, Women Reaching Women increasingly emphasized changing the treatment system to be more responsive to the special needs of women. Notably, the concerns they identified are also highlighted in the current literature on women and substance abuse (Covington, 2002). With AODA providers, members explained that women were dissuaded from seeking treatment for alcohol and drug problems for many reasons, including fear of losing their families, not having enough money for treatment, and the greater stigma and blame society places on women substance abusers as compared with men. They discussed other women's issues related to female substance abuse, such as traditional female socialization toward dependency and submissiveness and women's experiences with physical and psychological abuse, rape, and incest.

> They use a male model for recovery. There is no female model. Issues of family violence, bulimia, anorexia, incest, rape are not addressed in treatment.
>
> Premenstrual syndrome. I've known of several women who would relapse at that time, and that's never taken into consideration. I see Women Reaching Women as trying to make some changes in that.
>
> [Same speakers?]One woman had an eating disorder which, when she went through treatment, she was laughed at for. When she would talk about it along with her alcoholism, her counselor made fun of her and thought that she was denying her alcoholism. "Come on. You're just trying to get off the track. Your real issue is alcoholism, and you don't want to talk about that, so you talk about bingeing and purging." But that eating disorder was just as strong with her, and the place was not equipped to deal with something like that. . . .
>
> One woman said to me, "When I went into treatment, they said, 'In order to become well, you have to give up your power.'" And she said to them, "But you're talking about in order for males to become well, they have to start giving

up some of their power. That doesn't work for women." They made her feel like she was extremely weird.

A lot of women going through treatment, whether they're recovering women or affected women, are saying, "I felt crazy, and when I got there, I felt even crazier." Women Reaching Women is a project which says, "You're not crazy. The system that you went into was designed to meet the needs of the white American male. Your reality has validity. Because it's not the same reality as the white American male does not mean that you're crazy." The stories don't change. That's what keeps pushing us to develop a treatment model, to keep working on a treatment center, to keep pushing and pushing for change.

Members focused on the fact that women did not seek treatment due to fears of losing their children and the unavailability of child care, and that these issues are ignored in treatment.

If a woman's in treatment and it's 3:00 in the afternoon, and she starts looking out the window, and it's a rainy day or a cold day, I've seen it happen, clinicians will make the assumption that she's not invested in being in treatment. They don't even think about the fact that she's worried about, did someone pick up my kids or are they walking home and it's twenty below zero. That's why her attention's gone. It has nothing to do with how invested she is in being in treatment.

What do women do with their children if they need to go into treatment? Women are still the primary caretakers of children. Whether we agree that it's just, equitable, or in kids' best interest is not the issue here. It's a major barrier to women receiving treatment. There's no place for a woman with children to go that will provide care for her children. With women, you have children. Unless those women have some place they can put their kids without putting the kids in jeopardy, you're not going to get the women into treatment . . . . A lot of these women are single parents. The idea of going into treatment and getting into a child custody battle and having their children physically removed from them, you can't imagine the heartache. It truly is like having your heart torn out, just the idea of your children being taken away from you. . . . Getting help may be the very thing that her husband will use to take the children away, and that's happened.

In their discussions of goals and services, members incorporated concepts of equality *and* concepts of difference. They believed that gender equality was a prerequisite for meaningful change for their consumers. They demanded equal levels of concern and support as well as equal access to resources and services. At the same time, they asserted women's unique experiences and needs and pressed for the provision of different services than those provided for men. For the women they served, members sought an equality based on difference.

In stark contrast, when members discussed the internal operations of their organizations, themes of difference predominated. Their focus on gender differences was consistent with radical feminism's investments in the creation of woman-centered alternatives. Also, it may be that advocating within conservative systems on behalf of conservative clients necessitated a stance that rested on well-accepted, long-standing, liberal commitments to equality. Within their organizations, members were freer to reveal their beliefs about gender differences.

HIGHLIGHTING GENDER DIFFERENCES

We're not just focused on providing a service. We're also focused on how we provide that service and how our workers feel about it. It creates a more humane, a more womanly environment for the volunteers. (WTA)

Feminist service organizations were founded on assumptions of gender difference. The feminists who built these organizations asserted their legitimacy and expertise largely based on their shared problems and commitments as women. Their underlying assumption was that, by virtue of being women, they had unique and valid insights into the nature and effects of sexism. Further, by creating woman-dominated workplaces, they sought to function in ways that were consistent with what they viewed as women's positive values and attributes. Success was defined in terms of creating alternatives to what they viewed as dysfunctional male behaviors and dehumanizing male organizational forms.

Like many other feminists, members underscored female-male differences while revising traditional conceptions of these differences. Many socially valued characteristics associated with masculinity were judged to be detrimental to individual psyches, interpersonal relationships, and group functioning. Feminine qualities, devalued in society at large, were vested with positive meanings and revalued as preferable to masculine ones. As compared with men, women represented connectedness, not individualism; subjectivity, not objectivity; sensitivity, not aggressiveness; nurturance, not neutrality; cooperation, not competition; and compassion, not conflict.

In a variety of ways, members' accounts of their experiences embodied assumptions about gender differences. Throughout their interviews, members applauded feminist efforts to create workplaces shaped by what they viewed as positive female qualities. They valued expressing emotions, having supportive relationships, and validating the contributions of all members. They praised themselves by placing their methods in opposition to the hierarchical approaches they associated with male values and male ways of operating.

> Political dilemmas confront us constantly. I've been involved with a lot of non-profits and social change organizations, and I find that to be true in every organization. What I find to be different here is that people are willing to work on resolving those in a nonhierarchical manner. I was involved for years with a nonprofit agency where the same number of dilemmas arose, but the way they dealt with them was very hierarchical, very male-oriented. (WTA)
>
> Hierarchy, in my way of thinking, isn't what the women's movement is about. We're not women trying to fit into men's pants, but women who want a distinctly different method of communicating with one another. (ABW)
>
> We have a belief that expression of feelings is strength, not weakness. Outside of this agency, I see the opposite being true in our culture. It's the John Wayne syndrome of never showing feelings, and that's supposed to be strength. We don't buy that here. (RCC)

Seeking alternatives to the ways that power has traditionally been exercised by men, members criticized women who engaged in what they considered to be "male" approaches.

> When we experience internal rivalry, backstabbing, hostility, and the overpowering of one another, and the insensitive treatment of one another, I really question, is it a feminist agency more than it is not. Women are acting just like men. (ABW)
>
> One of the issues for me was the apparent lack of feminist consciousness among some of the members. They seemed to be acting more like a man would treat a woman. It was much more a feeling of trying to dominate, trying to use their power to their advantage. . . . One faction was feminist-oriented, wanting fairness, wanting open communication. Another faction was the more male-acting faction, wanting to make final decisions without any communication between them and others in the group, essentially wanting all the power, not trusting the other members in the group. (WTA)

Members recognized also that deliberately promoting qualities associated with femininity, like being empathetic and open about personal issues, could interfere with the smooth operation of their organizations.

> There's an expectation that we all have to tell each other everything about our personal lives. It would be better if we tried harder to respect each other's privacy. That would be a healthier work environment. (RCC)
>
> There's some leeway given for the emotional needs of the staff. You won't find that as much in more traditional organizations. Although we went too far. If someone was feeling bad, if they had some need at home, they would be

excused from their work. That has had to be balanced out. People have to accomplish their work but, within that, there's a great deal of flexibility in terms of their addressing their emotional needs. (ARC)

In addition to their deliberate incorporation of what they considered to be positive female qualities, members struggled to overcome the detrimental aspects of traditional female socialization, especially in relation to the exercise of power and dealing with conflict.

Sometimes we're overly committed to working stuff out instead of taking action when it's needed, especially women who are feminists, because we know how society has brought us up to compete with each other and view each other as enemies and threats. But wanting to break that down, we go to the other extreme. I'll take shit from a woman that I'd never take from a man. (WTA)

Learning effectively to deal with conflict, that's another thing that we, as women, don't do well. We haven't had a lot of experience dealing with conflict situations in a way that comes out feeling constructive. We tend to shy away from it too long until we blow up. . . . A lot of the struggles had to do with our experience of being brought up as women in this society. (ABW)

As women, we haven't learned to criticize and to take criticism. We're not trained in criticism, in accepting it and taking it matter-of-factly and getting back to work. (ABW)

Women have a hard time dealing with power. When you have it, you might not use it appropriately, or you might be afraid of it. Women's learning how to deal with power is a stepping-stone. (WTA)

Assumptions about gender differences were the force behind members' maintaining woman-centered work environments. Believing that women's values and interpersonal styles were very different from and better than men's, members saw their organizations as opportunities to work with like-minded women, relatively free of male influence. They believed that, by establishing groups internally free of male domination, their members could empower themselves to alter the forces that maintained female powerlessness. Similarly, they were confident that services provided by women to women enhanced their consumers' abilities to empower themselves.

Benefits of *Women Helping Women* for Consumers

Members pointed to numerous ways that consumers benefited from the all-women aspects of their organizations. Female staff and volunteers served as role models for consumers and could avoid the well-learned male-female interactive strategies that reinforced women's passivity and powerlessness. Being female increased members' ability to empathize with consumers and to understand and share experiences related to being female in a male-dominated society. Finding that they could rely on women for support and assistance, members hoped that consumers would learn to respect and trust other women and discover that women need not be dependent on male authority.

Members were often met with the argument that they should have male counselors in order to provide consumers with positive male role models and relationships through which they could work on their interactions with men. However, the potential benefits of consumers' having positive experiences with male counselors were considered less important than the advantages accrued by women's being helped by other women.

> We don't have any men on our staff. That's not because we don't like men, but because we want to teach women the strength they can get from other women so that they don't always have to look for their strength from some big guy. (ABW)
>
> Women offenders usually don't trust women. They're into, "Women are bitches and they steal your men. I've got to be tough with other women." It's very feminist to facilitate a trust among the women. Change comes with hearing that you're not alone and removing the isolation that the women feel. (ARC)
>
> The women are deeply concerned and interested in women taking control of their own lives, supporting each other through each other, as opposed to male support. It's women of strength helping women who don't know their own strength. (RCC)
>
> In our support groups, we talk about a lot of different issues, not just alcohol and drug abuse issues. One of the reasons that we set up the support groups separate from an AA or Alanon group is so women would have a chance to talk about those issues. Women seem to feel more comfortable in talking with other women about medical issues, child-rearing issues. (WRW)

In addition, the Rape Crisis Center and Women's Transit Authority were concerned about male staff and volunteers jeopardizing the trust, comfort, and safety of consumers.

> The first voice she hears should be a woman. She should not ever have to risk having a male answering the phone after a sexual assault. (RCC)
>
> Women are intimidated if they call and hear a male voice answer the phone. (RCC)
>
> There has been pressure on Women's Transit at times to allow men to volunteer. We just explain the safety issue, that it's not safe for men to know where women live. (WTA)
>
> Sometimes we're picking up women who have just been assaulted, or who have just narrowly escaped assault. Those women would not want to be met by a man when they had just experienced violence against them from a man. (WTA)

ARC House was the only exception. Since its founding, ARC House had hired two male counselors, both of whom were members of Ananda Marga and shared staff values about spirituality and creating a therapeutic community for residents. The first male staff member worked there for three and a half years. Then, after two years with only female staff, it hired another male counselor. Some members of ARC House wanted to maintain an all-female staff. Others asserted the importance of having a positive male role model for the residents.

> Some people say, "There has to be a man on the staff." That's bullshit. "Most of the women's problems are with men." I don't believe that. Most of their problems are acted out in relationships with men, but having a nice man on the staff has never worked wonders for any woman yet.
>
> Hiring a man was always a big issue. The women are working through very sexist roles themselves, so they relate to men very differently than to women. There was always a fear that the women would regress in dealing with their problems with a man. Two times, we made an exception. One was a counselor who was there from the very beginning, who the residents made an "honorary woman." Actually, he was good to have there because the residents saw that there is that kind of male, too, and that they could start asking their men to make some changes. He was a good role model for them to see. The same thing with the second one that was hired.
>
> Women's relationships with men, that is the primary factor in their involvement in the criminal justice system, so we do a great deal of work around that. The reason we finally hired a man was to bring those issues home. They did fine as long as they were around all women. They went outside and got involved with men, and it all fell apart. So, we were trying to bring the issue into the house where we could deal with it directly. I have mixed feelings about it, though.

Benefits of *Women Helping Women* for Members

In the four organizations that consisted only of women staff and volunteers, members commented on the pragmatic advantages of their working solely with other women in woman-centered work environments. Working independently of men, members learned to trust and rely on other women and themselves, to exert leadership, and to learn new skills. They could avoid having to deal with the oppressive attitudes and interpersonal behaviors males often exhibited toward females based on male socialization, and they could avoid the interpersonal games that they learned to play with men as part of female socialization. They were freer to behave in ways that were assertive, knowledgeable, and competent and at the same time, to draw on the more positive aspects of traditional female socialization to create intimate and emotionally supportive workplaces.

It's staff solidarity and women working together, and all the nice things that go along with that, that you lose when you have a male staff person. It's just different. It changes the whole feeling. The intimacy that you can have with an all-female staff is so much greater than if there's a man, and the power that you can feel in what you do is so much greater. It puts people in weird positions to have a man on staff. It brings up all kinds of other issues around power. You don't want to misuse your power around this person, but you want to make sure he doesn't misuse his. There's a constant being on your guard. (ABW)

We like to give women a chance to be leaders, and sometimes men want to tell us how to lead. Not only tell us, but be the leader. We like to think, "We want to try it for a while. We want to see what it feels like up at the front of the 'Take Back the Night' march" [a march held to protest sexual assault]. There's that controversy every year, men wanting to be in the front of the march. It's a perfect metaphor. Women want to be in the front for a while. It doesn't mean men can't ever be, but we want to see what it feels like at the front. (WTA)

Women supporting one another is so important for us to realize our potential as women. That's an important aspect of women becoming all that they can be. It's nice to speak in an all-female group, to speak without getting the funny looks or stares that you get with men in the room. I've been in meetings with predominantly men, and I felt like I was hardly heard. I wasn't paid any attention to because I was a woman and what I had to say couldn't possibly be important. Here, you don't have to feel like what you have to say is not important. (WRW)

In every organization, members valued the power and connectedness that they felt in an all-women workplace. In addition, some women sought out women-only work environments because of their anger toward men as representatives of the patriarchy and the personally demeaning and often violent experiences they and other women had with male employers, colleagues, teachers, clergy, therapists, family members, friends, and strangers: "A lot of women just didn't want to have to deal with men." (ABW)

Moreover, especially in Advocates for Battered Women, the Rape Crisis Center, and Women's Transit Authority, there were many lesbian feminists whose personal lives revolved around female partners; female friends; and a rich culture of lesbian feminist music, literature, dance, art, and theater. For these women, feminist organizations offered additional opportunities to work and socialize with other lesbians in politically meaningful activities. In addition, they could work with nonlesbians who were supportive of their life choices and political views, who had close ties with women in the lesbian community, and whose lives were similarly enriched by women's culture.

In two of these organizations, providing a safe space for members was a high priority. Concern about harassment of and male violence against workers was a primary justification for the women-only stance of the Rape Crisis Center and Women's Transit Authority.

We have a referral list of male therapists who work with male assault survivors. If a man calls and wants to talk with a man, we have numbers right there to give him. But we haven't trained men to work on our lines. . . . Volunteers sleep overnight. Given that we couldn't figure out how to screen out sex offenders, we weren't going to allow men there. (RCC)

Most people seem to understand and accept that we don't want to have male counselors, but they wonder if there's a way that we can have a male bookkeeper or a male business coordinator. One stance that we've taken is that people need to be able to feel that the Rape Crisis Center is a safe environment, and most people have accepted that. (RCC)

We don't know how to screen out rapists. The implication there is that all men are potential rapists, and men don't like that. No one likes to think their boyfriend or their friend or their uncle could be a rapist. But if you look at the statistics, those are the rapists, people who you know and who you've trusted. With as many volunteers as Transit has, there's no way to go through a screening process with male volunteers. Since safety is our main thing, we can't allow that. (WTA)

Members' desires to have women as paid staff did not hamper their meeting affirmative action requirements. Most men had neither the knowledge nor experience required to be hired, and few applied. The men who may have been qualified generally shared values with members and supported their *women helping women* stance.

Debates Over the Participation of Men

The theme of *women helping women* consistently guided members' decisions for both ideological and pragmatic reasons. For example, Women's Transit Authority emphasized that women should be helping one another and asserted the political significance of their demonstrating that women could take measures to protect themselves. However, members also stated that their organization valued men's support, particularly in the areas of publicity, fundraising, bookkeeping, and consciousness-raising among other men. Their stance was explicitly stated in their bylaws:

Only women may volunteer to provide the direct service of Women's Transit Authority. This is for two reasons: the safety of the volunteers and the riders, and for the strength that is gained when women work together. WTA does value and encourage the efforts of men to eradicate sexual assault. Within WTA men may become involved in areas approved by WTA, such as publicity, community relations, fund-raising, and outreach. Any action that reduces sexism, sex role stereotyping, misogyny, violence, and all that fosters and condones it, is a step toward ending violence against women.

Allowing men to assume minor roles within Women's Transit Authority exemplified members' modifying their politics in order to maintain support in the larger community. In its early years, many volunteers looked to Women's Transit Authority as a separatist feminist organization. The importance of attracting and maintaining funding led members to modify their women-only stance, however slightly.

> As we came to rely on public funding, we couldn't continue to be seen as a separatist organization. That was a dilemma for a while. There was a large group of volunteers who saw it as a separatist organization, and we couldn't let that kind of image be reinforced in the community.
>
> Personally, I don't think that was compromising at all, because the way you fight sexual assaults is to get everyone in the community involved. Unless men see it as an issue that affects them, we're not going to be able to effect the changes that we need to eradicate sexual assault. It was essential for us to have the support of men in the community. If men wanted to offer their services to us, if we could make use of them, I thought it was a very positive step.

A more central change resulted from the organization's decision to ask the city to supplement its services with cab rides. In 1983, the city gave Women's Transit Authority funding to offer women free cab service when it was unable to handle all of its calls within a reasonable time or when women needed rides outside of Transit's service area. Callers who were in danger remained the highest priority and were provided with rides in Women's Transit Authority cars. Although Women's Transit Authority still did not allow men to work as volunteers or staff, this new program meant that some riders would have male drivers.

> If we were going to send a cab to a woman, we'd ask her permission first and tell her the likelihood that it's a man is very great and does that bother you. Most women would say no but some women wanted a Women's Transit ride, and they would get it. That was a big change, because male cab drivers would be providing our service for us.

This issue required Women's Transit Authority to blend feminist philosophy about the importance of *women helping women* with its desire to improve its services in order to help more women. The positives were that the city validated and further legitimized the organization's work by funding this joint venture with cab companies, and it was able to greatly increase the range and efficiency of its service. The negatives were that offering women rides with male drivers could potentially change the intensive woman-centered spirit of the organization.

There was a sense that a lot of women did not want cabs. They wanted Transit rides because of bad experiences with men. But some volunteers felt that women preferred cabs because they were faster, and that lowered morale. Also, the sense of women empowered by women working for women changed, subtly, but it changed.

Having men serve as staff and volunteers was often debated in the Rape Crisis Center: "At different times, there were some of us who were more open to the idea of having men in different positions and some people who were adamantly opposed to it." At one point, members agreed to hire a man and a woman for a CETA-funded project to do prevention and education.

> We thought that it might be a neat idea to have a male-female team because they were only going to do education. They were not going to do any advocacy or counseling. We felt that all the different kinds of risks were minimized, so we told CETA, "This is what we're looking for in terms of educators who want to do this." We never specified sex, never got any men referred, so it became a non-issue. That was one time that we were willing to hire a man.

Over the years, there were recurring discussions over the organization's policy that only women should staff the crisis line; these discussions were usually initiated by new volunteers. Some women believed that male volunteers could be helpful to all callers; others argued that they needed men to talk with male victims. These perspectives were accepted as legitimate to raise, especially since other rape crisis centers around the country had men staffing their crisis lines, but they were quickly, sometimes forcefully, dismissed as inconsistent with the dominant belief system of the center: "Her needs, the survivor's, come first. That's the way it is. It's not going to change."

> We've talked about, should we have men working the lines, especially to talk with male victims. That argument has never gotten very far. The overwhelming response is no, because you don't know when a male will call. And frequently, male victims don't want to talk to a man, they want to talk to a woman. It's more than just the issue of women don't want to call and hear a male voice. That's the reason that's easiest to use. The truth is that most of the women who volunteer at Rape Crisis wouldn't feel safe.
>
> The women bringing up the issues are generally drowned out. They generally drop the issue when they realize how unsafe it is to bring it up. They don't get any support for the idea, and so they drop it. As people turn over, it may get trotted out again by a newer person who wasn't there the last time we went over it. I'm sure we've lost volunteers and potential volunteers when they have not felt supported for the fact that they feel men should be brought into the agency. They start feeling alienated from the rest of the group.

Most members of the Rape Crisis Center were passionately committed to *women helping women*. They believed that it was in the best interests of women victims to speak with women, and they remained concerned about the safety and comfort of their members. Unique among these five organizations, the Rape Crisis Center also related disagreements over having male members to two other concerns: (1) that the women who were most insistent about including men were "male-identified," and (2) that some volunteers incorrectly assumed that the Rape Crisis Center's women-only views were based on "man-hating" rather than the importance of *women helping women*.

As noted in chapter 2, being woman-identified was an explicit part of the ethos of this organization, and most of the women who worked there defined themselves as woman-identified, regardless of their sexual orientation or lifestyle. The women who argued persistently that men should be working at the Rape Crisis Center were often viewed as "male-identified," that is, as women whose self-definitions were tied to male cultural values, male approval, and the acceptance of male prerogatives: "Male identification is the act whereby women place men above women, including themselves, in credibility, status, and importance in most situations, regardless of the comparative quality the women may bring to the situation . . . Interaction with women is seen as a lesser form of relating on every level" (Barry, 1979, p. 172). In this setting, male-identified staff and volunteers were presumably heterosexuals, but male identification can exist among lesbians as well.

In the Rape Crisis Center, many members assumed that the women who most intensely objected to their no-men policy were actually opposed to members' strong ideological and personal commitments to women.

> There's volunteers periodically that view some things as too harsh, some philosophies as too strong and too radical. Oftentimes, it's come up in training sessions where we'll talk about our politics. Many women will be there that haven't thought about the men in their lives and how they would fit into our overall view of men. It can be real threatening.

Differences between woman-identified and male-identified women were exacerbated by the high levels of anger toward men that existed in the Rape Crisis Center. More than in any other organization, members of the Rape Crisis Center were constantly in the throes of crises involving male violence against women. They counseled women of all ages who were still trying to cope with being raped in the past; they assisted women who had just been assaulted and helped their families and close friends as well; they helped women face their attackers and deal with insensitive and sometimes cruel male doctors, police officers, lawyers, and judges; and they spent time that would be better spent in other ways handling crank calls from men. Members were well aware of the anger that their work stimulated and that feminist expressions of anger were often offered as evidence that feminists were "man-haters."

Accusations of "man-hating" were frequently flung at both lesbian and straight feminists during this time. Some people genuinely failed to understand that feminists were enraged due to their ever-increasing insights into female oppression and that this rage complicated feminists' relationships with both women and men, feminists and nonfeminists (Frye, 1983; Kaplow, 1973; Kearon, 1973; Shulman, 1998). They ignored the fact that feminists loved many men, including their fathers, brothers, husbands, and sons, and had positive and caring relationships with supportive male friends and lovers. For many others, however, accusing feminists of "man-hating" was a means of dismissing their concerns and discrediting their efforts: "The term 'man-hating' is often used by critics of the women's movement ostensibly in response to the male-exclusionary policy of many groups. More often it is a shorthand way of questioning the psychological 'normality' of the women in the movement. On this level the charge is dismissed by the women as a functional equivalent of 'red-baiting'" (Hole and Levine, 1971, p. 235).

Understanding the sources, legitimacy, and power of their anger, members of the Rape Crisis Center did not expect or desire to stop being angry. They were concerned, however, that some volunteers misinterpreted their anger; they also worked to minimize the impact of their anger on their interactions with male sexual assault victims.

> Sometimes, the volunteers will see the anger that others feel against men in general because of the violence against women. They may start feeling afraid that, to be part of this organization, you have to eliminate the men in your lives. Or they feel afraid that they're going to feel the same anger and they won't want men in their lives. That especially happens during volunteer training when some of the trainees are starting to feel great rage. Some will drop out rather than deal with it. We lose potential resources that way, when we're incorrectly perceived as man-haters because of our anger.
>
> The agency collects such a magnetic charge of anger against men that it's hard to serve men and it's hard to work with men. By the time you've heard half a dozen of the stories, you're ready to slit the throat of every man who comes in the door. We have to fight that because there are male victims of sexual assault who need us. We really believe that we should be serving anyone who's a survivor, regardless of sex. . . . Serving male survivors is difficult for us because we receive so many crank calls from men that our volunteers are horribly suspicious any time there's a man on the other end. They think it's funny. It's "Hi, I just raped my girlfriend, ha ha ha." Slam. One woman said there was some guy who called every hour on the hour and said obscenities until 3:30 in the morning, and she got no sleep. Some of our prank callers have real good opening stories too. We do, pretty frequently, have discussions about

how to deal with these men and how to get rid of some of the anger that comes from the crank calls. We do a lot of processing of the calls to help us serve men better.

It is likely that, for the volunteers whose fears of "man-hating feminists" dominated their responses to the anger they observed, *women helping women* became too closely tied with having to acknowledge gender differences in the perpetuation of and commitment to eliminate violence against women. Expressed anger toward men, regardless of its merit, would inevitably make it more difficult for these women to trust that the exclusion of men as workers was based on the benefits of an all-women workplace for women and not on hatred toward men. Also, as discussed in the following chapter, accusations of man-hating were closely tied with homophobia.

Highlighting gender differences, all of these organizations exemplify a particular form of feminist separatism. They were organizations controlled by women, in which women could work and receive help and through which women could increase their self-sufficiency and social power (Freedman, 1979; Frye, 1978; Valeska, 1975). Like the separatism of cultural feminists, this form of separatism celebrated qualities associated with being female, denigrated traits socially valued in men in male-dominated arenas, and emphasized the personally affirming nature of all-women groups (Taylor and Rupp, 1993). As with the separatism of NOW, men were permitted to play supportive roles. Like the early radical feminists, members of these five organizations viewed *women helping women* as a political strategy toward the long-term goal of gender equality (Ryan, 1992).

Also like the early radical feminists, members viewed their work in terms of the different attitudes, behaviors, and experiences of women and men. They struggled to overcome the debilitating aspects of traditional female socialization and to productively incorporate the many qualities associated with being female that they valued. Rejecting the ways in which, historically, men have exercised power, members challenged themselves to develop alternative workplaces based on their understandings of women's strengths. In addition to the broad goal of empowering women, members identified numerous specific benefits of all-women service organizations for members and for consumers, including providing positive role models; increasing women's trust in women as a group and thereby increasing their confidence in themselves as women; promoting women's safety and comfort; and creating validating and supportive work experiences for women.

The overall stance among members of these organizations was that significant differences exist in the status, power, and life options of women as compared with men, and that these differences were a determining factor in women's psychological distress, personal difficulties, and victimization.

Understanding gender inequality as a source of women's problems, they promoted goals of gender equality, but not an equality defined in terms of women's obtaining the same services as men. Instead, members sought equal opportunities and resources for women to receive services that addressed issues, needs, and circumstances that were very different from men's. Members maintained a multifaceted perspective on gender equality and gender differences in their understandings of women's experiences and in determining their politics and programs.

Chapter Four

Building a Sisterhood
Based on Difference

For those people working here who are neither lesbians nor minorities, the burden is on them to learn and to participate in making the changes that are necessary, to understand how we're homophobic, racist and sexist. You don't just learn it and then you're done learning it. It's an ongoing education that seeps in, in bits and pieces. Then you can apply some of it, and then you have to go back and learn some more. (ABW)

The phrase *women helping women* reflected women's growing consciousness of the oppression women experienced as a group and signaled the alliances among women that formed the basis of a national movement. However, just as commitments to *women helping women* served to highlight differences between women and men, this notion also served to obscure differences among women. Feminist ideals of building a movement based on commonalities among women stood in direct opposition to the multitude of significant differences that exist among women. Paradoxically, feminists' expectations of women joining together as sisters to form powerful political coalitions based on common concerns and goals could be realized only by understanding and addressing differences. Feminists had very different backgrounds and experiences based on age (Bell, 1975; Faulkner, 1980; Macdonald, 1983); disability status (Browne, Connors, and Stern, 1985; Fine and Asch, 1988); and income level (Lefkowitz and Withorn, 1986; Seifer, 1976). Particularly painful divisions among women in the movement were based on anti-Semitism, racism, and homophobia (Beck, 1983, 1984; Bulkin, Pratt, and Smith, 1988).

In each of these five organizations, members sought to understand and address differences among women while maintaining the concept of *woman* as their primary identity. Their strong identification with women as a group and their deeply held beliefs that changing women's lives was the central project of their work created two opposing forces. On the one hand, being inclusive was an expectation they held of themselves as feminists. To successfully work on behalf of women as a group required that members represent women in their diversities and address significant differences among women.

> In the first months, it became clear that the calls we were getting were so diverse that we needed a mass representation of people. We were very, very happy when a woman in her 60s applied to be a counselor. Another woman, as a high school graduate and probably the only one who had kids, represented a strong portion of the public that we were trying to reach. By her talking with her friends, we could figure out ways to reach more people. (RCC)
> One of our goals is to reach out to our ridership to recruit women of color. Not just to say, "We have more women of color working for us now," but because our ridership should have power in the organization. (WTA)

At the same time, members recognized that remaining a distinctly feminist organization required their having shared values and goals. The greater the diversity among members, the greater the possibilities of dissension, disillusionment, and the dilution of their philosophy.

> We ended up looking for people for the board who were just like staff, which has created its own problems in terms of how the organization looks and the breadth of skills and information that is brought in. But at least we created a trusting environment and base from which to function. (ABW)
> We don't want to be this elite group of women, but we're proud that it doesn't take a long time to come to consensus. If we do get diverse groups of women in here, it's going to take a long time to make certain decisions. That's the ironic part about it. We want to be so loving and bring in all these wonderful women and make everyone feel at home. But at the same time, it would really bug a lot of people if we drew out things for weeks because some people disagreed with everybody else. (RCC)

Heightened sensitivity to the potential problems associated with increased diversity created tensions as members considered broadening their memberships. For example, the Rape Crisis Center was proud of its explicit commitment to a radical, woman-centered approach to feminism. It emphasized the deleterious effects of male supremacy, especially male violence against women, and it celebrated social, emotional, and sexual bonds among women. Correspondingly, it recognized that members' politics alienated many traditional white women and many women of color. The organization's challenge was to determine if and how it should alter its politics in order to attract women who did not share its woman-centered views.

The dilemma is that, by being a strongly feminist organization, we are shutting out a lot of women, both as clients and as volunteers and staff. They won't call themselves feminists, or they define themselves as feminists in a different way. I'm thinking specifically of women of color and traditional heterosexual women and women over 40. They feel alienated because of our radical feminist viewpoint. We are really strong about empowering women. We're not as strong about empowering men. We blame men a great deal, and a lot of women are uncomfortable with that. There's no deliberate shutting out of those populations, but the gap is there. We're missing the perspective from all those women . . . Right now, we are having discussions about how we can attract more women in these populations. What we've run up against, in the same discussions in the past, is a realization that the value systems of those groups are different from the core group at the center. No one wanted to change her values, but everyone wanted those women to come in. What we're going to have to argue about is what we're willing to change in order to attract those women . . . We just have to do more communicating to work on it.

"We just have to do more communicating to work on it" reflects a long-standing and central feminist strategy. Much like the early radical feminists, members relied largely on discussions of their own experiences and the experiences of other women to derive their own versions of feminist thought and practice. They believed that, as their memberships became more diverse, their philosophies and strategies would increasingly take female diversity into account.

PERSONAL EXPERIENCE AS A SOURCE OF KNOWLEDGE

Given members' highly personal approach to the political, issues of difference were most consistently and effectively addressed when differences were represented among the members of the organizations. Based on their understandings of *the personal is political,* members needed to incorporate a diverse range of the personal in order to derive the political.

When you don't know what the other side is like through your own experience, whether it's through unemployment or being black or not having the class privilege of that kind of education, you don't appreciate the differences. (ABW)

Even though I would not want to be prejudiced, I may be unconscious of certain prejudices. That's why it's important to have lesbian staff and minority staff. You may think that you're being nonprejudicial, but you aren't. (ARC)

It's hard to combat all those "isms" when you don't have people of other cultural backgrounds to show you your classism or your own racism. We've done a whole lot better on homophobia, and that's because there are a lot of lesbian women in the organization. (ABW)

I don't think now, even if all of us were heterosexual, the emphasis on services to gay women would be lost. It's now a part of the program. But it's the
bringing up of issues and how they're dealt with that is often dependent on
who's here. (RCC)

Relying on "mandatory presence," that is, relying on members of oppressed groups to raise the issues that are of concern to their groups, can be a
dominant group strategy to avoid members' own responsibility to understand
and address various forms of oppression. However, in the context of feminist
values, mandatory presence is a crucial means of raising consciousness, creating dialogue, and increasing group responsibility (Apuzzo and Powell,
1981). In these organizations, all members were expected to bring their own
experiences to bear on policies and practices. They were each burdened with
expectations that they would reveal their own sensitivities and needs, even
when the promised understanding, empathy, and support did not materialize
in response.

Most members were middle-class, but there was no mention in the interviews of problems between middle- and working-class members or between
members and low-income consumers. These organizations were affected,
however, by differences among women based on sexual orientation and on
race. The very different histories, cultural values, and priorities of white feminists and women of color hampered members' efforts to create culturally diverse organizations. In contrast, members had considerable experience in
dealing with differences based on sexual orientation since both lesbians and
nonlesbians joined these organizations in order to pursue and advance their
politics.

THE PARTICIPATION OF LESBIANS

Gay/straight issues have been dealt with by recognizing that lesbians have been
at the forefront of the whole movement, respecting that, and giving people credit
for that, and making statements to the community about how lesbians are taking
that kind of risk. (ABW)

Throughout the early years of the movement, tensions were ongoing between lesbians and heterosexual women. For example, in 1969 and 1970,
there was considerable turmoil within NOW over whether its association with
lesbianism would discredit the organization: "The fears and anger of both fac-
tions almost caused the demise of the New York chapter in the spring of
1971" (Hole and Levine, 1971, p. 94). By its 1971 convention, however,
NOW had passed resolutions that affirmed a woman's right "to define and

express her own sexuality and to choose her own life-style," that identified "the oppression of lesbians as a legitimate concern of feminism," and that supported "child custody rights of mothers who are also lesbians" (Carden, 1974, p. 113). The tensions subsided further within NOW when, in 1973, it called for legislation to end discrimination based on sexual orientation (Freeman, 1975). Still, the gay/straight split among radical feminists continued, with many heterosexual radical feminists choosing not to be involved in radical feminist activities (Echols, 1989).

Tensions between these two groups of women were based on straight women's homophobia, lesbian separatism, and lesbian demands that feminists address heterosexuality as an institution that oppresses all women. Lesbians and nonlesbians are oppressed not only by sexism but also by heterosexism, a belief system that values heterosexuality as superior to and more natural than homosexuality (Boston Lesbian Psychologies Collective, 1987; Kitzinger, 1987; Lorde, 1984; Martin and Lyon, 1977; Vida, 1978). As Adrienne Rich explained in her classic article "Compulsory Heterosexuality and Lesbian Existence,"

> . . . the issue we have to address as feminists is, not simple "gender inequality,"
> nor the domination of culture by males, nor mere "taboos against homosexuality," but the enforcement of heterosexuality for women as a means of assuring male right of physical, economical, and emotional access. One of many means of enforcement is, of course, the rendering invisible of the lesbian possibility. (1980, p. 647)

As a lifestyle and subculture in which women function relatively independent of men, lesbianism challenges cultural mandates that women seek personal fulfillment and economic security through heterosexual bonding. Thus, by creating hate and fear toward lesbianism, heterosexism maintains gender inequality. Homophobia and fear of being labeled homosexual serve to keep women (and men) within the confines of traditional gender roles. This process was described in 1970 in the widely circulated position paper written by the Radicalesbians, "The Woman Identified Woman":

> As long as the label "dyke" can be used to frighten a woman into a less militant stand, keep her separate from her sisters, keep her from giving primacy to anything other than men and family—then to that extent she is controlled by the male culture. (1973, p. 243)

Just as many heterosexual feminists' homophobia separated them from lesbian feminists, many lesbians attacked the life choices of straight women. Lesbian activists frequently asserted that straight women's sexuality was a sign of their oppression and that heterosexual women were choosing to collaborate with their oppressors, that "feminism is the theory, lesbianism is the practice" (Freeman, 1975, p. 138). Particularly in the 1970s, antagonism and distrust among lesbians and nonlesbians often overwhelmed, and sometimes destroyed, feminist groups.

In these five organizations, however, members' experiences reflected long-term and productive relationships among lesbians and nonlesbians. Their success was at least partially due to the political and social environment in Madison, a city that added sexual orientation to its equal-opportunity ordinance in the mid-1970s. Madison's representative in the state legislature sponsored the bill that, in 1982, made Wisconsin the first state to pass a gay-rights bill. In Madison, there were multiple opportunities, political and nonpolitical, for strong ties to be established among lesbians and nonlesbians.

Lesbian and nonlesbian feminists could find many points of unity in organizations that emphasized female-male differences, incorporated woman-centered political analyses, and endorsed woman-centered workplaces (Taylor and Rupp, 1993). Most members took for granted that their organizations would and should include lesbian women as staff, volunteers, and board members, and homophobia was consistently, if not always effectively, addressed.

Members referred to the many lesbian-specific practices they had developed for their consumers. Advocates for Battered Women organized support groups for battered lesbians in the community. It changed its intake form so as not to be geared only to heterosexual relationships, and it had counselors available for women who asked to work with someone who could handle lesbian issues. The Rape Crisis Center trained its volunteers to assist lesbians, and, if requested, it paired lesbian victims with lesbian counselors. In talking with callers, members would say, for example, "Do you have a partner who's supportive?" rather than refer to a "boyfriend" or "girlfriend," and in groups, they would make sure "that clients are accepting of people having different sexual preferences." ARC House members asserted the importance of having gay staff to work with and provide role models for gay residents. However, most members' comments about lesbian/straight issues revolved around developing levels of safety and comfort for lesbian members and consumers.

Like other shelters (Schechter, 1982), Advocates for Battered Women struggled with issues involving having lesbian workers and homophobic residents. Their concerns centered on how lesbian staff and volunteers could be honest and open about their own lives and respond to homophobic comments and, at the same time, maintain positive relationships with homophobic residents. The stance of the organization was defined in a written statement, "Principles of Unity on Sexual Preference":

Violence against women is one aspect of a whole system that oppresses women, people of color, working class, poor people, and people of differing sexual and affectional preference. Conditions for all women will not improve until this systematic oppression is ended. ABW recognizes the leadership and activities of Lesbian women in the movement and within our agency and takes an active stance against homophobia and Lesbian baiting. ABW shall seek to provide a safe, secure and positive environment for Lesbians and bi-sexual women who work within our agency and those who use our services. We shall work against the social attitudes and institutional barriers that prevent full participation of Lesbian and bi-sexual women in society—as parents, workers, friends and as intimate partners.

Advocates for Battered Women addressed homophobia primarily by upholding the general principle that all women in the organization needed to be able to feel comfortable and safe, "regardless of what the issue is." The concerns of lesbian volunteers and staff were dealt with by emphasizing "the rights of people to make choices" and "accepting and acknowledging individual differences and trying to put them aside to work on a common goal." As one member stated, "Both the staff and the board are committed to being supportive if something does come up."

In contrast, the Rape Crisis Center brought lesbian participation to the foreground, extolling the active participation of lesbians in the organization and emphasizing that homophobia was unacceptable: "We address homophobia wherever we see it. It is not tolerated in our organization." In this organization, homophobia was most evident among new volunteers. In their trainings, members focused on eliminating homophobia by trying to reduce volunteers' misconceptions and fears. If education and support were not effective, then homophobic volunteers were asked to leave.

The lesbian caucus took over a portion of our training, doing consciousness-raising about dealing with lesbians who are your co-staffers and your colleagues and how to assist lesbian client victims. It's a special evening. People telling their stories of growing up and coming out and sharing what it's like to be gay in reference to their whole lives, and then also in reference to being a member of the center . . . We do actually raise the consciousness of the women in training, and the ones whose consciousness is not raised, who remain homophobic, are not taken into the organization. Before it became a part of the training, it was dealt with solely by the lesbians. At this point, we have very supportive straight sisters who will also challenge homophobia when they see it. So, it's not left just to the lesbians to have to fight it.

We're very aware that it may be the first time a number of the trainees have ever confronted the issue. So, we have to do it in a careful way, but also in a committed way because we have had some incidents of homophobia that have been real painful and just not acceptable.

Problems between lesbians and nonlesbians often centered on the issue of allowing men to work at the Rape Crisis Center. Throughout the movement, women's political views about men were often assumed to be directly tied to their choice of sexual partners (Koedt, 1973; Shulman, 1980). Heterosexual women who insisted that men be included were often viewed as being homophobic, and lesbians who insisted that men be excluded were most often the women accused of being man-haters.

> There have been and are individuals that are threatened by the majority attitude of "We don't want men as part of the organization." I've seen both volunteers and staff who are more male-identified or less woman-identified than the majority of people and feel angry and hurt when they try to bring up as an issue that we ought to recruit men. Occasionally, that has taken the form of dyke-baiting, some straight women calling other women "man-haters." The issue is homophobia.

Members of the Rape Crisis Center also mentioned addressing the discomfort that heterosexual women could experience as the minority group in a woman-identified organization; and they discouraged heterophobia, that is, prejudice toward heterosexual women's lifestyles and sexual preference.

> One of the criteria of being a volunteer or paid staff is that she must address her own homophobia and talk about that and be able to work with women who are not the same as she is. The same goes for heterophobia.
>
> There are a lot of lesbians and bisexual women who work here. Ironically, the problem is not making a safe place for them. It's making a safe place for heterosexual women who derive most of their support from men. Rape Crisis is a strongly woman-identified group of women who don't hate men, but who don't need men in their lives. Because of that, the women who do have men in their lives are sometimes threatened, extremely threatened. We have a lesbian caucus for the lesbian women. We were just talking about maybe heterosexual women should have a support group.

As in the Rape Crisis Center, members of Women's Transit Authority expressed great pride in and admiration for the many lesbian women who had provided leadership in their organization. However, in this organization, homophobia was not a major issue. As drivers, volunteers could maintain distance between themselves and other members. Also, the range of issues through which prejudice might be expressed was much narrower. Members did not need to address relationships with clients, and the safety issue in and of itself was sufficient to handle questions about having male workers.

> Most of the people involved in the organization were fully aware and fully accepting of lesbian lifestyles. Internally, with the people who were most active, it

wasn't an issue. It became an issue when you started going beyond that inside group. It became an issue with some volunteers . . . In our trainings, we talk about how many different kinds of women there are at Transit so that women have a sense that there are lesbians and straight women working with us before they sign their contracts to volunteer. We handle it in another way, and that is to be very proud that many of the women working for us are lesbians.

When I was involved, the staff made a point of saying, "There are lesbians who are active in this group. Lesbians helped found this group, and we're very grateful for the lesbian energy that's made this group go. This group used to be called 'Lesi-lift,' and it's something that you as a volunteer have got to deal with." That's grand. It's a focused way to enable people to face their own homophobia.

Members of Women's Transit Authority commented that it often would be the heterosexual women who were uncomfortable as the women in the minority, on the outside.

I wonder myself if sometimes there's tension between the lesbians and the women who are not oriented that way. It's a safe place for lesbians to be, and they feel very free in expressing their sexuality there. There's been a couple of times when other women were put up tight by that.

There's some volunteers who are extremely uncomfortable when lesbians joke among themselves, like on their shift. Some straight women get uncomfortable about that and quietly quit or switch to another shift.

Both ARC House and Women Reaching Women took a relatively straightforward, nonjudgmental stance on lesbianism. They concentrated on providing support and creating options for their consumers, which included supporting women's sexual preferences.

There was always a percentage of the residents who were gay. Some of the counselors were also gay and politically active and that was very good for the residents. It was always an issue we were conscious of, to make ARC House safe for women who had any sexual preference. We were a house where all sexualities were accepted, where they could choose the partners of their choice, or they could talk about it freely in therapy. It has never been a major problem. (ARC)

A number of years ago, it created a real rift. There were some women who did not want to be involved if there were going to be lesbian women involved. Ultimately, how it was handled was saying that the project was designed to meet the needs of women, all women. If you couldn't work together with other women, you would just have to find another place to do your thing around women's issues in this field. I don't really see it as a major problem right now. Periodically, you'll see new people coming into the project and it's like, "Oh, okay, there's some lesbian women around here," that kind of thing. They either choose to stay or leave. It's their choice. (WRW)

In these organizations, woman-centered goals and feminist frameworks provided a rich, multifaceted context within which lesbian and straight women could join together. Lesbians' participation ensured that issues of sexual orientation would be addressed. In contrast, most white feminists and most politically active women of color held different priorities and goals and were aligned with different social movements (Joseph and Lewis, 1981; Murray, 1975). Members of these organizations needed to overcome many barriers before they could rely on face-to-face encounters and small group discussions for consciousness-raising on issues related to race and racism.

THE PARTICIPATION OF WOMEN OF COLOR

There's a lot of racism at our agency, just like there is everywhere. We're trying to address that now so that we can create a better environment for women of color when they do choose to work with us. (RCC)

Over many years, within each of these organizations, members had come to a broad consensus about the nature and importance of gender differences and differences among women based on sexual orientation. In these areas, they had developed relatively coherent belief systems and relatively effective practices. In contrast, these interviews occurred at a time when members were in the early stages of addressing differences among women based on race. Thus, their comments primarily reflected the issues with which they struggled, their commitment to deal with issues of race and racism, and their determination to increase the presence of women of color within their organizations. The challenges they faced were not unlike those confronted by the women's movement in general.

Although highly underrepresented, women of color had been active in the women's movement from its earliest years. For example, Pauli Murray, a black civil rights lawyer, was a founder of NOW, and Aileen Hernandez, a black union leader, was a founder and early president of NOW. Shirley Chisholm, a black congresswoman, was an early leader of the National Women's Political Caucus. In the 1970s, women of color established the National Black Feminist Organization, the National Alliance of Black Feminists, the National Association of Black Professional Women, the Mexican-American Women's National Association (MANA), and the Organization of Pan Asian American Women. A conference on the linkages between racism and sexism was cosponsored in 1976 by the National Black Feminist Organization and Sagaris, an independent institute for the study of feminist politics (Apuzzo and Powell, 1981).

Moreover, in the 1970s, the writings of women of color were already identifying the interconnections between racism and sexism. Some examples include "Double Jeopardy: To Be Black and Female" by Frances Beal (1970); *The Black Woman: An Anthology* by Toni Çade (1970); "Racism and Anti-Feminism" by Shirley Chisholm (1970); "A Historical and Critical Essay for Black Women" by Patricia Haden, Donna Middleton, and Patricia Robinson (1970); "Black Liberation and Women's Lib" by Linda La Rue (1970); "A Response to Inequality: Black Women, Racism and Sexism" by Diane K. Lewis (1977); "The Liberation of Black Women" by Pauli Murray (1975); and *Woman Power: The Movement for Women's Liberation* by Cellestine Ware (1970).

Still, at this point, the politics and investments of feminists and women of color were widely viewed as antithetical to one another (Dill, 1983; Garcia, 1989; Simons, 1979). Most women of color were highly suspicious of the women's movement. The efforts of the early radical feminists were based on theories about female oppression and on methods of educating and supporting women that were derived largely from their experiences in small groups, groups that consisted primarily of white, middle-class women. Based on these experiences and on white ethnocentrism in general, white feminists generalized from their own experiences to develop theories and practices that they believed universally applied to women as a group. They spoke of *women* as if this category captured the critical experiences of all females. They expected that conservative white women and women of color would increasingly recognize the nature of shared female oppression under patriarchy and the importance of women joining together to critique and resist male domination.

Feminists' determination to combat male supremacy and resist female subordination was understood by most women of color, however, as directly contradicting their investments in increasing the power of men in their communities. For many women of color, feminism's emphasis on male privilege appeared irrelevant, counterproductive, and presumptuous given the racial oppression of men of color and the privileged position of most white women as compared with women and men of color. Correspondingly, many white feminists believed that racism was not their issue. bell hooks described additional sources of tension:

> Many feminists continue to see [racism and sexism] as completely separate issues, believing that sexism can be abolished while racism remains intact, or that women who work to resist racism are not supporting feminist movement. Since black liberation struggle is so often framed in terms that affirm and support sexism, it is not surprising that white women are uncertain about whether women's

rights struggle will be diminished if there is too much focus on resisting racism, or that many black women continue to fear that they will be betraying black men if they support feminist movement. (1990, p. 59)

In the 1970s and 1980s, the writings by women of color began to challenge the basic premises of feminist theory, proposing alternative theories that analyzed differences among women based on race and class. This body of literature asserted that defining male domination as *the* source of female oppression blatantly ignored the experiences of women subjugated by racism and closely identified with the oppression of men of color. It emphasized that patriarchal domination is only one form of social domination, a form in which men oppress women. Under other systems of domination, women can be the oppressor and men and other women the oppressed. This literature began to identify how the interconnections of patriarchy with other social inequalities create different systems of subordination for different groups of women (Garcia, 1997; hooks, 1981; Hull, Scott, and Smith, 1982; Joseph and Lewis, 1981; Lorde, 1984; Moraga and Anzaldua, 1983; Smith, 1983).

The different perspectives and priorities of white feminists and women of color certainly contributed to the overall whiteness of these organizations. Also, the fact that these organizations were located in a predominantly white community helps explain why there were few members of color. Women's Transit Authority, Advocates for Battered Women, the Rape Crisis Center, and ARC House had one or two minority staff and a small number of minority volunteers. Except for Women's Transit Authority, they had one or two women of color on their boards. The sole staff member of Women Reaching Women was white. As a statewide organization, Women Reaching Women was able to establish chapters in areas of Wisconsin with large minority populations. Its volunteers of color were primarily associated with its Native American chapter and its "Rainbow Chapter," which consisted of African American, Hispanic, and Native American women and white low-income women.

In discussing the low participation of women of color in their organizations, members pointed to three factors: inadequate outreach efforts, racism, and differing understandings of the nature of female oppression. Once again, members were in uncharted territory.

Racism very often competes with sexism because of everybody wanting to get the very best that they can in terms of support and clarity. Who's the most oppressed? How does the system use us? It's difficult because the oppressions that people could and do have unity on are pitted against one another, competing for who's worse off, who's got the right answer. If somebody is accusing the system of being racist, do they have anything in common with someone who's accusing the system of being sexist? If so, what are the distinctions? My perspective of feminism is that you cannot address one without addressing the other. A lot of people are afraid of it because there aren't any obvious answers. We are the ones who are paving the way and creating the answers. (ABW)

Members believed that one barrier to the development of shared understandings was the racial composition of their organizations. Being predominantly white was viewed as a major factor for their remaining predominantly white.

Rape Crisis was "one of those feminist organizations that was started by a bunch of white women," and I'm sure that's what it looked like. I don't think we were conscious of having to outreach to the community because we were more conscious of changing the laws. By the time we got around to being conscious of the need to do much more active outreach, we had been around for several years, highly visible and highly white, so it made the outreach a lot harder.

Transit's mostly been an all-white organization, and because of that, has not been able to successfully recruit many minority women to volunteer or to paid positions. There have been a few minority women who have volunteered in the past, but it's been a very small number. We recently hired a black woman as a staff person, but it's clearly a mostly white organization. But because we haven't had many minority women involved as volunteers or paid staff, we haven't gotten more minority women involved.

In response to this dilemma, members placed much of their energy into outreach activities, to inform women of color about the problems addressed by their organizations and to encourage them to join. They expected that having staff, volunteers, and board members of color would result in the participation of more women of color. Often, members expressed disappointment in and impatience with their slow progress in achieving racial diversity.

There have just begun to be some minority chapters. But for some period of time, minority women were not attracted to this project at all. Some of the fault lies with the minority community itself. Some of it lies with the majority community. It's not every day that you run across women like their project director who purposely reaches out to minority women and tries to get them involved. Sometimes that's what's needed. (WRW)

We've had very little minority representation among Rape Crisis volunteers and staff. Among our clients, we have a percentage of minority people that is reflective of the percentage of minority people in this community. It is disturbing and negating that we can't get at least that reflected among the volunteers and staff. (RCC)

There are a number of minority riders, which is good. We've done good outreach in the community in terms of letting a variety of women know about our service. Our biggest downfall was that we didn't have any minority employees, and there were very few minority volunteers. Until now, we've just sat back and hoped, "Gee, it would be nice if these women came to us." But we've got to go out and ask them and make it an organization that can benefit them specifically. (WTA)

Are we just waiting for battered women to come to us? If that's the case, the minority community is not likely to come running to us if we don't do some outreach, express our interest in working with women of color, and ask them how we can work better with them. We are working on that now, but we've been around long enough that it's unfortunate that hasn't happened sooner. (ABW)

I'm concerned that there has never been a full-time black woman on the staff. If you don't make a conscious commitment in a community like Madison, it's easy to say, "I don't know anybody" and to overlook it. There has to be a conscious, stated effort that makes a commitment. (ARC)

For the Rape Crisis Center, additional barriers were created by the differing ways in which some white and black women viewed rape. The antirape movement assigned responsibility for rape to men and male culture. For white women, rape was a form of violence against women sanctioned by male supremacy. However, rape held other cultural meanings within the black community (Davis, 1981). False accusations of rape had long been used by whites specifically as a means of legitimating violence against black men and, more generally, as a way to enforce and reinforce racism. Members of the Rape Crisis Center were very aware that their philosophies and those of some black women appeared to be diametrically opposed.

Women of color sometimes have blamed women for rape. Not just white women. They've blamed the women, period. It's a conflict because the radical feminist women do not want to change their political philosophy on why men rape women. They do not want to blame women for it, and they're not going to change that. I'd like to see women of color working for women of color, but it's going to take a while. We will find women of color who do agree with our politics. We may not find many.

When we get into discussions with members of the black community about rape, we get a lot of "women lie" type stuff. A lot of times black organizations call on us to denounce the fact that a black man is once again being accused of sexual assault. That's a dilemma because, while we know the history of the word "rape" and how it's been used against black males, we are always on the victim's side, no matter who she accuses of assaulting her.

Although white feminists recognized that male dominance prevented men from fully understanding the experiences of women, many failed to see the ways in which white racism shaped their assumptions and clouded their vision about women of color (Frye, 1983). It was not sufficient to understand how economic deprivation, racial prejudice and discrimination, language barriers, and racial violence shaped the lives of women of color and exacerbated the effects of sexism. White feminists needed to address their own racism and racism within the women's movement. As one member of Women's Transit Authority observed:

> It's almost like what I get pissed at men laying on me. I was defining what I wanted from them, instead of asking them if they wanted to give any support. I have to deal with the "I'm privileged because I'm white," just like I want men to realize that they're privileged because they're male.

At the time of these interviews, the Rape Crisis Center was in the midst of a deliberative effort to address issues of race and racism. Its members described an incremental and shifting process through which they gained clarity and developed strategies: "We're all very committed to it, and we've started doing the work on it, and we'll just keep doing it. If it doesn't happen, it won't be because we didn't try."

> We do a lot of information sharing with the Urban League, educating them and having them do in-services for us. I don't think the issue of racism will ever totally be resolved, but there's a lot of steps we can take. How we're going to do that is to come out with a public statement on racism, do much more outreach into the black community as far as gaining allies, and two-way education.
>
> We've done a lot of dialoging in the last 18 months with the black community about why black women won't volunteer here. We wanted to set up a hotline run by minority people for minority people, and they didn't want it. They wouldn't come to the training sessions. We have minority victims, but we couldn't get minority people to take care of minority victims. It had a lot to do with white people saying, "This is an issue. You've got a problem." We tried to tackle it and discovered we were tackling it in the wrong way.

In response to their lack of success in attracting women of color, members of the Rape Crisis Center focused their efforts within their own organization, again using consciousness-raising but this time to examine their racism.

> Earlier this year, the two staff members of color were paid by the agency to attend a conference in New York City on racism within the antiviolence movement. It gave them lots of ideas which they are bringing back to the agency. They are going to do a mandatory in-service on racism. The plans are to have three special meetings for everyone in the agency, and there will be small group work done on confronting our own racism. It's going to be an educational tool, because a lot of women don't believe they are racist. The first step is to recognize how racist we are. Then, from there, to determine what we need to do to get women of color into the agency.

In each of these organizations, members' comments reflected their own histories and culture and the enormity of the task before them: to address their own racism, an approach that was rarely mentioned in society at large and for which there were few models, and to add a particularly volatile concern to their already difficult task of translating feminist principles into effective forms of feminist practice.

IDENTITY POLITICS AND ISSUES OF DIFFERENCE

> We're going to have to be more open to differences. But what we're learning is that it's okay to have values and philosophies around certain things. We're fig-uring out what those important issues are and what people need to agree with in order to work here. We don't all have to be white, middle class, young women. We can have a lot of different kinds of people working within the agency that will agree with those basic values and philosophies. (ABW)

In each of these organizations, members struggled to create policies and prac-tices based on shared experiences, common oppressions, and unifying needs. Their political commitments revolved around women as a group, with power differences between women and men their primary focus. Within this frame-work, they pursued the difficult task of addressing differences among women. They most effectively handled issues of homophobia since lesbians and woman-centered heterosexual women were well represented among their members. They had less success but were proactively dealing with the differ-ences that separated them from women of color.

Members' emphasis on shared female experience was a form of identity politics, that is, their political analyses and activism were derived primarily from their shared identities and oppression as women. The concept of iden-tity politics was introduced in the 1977 "A Black Feminist Statement" writ-ten by the Combahee River Collective.

> We realize that the only people who care enough about us to work consistently for our liberation is us. Our politics evolve from a healthy love for ourselves, our sisters and our community which allows us to continue our struggle and work. This focusing upon our own oppression is embodied in the concept of identity politics. We believe that the most profound and potentially the most radical pol-itics come directly out of our own identity, as opposed to working to end some-body else's oppression. (1983, p. 212)

Identity politics assumes a highly positive and self-validating identity and unity among people who share a particular form of subordination (Bulkin, Pratt, and Smith, 1988; Fuss, 1989). From a pragmatic point of view, identity politics acknowledges that people with identities and specific oppressions in common can usefully organize as a group to press for political changes that most directly affect them as a group. In the case of women, identity politics is based on the idea that women's oppression under patriarchy can be the basis of their developing an identity as women, which in turn can determine shared political interests and investments. As Linda Alcoff explained:

> One's identity [is] always a construction yet also a necessary point of departure . . . just as Jewish people can choose to assert their Jewishness, so black men, women of all races, and other members of more immediately recognizable oppressed groups can practice identity politics by choosing their identity as a member of one or more groups as their political point of departure. This, in fact, is what is happening when women who are not feminists downplay their identity as women and who, on becoming feminists, then begin making an issue of their femaleness. It is the claiming of their identity as women as a political point of departure that makes it possible to see, for instance, gender-biased language that in the absence of that departure point women often do not even notice. (1989, p. 322)

With a growing consciousness of differences among women, members of these organizations engaged in the long and difficult process of understanding and addressing differences while maintaining the overall concept of *woman* as the identity through which they would function. Their purpose was to address the ways in which homophobia, racism, and other prejudices had direct and negative effects on their services and operations. Dominant group members needed to take into account multiple forms of oppression and their own participation in the subordination of lesbians and women of color. Under these conditions, they would be able to attract lesbians and women of color who were similarly invested in *women helping women,* constructing a unity within the organization based on shared interests and commitments and respect for differences among women.

With diverse understandings of many aspects of gender, members moved toward consensus on those concepts of *woman* that were most important for organizational survival. Amid and through their tensions and deliberations, there emerged over time organization-based ideologies constructed around views of women that were both partial and pragmatic. Placed in the foreground were understandings about female identity and experience and gender inequality that were most important for interactions among members, external political processes, and goals and services. Their steadfast focus on being *women* was a source of strength and knowledge for their particular form of feminist practice.

Chapter Five

The Impact of
Funders and Fund-Raising

> Funding sources' demands have caused a lot of tension, but they're productive
> tensions. They've helped to create a clearer idea of what you need to know to
> operate. (WTA)

The requirements of funders are generally discussed in the literature in negative terms, as pushing feminist organizations toward less political missions and structures. For many feminist service organizations, funding requirements led to changed priorities, goal displacement, and co-optation (Ahrens, 1980; Ferree, 1987; Johnson, 1981; Morgen, 1986; Pride, 1981; Sullivan, 1982; Tierney, 1982). In other instances, institutionalized funding had positive effects on organizational development (Koss and Harvey, 1991; Matthews, 1989, 1994; Reinelt, 1994, 1995; Rodriguez, 1988; Simon, 1982). These five organizations were fortunate in that they did not have to compromise their basic values and goals to obtain funding. Still, inevitably, their programs were influenced by funding sources and the demands of fund-raising. As Charlotte Bunch observed, "We learned, as women everywhere have learned, that the demands of economic survival establish the parameters for the pursuit of dreams" (1981, p. xxii).

In all of these organizations, demands for their services increased rapidly as more and more women in the community learned of their existence and as other service providers became familiar with and respectful of their work. As they learned more about the nature of the problems they were addressing, members requested and received higher levels of funding to support more consumers, an expanded range of services, additional paid staff, and the recruitment and training of more volunteers. Increased funding was accompanied by heightened scrutiny and requirements. However, in many respects, the changes associated with obtaining higher levels of funding were viewed as inevitable, reasonable, and even useful. Funders insisted that organizations maintain statistics on service utilization; prepare financial reports; conduct staff and program evaluations; and engage in long-range planning. These features facilitated members' incorporation of sound business practices and provided the basis for fiscal accountability.

> Most of what is required by funders is simply good business practice and nothing else. We should be doing it even if they're not breathing down our necks. I'm not sure that we'd do things a whole lot differently if we didn't have the requirements. (ABW)

Demands of funders were viewed also as a contributing factor to the increased bureaucratization of these organizations (Matthews, 1995; Morgenbesser, Notkin, McCall, Grossman, and Nachreiner-Cory, 1981; Ristock, 1990; Schechter, 1982). Funders expected a visible spokesperson who could be held accountable, and they expected decisions to be made efficiently. As funders became "more and more stringent about what they wanted," members increasingly turned to their boards to handle the complexities of dealing with funding sources. Maintaining adequate levels of funding required that members devote considerable time to data collection and fund-raising activities and participate in contract billing systems that ignored the work of volunteers and emphasized one-to-one counseling. Although these organizations maintained a dual focus on social services and social change, funders primarily supported the provision of social services. Many social change efforts were conducted in addition to, not as part of, the full-time work for which staff were paid. Also, funding did not take into account that internal administrative tasks, fund-raising efforts, lobbying, and public speaking were handled by many staff, not only those who held administrative titles.

> Funding sources have concerns for efficiency and output. We contract to provide a certain level of services, and the number of hours or the number of clients we should be able to serve is calculated for organizations that have hierarchical structures, and maybe have two or three administrators, and the other people do nothing but direct services, and that's not the way we function. That builds in a high service level that people have to do in addition to other things, and that can be hard. (RCC)

In Advocates for Battered Women, ARC House, the Rape Crisis Center, and Women's Transit Authority, learning fund-raising strategies and creating data-collection systems to justify continued funding were essential but very difficult first steps. Fund-raising was extremely time-consuming, and the inability to predict funding levels from year to year created very stressful work environments. The organizations had multiple sources of funds, each with different reporting requirements. Looking at the unmet needs of their consumers and their own heavy workloads, members resented the time and game playing involved in obtaining and renewing funding, especially when they repeatedly needed to convince condescending and cynical funders of the need for their services.

> It's incredibly stressful and draining to have to worry about money. I deliver services, and then I have to go out and beat the bushes for money to keep my salary. It comes down to putting in 14-hour days. You work all day on your caseload, and then you have to go to some funding meeting and grovel for money when you spent the afternoon with some woman who's been raped. I do this incredibly painful job, and then I have to grovel in front of some politician about why they should pay some unit cost that's less than what they should be paying. (RCC)
>
> I always felt angry that besides doing all these goddamn forms for them to get their money, that you also had to be responsible for raising their consciousness. I mean, it's okay, but when it happens year after year and time after time, the same questions, "Why can't men do this?" There's always someone who says, "Do you take those women to bars?" Someone saw a prostitute get into one of our cars and thought that we should screen all women according to where they work. Some of them don't think it's right for taxpayers' money to be going for taking women home from bars. So we would say, "Yes, we do not question where women are going or coming from, and it is important to pick up a woman from a bar. She's even more vulnerable if she's been drinking." (WTA)

Members devoted extraordinary amounts of time to educating, lobbying, anticipating problems, responding effectively and credibly to both legitimate criticisms and prejudice-based opposition, resisting cuts in funding, and identifying opportunities to expand.

> We do a lot of political work. We have to know everything that's going on all the time. We have people that alert us when there's a problem before it gets too bad. We develop positive relationships with funders, police officers, social workers, legislative people. We do educational work constantly. But to be honest with you, I think what we're required to do is way above what we should be doing. My fear is that, if we didn't do it, we wouldn't survive. (ARC)

ARC House successfully retained funding at points when it had been eliminated, for example, when it convinced the legislature to release money into Corrections for its halfway house after "all the money was taken away by Corrections and given to the male houses." It also successfully retained funds from sources that were prepared to withdraw their funding based on the mistaken belief that Ananda Marga was a cult. Members corrected popular misconceptions about Ananda Marga and kept funders well informed about the organization's actual goals and methods.

A major success for Women's Transit Authority was obtaining funding from the city in 1983 for its expanded service program. As discussed in chapter 3, this program allowed Transit to expand its services by using local cabs. The impetus for this funding was the murder of a female student on the University of Wisconsin-Madison campus in July 1982, a tragedy that led to a community-wide outcry for additional transportation services. In response, a city committee suggested providing half-fare cab coupon booklets to women. Women's Transit Authority pointed out that this strategy still required women to be able to pay and that women would need to purchase the coupons in advance, which would not help them during emergencies. The organization submitted a proposal suggesting, "Instead of creating a new service, why not put the money into Women's Transit?"

It had the support of the mayor, members of the City Council who were friends of coordinators and drivers, and individuals from the university administration. Still, a decade after Women's Transit Authority was founded, conservative funders were raising familiar questions about whom they served. One woman who testified on the organization's behalf reported what she described as "a bizarre story."

I was down at the City Council, testifying on behalf of the program. One of the very conservative city councilmen really had his back up, and he was saying things like, "Suppose this kind of woman gets a ride or that kind of woman gets a ride." Finally, he said, "Supposing a lady of the evening," this is archaic language for a prostitute, "Supposing a lady of the evening rides on Women's Transit, what do you think of that?" I said, "If a lady of the evening rode Women's Transit and therefore was prevented from being murdered or sexually assaulted, I thought that it would be an extremely good use of tax dollars. Any investigation of a sexual assault or a murder costs at least several hundred thousand dollars of police time" . . . He went on to say, "Supposing somebody like Gloria Vanderbilt rides on Women's Transit?" I said, "First of all, the same principle applies. I would hope that, if Gloria Vanderbilt had lost her wallet and needed safe transportation, she would call Women's Transit. Hopefully, the driver would identify her as Gloria Vanderbilt and encourage her to make a donation at the Women's Transit office."

Even with a generally supportive funding source, members of feminist organizations and their advocates needed to be prepared to answer the questions of cynical decision makers in a manner that would not undermine their existing support and jeopardize approval of their requests.

The City Council approved Women's Transit Authority's proposal. The expanded service program allowed Women's Transit Authority to offer women free cab service when they had waited over 45 minutes for a Transit car or when they requested rides outside of Women's Transit Authority's boundaries but within city limits. Calls from women in danger were still handled only by Women's Transit Authority cars.

The staff were dismayed and angered that it took a woman's murder to stimulate community concern about women's safety and to focus public attention on Women's Transit Authority. Further, they were concerned that the community viewed the expanded service program as a "solution" that absolved the community of further responsibility for dealing with male violence against women.

> I was amazed and disgusted at the same time that the media were all calling us that one day, wanting to know what our response was. We felt there was some victim blaming going on, "If she would have used Transit . . ." All the TV stations, all the radio stations, suddenly wanted to talk to us. We had to beg them prior to this to air our PSAs. We had to send them letters, call them up on the phone, and beg. We talked about what mixed feelings we had, that a tragedy resulted in people saying, "Yeah, we'll give Transit more money," as if somehow that took care of it. We were glad for Transit because more money and staff were needed, but sad that it had to come from such an incident.

The expanded service program nearly doubled Women's Transit Authority's ridership and allowed it to offer services to low-income women on the outskirts of the city. It used about 15 cabs a night, reducing the 75-minute wait time to 30 to 45 minutes. In addition, this program increased the organization's visibility in the community, which was mostly positive, but not always: "People who didn't like us before didn't like us any better now, because not only were women getting free Women's Transit rides, they were getting free cab rides." Members were particularly pleased that they had produced "an environmental change."

Members also had to consider the impact on their funding of political actions not directly related to their work. Especially for those organizations with close ties to other feminist groups, it was important to maintain credibility within the general community *and* within their feminist network.

> We end up with one foot in both camps. We have to keep the status quo happy, and we have to keep the feminist, politically left community happy. If we're approached by a leftist coalition to "Let's do something to disrupt X, Y, or Z," we have to decide how visible we're going to be and what we're going to base our decision on without alienating this coalition. Whatever we decide to do, we can't go against any of our funding contracts, and we have to be concerned about our image in the media. The Rape Crisis Center is both mainstream and nonmainstream. In a town like Madison, you have to find a way as an agency to keep both sides happy, and it's not easy.

Making political statements and endorsements was frequently mentioned as an issue in Women's Transit Authority. Supporting another group's endeavors, advertising in specific newspapers, or choosing a place to hold an event were all viewed as political decisions. The issue was whether to focus only on issues directly related to its services or to involve Women's Transit Authority in other political activities that "have something to do with solidarity of women all over the world."

Many members were strong supporters of other issues related to leftist or feminist politics, or both, and were interested in lending organizational support. At the same time, they were concerned that their association with other political causes might jeopardize community support and funding. Although many candidates for public office and for leadership in the Wisconsin Student Association (an organization that provided some of the organization's funding) included support for Women's Transit Authority in their platforms, endorsing individual political candidates was viewed as unwise. Women's Transit Authority endorsed few activities outside of those that dealt with violence against women: "The organization has very carefully avoided stating anything except that it was for giving women mobility and against a rape culture. That has been our point of unity. We have a limited focus, and that's what works for us." Some members viewed this as a very conservative strategy.

> We've had problems with deciding if we should endorse certain happenings. Do we want to stick our necks out? How will that change our image? There's diverse attitudes within Transit about what to do, but basically, it's conservative. We stick to just our functions so that we continue to be funded. We do not feel free to endorse certain events or take part in them for fear of being seen as too radical. That's because of funding sources. We're very concerned about our image.

Other members of Women's Transit Authority believed that their approach was not only appropriate but also an example of an important process, that is, being able to move beyond one's own personal politics to look at how an issue could affect the organization as a whole.

In all five organizations, members did not pursue funding sources that were inconsistent with their politics. They would, however, temper their language and de-emphasize ideology. In terms defined and understood by funders, members focused on the need for and the effectiveness of their services.

> We get our funding because we do what we say we're going to do. When we go out for money, we tone down the politics. We talk about services and get out the statistics. You've set your goals, and you've met your goals, and X amount of clients weren't served because we need another counselor and X amount of money. We go about it very matter-of-factly. (RCC)

So far, we've been fairly successful in tiptoeing around some of the advocacy
or more social change things that we do because that scares them a lot. Our
funding sources know that we're different than conventional social services, and
they allow us to be different because they can see that we're effective. (ABW)

I don't think it's changed our political stance, but it's made us present it in a
more palatable, more understandable manner. We try to speak their language and
educate, trying to win support that way. We'll get a certain amount of flack for
spending time on women learning about nutrition or about their bodies. That's
been dealt with by the project sticking to its guns and getting results, by providing statistics on our success rates. (ARC)

There were also instances in which members resisted funders' demands or
gave up funding rather than acquiescing to requirements that would undermine their basic principles. For example, after one year of funding from the
county, Women's Transit Authority was informed that it needed to report detailed information on its riders, including names, addresses, ages, and incomes. The provision of this data would be required for all agencies receiving Title XX monies for 1979. Members of Women's Transit Authority
believed that collection of this data was unnecessary, would be a burden on
their drivers, and constituted invasion of their riders' privacy, and the county
did not provide funding for a second year.

We felt that was confidential information. We didn't want to report it to the
county or to keep it ourselves. It invaded women's privacy, and there was no
need for it. As a result, because we weren't willing to agree to that, we did not
get money from the county for the second year. It was frustrating because we
had spent a lot of time on it, but people bounced back pretty well.

When this same mandate from the county required that the Rape Crisis
Center provide the names of consumers assisted by paid staff, the Rape Crisis Center requested permission to use pseudonyms. The county responded by
asserting that state and federal laws required names. Rather than retreat from
ensuring consumer confidentiality, the Rape Crisis Center decided to negotiate for a waiver from the state and federal government and, if that was not
successful, not to provide advocacy services at all: "The risk was there that
we would lose that whole service component, and that was hard for the center to decide, to take that risk."

We decided that we'd never make a threat about not providing services unless
we were ready to live with it. To say, "If you don't fund this, we won't provide
this service" was a very serious thing to do. We always wanted to provide services somehow. So, there would always be long philosophical meetings. What
do we say we will do if they don't provide this funding? What will we say we

will do if they do provide it? That was always part of the process. We got a waiver saying we could use pseudonyms. Otherwise, we had chosen not to accept those funds. People have a right to tell who they want to that they've been assaulted.

The Rape Crisis Center negotiated a system wherein it would use pseudonyms, "a dead feminist for every month. Like for the month of February, Susan Anthony was the pseudonym for all of our clients, because her birthday is in February. Then, we used letters of the alphabet for the middle initial, so we'd have Susan A. Anthony, Susan B. Anthony. We maintained the master list of who Susan A. Anthony really was, but they couldn't have that list, and they accepted that."

In Advocates for Battered Women, fund-raising successes caused unanticipated difficulties. Its budget increased from $11,500 in 1977 to $180,000 in January 1978. Its staff had increased from three part-time positions to eight full-time positions and one part-time position. In April 1978, the shelter opened with a new group of volunteers and a largely inexperienced staff. The staff tried to do as much as they could in a wide range of areas; worker roles and responsibilities changed frequently.

> Organizations should start out with people being very clear about what their responsibilities are and what somebody else's are. We never had that. Besides that, it was always up for grabs. Every three minutes, somebody wanted to play merry-go-round with jobs. It was really tiring. We had so many meetings during that year and changed positions so many times, I don't even remember what I was. I just remember endless conversations about how we could label what we all were doing.

As discussed in the following two chapters, the development of Advocates for Battered Women was marked by controversies over service priorities and organizational structure into the mid-1980s. Having fewer staff when the shelter opened may have provided members with more time to develop shared understandings of goals and priorities and to thoughtfully expand staff roles and services. Slower development may have led to more stable development.

ARC House was the only organization in which a funding source significantly influenced organizational goals and methods. In its four-year grant from the Wisconsin Council on Criminal Justice, funding levels decreased each year. Correspondingly, each year, its funding from the State Division of Corrections increased. After the grant ended, the Division of Corrections regularly provided over 75% of the organization's funding.

In contrast to members' investments in working as a therapeutic community, Corrections was interested solely in "community adjustment," that is, residents' obtaining their GEDs, employment, and housing. In addition to their counseling residents about these issues, Corrections expected staff to work as case managers, linking residents with other agencies for vocational counseling, education, training to increase employability, and assistance in finding employment and housing. In its second year, ARC House began to place more emphasis on the vocational aspects of its program.

> That was the first crisis we pulled through. We could have collapsed at that point and been one of those experiments that didn't make it. We saw the need for the change, but that's what we were being paid for too.

In most respects, members believed that the shift from a therapeutic community to a transitional-living facility was a positive one. It was consistent with their own broadened understandings of the aspects of women's lives that needed to be addressed in order for those women to become emotionally and economically independent, ARC House's primary goals.

> You're always trying to get the balance. You lean toward a therapeutic community approach, and you find that the women are getting in touch with their feelings and working on heavy issues, trying to undo their dependency on men and being in destructive relationships. But it seems like they're never ready to leave. That's what happened before. The criminal justice system said we kept them too long, "They wouldn't be kept that long in prison." You have the world breathing down your neck saying, "Is this woman ready for a job? Does she have her diploma?" It is a fact that she's going to have to go out and make it. And so, you go back the other way, into more case management, and everybody's got their GED and a job, but they're in trouble again because their self-esteem is still a mess. I don't see that there's a resolution to that dilemma. It's always a struggle. As long as that struggle is happening in a conscious way, then that's okay.

In 1979, ARC House established two specialized positions. One counselor had increasingly focused on vocational issues; her role evolved into a vocational counselor position. In addition, ARC House had decided to add an AODA component to its program. It had become very apparent that a high proportion of the residents had problems with drugs and alcohol. With a two-year grant from the State Bureau of Alcohol and Other Drug Abuse, the organization hired an AODA counselor. After two years, its AODA position was funded through the Division of Corrections. Still, Corrections was most invested in its vocational program.

ARC House was incorporating aspects of two very different systems. The AODA system emphasized treatment, self-help, and long-term support for people in recovery. The criminal justice system focused on protecting the community, punishment, and time-limited rehabilitation. With the criminal justice system's valuing only short-term assistance directed toward "community adjustment," ARC House's challenge was to convince Corrections of the importance of maintaining women as residents for sufficient lengths of time to adequately deal with their personal issues and chemical abuse.

Corrections wants to see that the women have a job and are earning money before they leave and are on their feet financially, and for very good reasons. Those changes are very positive ones, and I don't question them. But that's the only place they tend to pressure us. They're not as interested in the drug and alcohol issues and the issues around incest and dependency on men. The difficulty has been in having people recognize the importance of the personal-growth aspects of the program and that there are all kinds of issues that the men's programs don't ever have to deal with . . . If we were just a criminal justice project, we would only have a vocational program. On the other hand, the drug and alcohol field tends to go totally in the treatment direction, keeping somebody in-house looking at their issues for six months or so, and then talking about getting a job. We have to balance all that and somehow come out smelling like a rose to all of them and feeling okay about ourselves and being successful with the clients on our terms and everybody else's terms, which is crazy making.

I'm surprised they survived, to tell you the truth. They really sent shock waves through the whole system. It wasn't so much that it was sponsored by a meditation group, and it wasn't necessarily the feminist stuff that was bothering them. It was the kind of programming that was being promoted that was freaking everyone out. Now, it's more state-of-the-art. But at that time, they were horrified. They thought that we were being conned right and left because "we were soft on criminals" . . . Programming in Corrections was largely vocational, and if you did any kind of therapy or anything that in the drug and alcohol system would be acceptable, it was very suspect. We had to do a lot more educational work and work harder on our credibility in order to maintain the kind of innovative programming we wanted. We haven't knuckled under in terms of innovative programming, but it takes a lot more political work to keep it.

With only one paid staff position and limited funding for its activities, Women Reaching Women was the most financially vulnerable of these organizations, being dependent first on a federal grant and then on block grants from the State of Wisconsin Bureau of Alcohol and Other Drug Abuse. Beginning in its second year, 1979, Women Reaching Women had provided some funding to individual chapters, including part-time salaries for five volunteer coordinators around the state. Due to cutbacks in WAAODA, these part-time positions were eliminated three years later, in 1982. Not being able to pay chapter coordinators hampered Women Reaching Women's recruitment of new volunteers, community outreach and educational efforts, and fund-raising to support chapter activities: "It's very difficult to set up volunteer organizations with a volunteer coordinator who's volunteering."

Without its own executive director and board, the organization was largely dependent on the fund-raising efforts of WAAODA's executive director and the funding priorities set by the WAAODA board. Given that WAAODA was having its own share of financial difficulties and that Women Reaching Women was not among its priorities, members had few options for expanding funding. By the mid-1980s, Women Reaching Women could not cover volunteer expenses for travel, long-distance telephone calls, or supplies.

I find myself even cutting back my trips into Madison because of the gas expense. My goal right now is to find an agency that will let us go under their umbrella, so we can use their tax-exempt status and hopefully raise some money. Even if we paid gas mileage to the people that volunteer, then it isn't an out-of-pocket expense for them. Time is very valuable, but gas mileage, that comes right out of their pocket. Ultimately, I'd like to be able to pay them for their time. It would certainly be nice to pay qualified people to handle jobs that corporations pay mucho dollars for.

Only 4 chapter coordinators, out of 25, were paid part-time, and they were funded through local agencies or councils. Local agencies and AODA councils were important sources of support but could also constrain their work.

When Women Reaching Women is unencumbered, when it does not have any paid staff or it's not housed in the council, it can fly on its own. It can take on issues without fear of repercussions. The weakness is legitimacy. Without being under an umbrella in a local situation, they have to work twice as hard to get out the message that they're here and to be accepted. At the same time, once they go under the umbrella of an organization, they have to respond to certain parameters that organization has. In one county, the coordinator was paid for 10 hours, so the council on alcoholism felt that the program should be a 10-hour-a-week program, and Women Reaching Women can't be a 10-hour-a-week program. It's much larger than that. The tension was incredible.

Members of Women Reaching Women were discouraged and angered by the stresses, both financial and psychological, that accompanied insufficient funding. They agreed that, for the long-range survival of the project, the work of chapter coordinators needed to be compensated and chapters needed funding to support their activities.

Although all of these organizations would have benefited from additional funding, they provided services at no cost to consumers. Not charging women was a matter of principle and of recognizing the low-income status of many of their consumers. Some chapters of Women Reaching Women did request two or three dollars a session for their support groups, "for postage, paper, coffee, just to keep them going," but no woman was excluded because of her inability to pay. When employed, ARC House residents were expected to pay a minimal room and board fee to have the experience of budgeting and feeling more independent. Until the organization moved into its new facilities in 1983, Advocates for Battered Women charged a nominal fee of $2.50 in response to funding requirements, but no woman was turned away or pressured to pay, much to the dismay of funders who consistently questioned why they were being asked to cover these costs.

> Women who are being beaten have a right to shelter and safety. The community has a responsibility to provide those services and an obligation to pay for those services. Women who are in crisis shouldn't have to be concerned about whether or not they can pay.

Similarly, although it "caused trouble with our funders," members of the Rape Crisis Center did not believe it was appropriate to charge consumers: "If you get victimized, it's not your fault. You've already been victimized. Enough losses."

> We, as a society, owe women support when they've been sexually assaulted. Sexual assault is wrong. It's a violent act which no woman deserves, and therefore she should not have to pay to get over it. She should be able to receive all the support she needs without having to pay money for it. There are some women who would love to see the perpetrators pay for it.

In general, ARC House, Advocates for Battered Women, the Rape Crisis Center, and Women's Transit Authority were funded at levels that enabled them to effectively pursue their missions. Except for Women Reaching Women, funding levels increased, as did their sources of funding. Members' skills in achieving credibility among funders and in documenting the need for and effectiveness of their services were obviously essential to their survival. However, two other factors were also critically important in defining these organizations as "adequately funded." The first was paid staff's willingness to assume responsibilities well beyond their formal job descriptions and the work for which they were paid. The second crucial element was the active participation of large numbers of dedicated volunteers in Advocates for Battered Women, the Rape Crisis Center, Women's Transit Authority, and Women Reaching Women.

In the early years, unpaid labor established the necessary foundations for the continued growth of these organizations. Over time, volunteers continued to contribute vital support, energy, and labor. They delivered core services; assisted in the preparation and defense of funding proposals; did public speaking; performed administrative and office work; participated in training new staff and volunteers; spoke on radio, television, and with members of the press; and participated in internal decision making. Their work was indispensable.

Members expressed some ambivalence over their reliance on volunteerism. Were they exploiting women by having them perform duties that under other circumstances would be funded? Were they conforming to social norms that generally relegated women to unpaid labor in their communities and in their homes? Were they preventing the participation of low-income women and women of color because, as a group, those women were more likely to need full-time employment?

Their predominant stance, however, was to assert with pride the importance of volunteers within their organizations. Their volunteers were highly respected within and outside of their organizations; they assumed major responsibilities and had considerable autonomy. Many were learning new skills and achieving levels of independence and power they had not previously experienced. It was personally fulfilling for many to be taking an active part in a spirited and increasingly influential women's movement.

> It fits my politics. I want to make changes in women's lives, that's important to me. I am feeling much more powerful myself and realizing that the key to change is participation. You don't change anything unless you participate. It may take a while, it may be difficult, you may struggle, you may get burned out, but change doesn't happen unless you participate. (RCC)
>
> The volunteers, who are at the bottom of the usual hierarchical totem pole, are actually the ones who make the organization. If they didn't exist, it wouldn't exist. The people with the least amount of power traditionally are the ones who keep the place alive and functioning. (WTA)

Through a combination of passion, courage, political savvy, and hard work, members were able to sustain the political missions of their organizations. They effectively balanced their commitments to social change and their need to maintain funding: "We've had to adapt to funding requirements, but we haven't had to sacrifice our basic feminist values or our fundamental political analysis and orientation to the work that we do." (ABW)

Chapter Six

Providing Social Services/
Pursuing Social Change

I don't know if the struggle of being a social change agency will ever be resolved. It will always be a struggle. I hope it will always be a struggle is what
I'm really saying. If we give up, that's what's going to be sad, because we'll become more of a social service. So, I hope we keep struggling. (ABW)

In these five organizations, members maintained social change and service
delivery as interconnected missions. *Understanding gender inequality as a
source of women's problems* provided the foundation for their investments in
promoting both individual and social change for women. The social change
missions of these organizations were most obvious in members' efforts to alter community attitudes, influence legislation and social policy, and change
conventional service systems. However, feminist commitments to social
change also provided the foundation for their direct services to individual
women. *Understanding gender inequality as a source of women's problems*
ensured that the limits of individual change strategies remained clear to members and consumers. Ultimately, meaningful change for individual women
would require meaningful social change for all women, including, for example: the availability of adequate and affordable housing, child care, and educational opportunities; increased employment opportunities, financial and legal assistance, and pay equity; improved health care, including maintaining
women's right to an abortion and federal funding for family-planning services
and abortion; and social programs and policies that protected women from
victimization in their communities, workplaces, and homes.

Women's Transit Authority primarily stressed the principle of *self-help.* In the
other organizations, members sought to *empower consumers through self-help
and sisterhood.* Members shared their experiences as women with consumers,
worked to minimize power differences, and provided consumers with support
and validation. They also *empowered consumers through consciousness-raising,*

helping them to understand the influence of social circumstances and cultural values on their personal lives. As appropriate, members offered consumers information about discrimination, gender-role socialization, and female victimization, and they encouraged women to explore a range of options beyond culturally prescribed behaviors and roles. They assisted women in working to reverse the powerlessness inherent in their social position by becoming more assertive and self-directed, and in some circumstances, more economically independent. They encouraged women not to blame themselves for their own victimization or for their inability to overcome societal constraints.

DIRECT SERVICE DEBATES AND DILEMMAS

Advocates for Battered Women

Advocates for Battered Women assisted battered women primarily by providing crisis intervention, support, information and referrals, and counseling. Members continuously debated whether self-help was the only appropriate method for their work with battered women, what forms of assistance constituted self-help, and if providing counseling moved Advocates for Battered Women too far in the direction of becoming a conventional agency.

> There has always been a therapy or self-help argument that goes on around here. Some people feel that anything more than an informational counseling session with a woman is therapy, and it's not what we do. Do we want to do counseling with women or are we there strictly as an advocate to say, "I'm here. If you want to work with me, fine. If you don't want to work with me, fine. Our main concern is that you be safe and get any information that you need." That has been seen as the struggle between becoming more traditional, like a social service agency, by counseling battered women versus just making sure we have a place for them and give them the information that they might need. Those arguments and discussions have always been healthy. They've always kept us striking a healthy balance.

A major controversy concerned the extent to which Advocates for Battered Women should be working with women and their children as a family unit. In the early 1980s, a research grant funded an 18-month project to assess how battered women's shelters could assist families where there had been violence. Under the leadership of the woman who had obtained the funding, Advocates for Battered Women began working with mothers and their children as a family, with some staff assuming that this program would become an integral part of the organization's services. Toward the very end of the project, however, the majority of staff decided that shelter services would return to their original focus, that is, helping battered women.

It wasn't until the last month that people said that the program was too therapeutic, and they didn't want it to be integrated into the organization. People were
all bent out of shape about the influence it was having on the direction of the organization toward therapy.

There was a lot of paranoia on the part of some staff in the shelter that we
were moving toward more traditional approaches to violence and woman abuse,
that we were looking at family systems and how the violence was perpetuated
and how we could intervene in the family as opposed to looking at the political
and social reasons why that woman was being abused. Most people would see
that as a more traditional time, when we were asking the woman to take a look
at the whole cycle of violence within the family.

The energy behind this debate concerned the political conservatism associated with the family systems approach and the more radical politics associated with emphasizing the plight of battered women and women's self-help
(Withorn, 1980). Throughout the battered women's movement, there was
concern that focusing on "domestic violence" and assisting "the family" di-
verted attention away from woman abuse, thereby undermining public concern and funding for battered women (Schechter, 1982). The emphasis on
"family violence" ignored the relationships between gender inequality and
male violence against women (Kurz, 1989).

Advocates for Battered Women returned to "a less traditional form of
working with women in the shelter." The woman's advocate and staff from
the children's program worked with the mother and her children on a case-by-
case basis, when parenting was identified as a problem by the mother or by a
child. Otherwise, they provided the children with supervised activities.

Advocates is a crisis center. That means we don't work with the family, that we
are here for the woman. If she happens to come with kids, we have activities for
the kids. We should focus on women and let them identify what their needs are.
If they identify their children as an area that they would like some help on, then
that is when we decide to work with kids.

By the mid-1980s, Advocates for Battered Women had created a new program for children in the shelter. Male volunteers and work-study students and
female staff and volunteers worked with the children, focusing on improving
their self-esteem and social and problem-solving skills. Most members retained the view that emphasizing woman abuse and assisting women was a
strength and a core part of the organization's mission.

Unlike any other organization in this area that deals with battered women and
their families, there's an emphasis on the woman in this shelter program. It's designed to meet her needs, to help her deal with her problems, to give her the

knowledge and skills that she needs, to provide her with an emergency service that isn't available anywhere else.

In returning to a less traditional approach, staff decided also to place a greater emphasis on self-help.

> In the past, an advocate would spend a lot of time with individual battered women and their children. The decision was made that individual advocates did not need to be in the shelter eight hours a day. Staff would work with battered women when they requested it. It cut down the time in telling her what's available and how the place works. We wanted to get away from battered women feeling like their advocate had all the answers.

Battered women in the shelter would receive less general information and ongoing support from staff. Specific assistance would be provided as needed. Volunteers would continue to support shelter residents and provide 24-hour crisis line services. Staff would devote more time to walk-in counseling for nonsheltered women.

The Rape Crisis Center

For the Rape Crisis Center, the most significant service issue was dealing with the continually expanding numbers of women asking for assistance and having no funds to increase its staff.

> We don't have waiting lists. It's immediate response to a survivor. They'd just keep coming in the door, and they'd just keep getting assigned to direct service staff. We didn't deal with setting limits until people started to get sick. They'd get cold after cold after cold or have double binds that you couldn't possibly get out of. Like being at the funding presentation wearing the beeper and having the beeper go off and thinking, "Now what do I do, try to get money for the agency or run down to the hospital?"
>
> That's the major debate right now, "What do we do with new people when no one has any more time to give? How much time can you expect from any one woman?" We pay people to work 40 hours a week and then we're closer to 80. Volunteers that contract to work 40 hours a month sometimes end up doing double that or more. At what point do you say no?

Since 1974, volunteers had handled the crisis line and staff had assumed responsibility for face-to-face counseling, advocacy and accompaniment, and crisis intervention. The staff prided themselves on consistently being there for their clients, placing no limits on the time required. In addition to their work during the day, staff were on call nights and weekends to assist women who chose to report. They would "go to a hospital or to a victim's home or to a police station and do whatever was needed."

Any time anybody wanted to report to the police or was thinking about getting involved in that process and wanted an advocate, we got called, because the crisis center volunteers weren't trained to do advocacy. You could have a real intense day, go home, and get called in the middle of the night and have to go out again. That got ridiculous because nobody could function.

To address this problem, in 1980, volunteers assumed the additional responsibility of face-to-face crisis intervention and advocacy from 7 P.M. to 7 A.M. The staff would begin working with the victim the next day. This change reduced the workload of the staff, but it also changed a long-held and valued practice of having one staff member remain with a client from the initial contact on, throughout her dealings with the criminal justice system and for as long as the client requested services.

The volunteer counselors are now trained to go through the first part of the legal process. That was a painful decision because there's all sorts of stuff that happens when somebody first reports that can be critical to what happens in the rest of their criminal justice experience. It meant giving up some power to control that. It meant giving up some continuity. It meant that no longer would a woman meet a counselor one night who would be with her for the rest of the time, and that could be two years. It was giving up a part that was important, but it was absolutely necessary.

Continuity was also disrupted by having victims rely on the staff as a group rather than having one advocate throughout: "All of a sudden, we'd have two court cases in two different branches at the same time, so we had to have advocates switching off. We never had that before, not being able to guarantee continuity."

In addition to increasing the advocacy responsibilities of their volunteers, by the mid-1980s, Rape Crisis Center members were considering various options for setting limits on their services, including increasing their use of groups, prioritizing calls and having waiting lists, deciding how frequently clients could be seen for counseling, limiting clients' access to paid staff by not giving out home phone numbers, and not offering three- and four-hour counseling sessions. Members' willingness to change based on ongoing assessment of their services, with feminist principles being a determining factor for their decisions, has been identified as a characteristic of highly effective rape crisis centers (Koss and Harvey, 1991).

Women Reaching Women

Gaining acceptance at the local level was the major challenge for Women Reaching Women. Many people in their field had long-term connections with and deep loyalties to Alcoholics Anonymous (AA), the dominant self-help organization for alcoholics, and to Alanon, a self-help organization for family members of alcoholics, including spouses, partners, and adult children of alcoholics.

> In AODA, there are turf issues all over the place. They fight some very resistive people right now. A lot of men who are AODA coordinators in a given county, for instance, don't feel safe with Women Reaching Women. As men become more accepting, the doors will open.

Women Reaching Women had to establish itself as meeting a different need, as fulfilling a different purpose, and as willing to work in cooperation with the AA/Alanon community. Establishing positive relationships with AA and Alanon was often the first step in creating a new chapter.

> There was some concern from the AA and Alanon community that there was no need for such an organization because AA and Alanon can cover those needs. Before even getting started and doing any distributing of brochures or going to the newspaper, we convened a group of representatives from AA and Alanon, people who have agreed to break their anonymity and meet with outsiders, and we explained the program to them. We talked to them about the program and the reasons for having the program, and they began to realize that we were not going to be taking away from AA. As a matter of fact, we were going to bridge a gap and work with them. That seems to help a lot, to focus on working in cooperation with the AA community.

Women Reaching Women's primary functions—that is, raising public awareness of the particular problems and needs of female substance abusers, helping women gain access to treatment, and changing the treatment system to better meet women's needs—did not overlap substantially with AA's goals. Furthermore, Women Reaching Women's work directly benefited traditional treatment agencies and AA. Some chapters of Women Reaching Women established child care projects for women in treatment, in aftercare, and in AA. Through their First Friends projects, they provided information about and accompanied women to their first meetings of Alcoholics Anonymous, Alanon, or Alateen, a self-help organization for teenage relatives of alcoholics.

> First Friends is the most important aspect of our chapter. So many women are frightened of going to these meetings, partly because of the small percentage of women, but for other reasons too. The human services people in our community

are excited about having someone to call, rather than just saying to a client, "Go to an AA meeting tonight."

However, their all-women support groups, and especially their Women for Sobriety groups, could serve as alternatives to AA. Women for Sobriety emphasized increasing women's self-esteem and their understanding of the psychological stresses and family relationships of women alcoholics. As described by Jean Kirkpatrick, the founder of Women for Sobriety, "The Women for Sobriety program is an affirmation of the value and worth of each woman. It is a program that leads each woman to asserting her belief in self, a program that leads her to seeing herself in a positive and self-confident image. She will see herself as forceful and compassionate, assertive and warm, capable and caring, resourceful and responsible" (1980, p. 172).

We often set up Women for Sobriety meetings, which is an alternative or addition to AA. It's a women's meeting totally. In AA, the steps are things like, "I'm powerless over alcohol." AA was designed for men. In order for them to become healthier, they do need to give up some of their power. But for women to say, "I'm trying to get well, and I give up my power" doesn't work. That's probably one of the primary differences in terms of Women for Sobriety. It's a real affirming program.

In Women Reaching Women, the idea is women taking charge. That idea can actually counter the principles of AA. Women are not brought up to be independent, so telling us we're powerless feeds right into that. I don't think helpless is the way we're supposed to remain.

For projects housed in agencies that are very conservative and traditional, generally speaking, they can't start with a Women for Sobriety chapter. I'm not saying that they can never do it, but that's not the first thing they should do if they want to survive and make an impact.

Within Women Reaching Women chapters, there were some tensions due to women's different views of AA. Some women were critical of AA and defined Women Reaching Women as a clear alternative. Others used Women Reaching Women groups in addition to AA and were uncomfortable with women's criticisms of AA.

There are women who use this group as an alternative to AA rather than in addition to AA. There are tensions when these women are critical of AA. I had that experience, and it scared me for a while because AA helped me. I see Women Reaching Women as an addition. I've got a firm base in AA, but in order to develop myself further, I was looking for the feminist support. When I'm hearing them countering something that I feel a sense of loyalty to, I do have problems with that. And in AA, it's like "No, this gives me all I need." There are different philosophies, and sorting that out is difficult.

By the mid-1980s, through numerous individual contacts and meetings at the local level, Women Reaching Women had convinced many AA groups and AODA organizations of the usefulness of its project. It alleviated fears of competition by stressing the ways in which its services increased access to and facilitated the work of other AODA groups. This was critically important since its chapters relied largely on referrals from established AODA service providers and cooperation from members of county AODA councils, AA, and Alanon. Also, many chapters relied on these groups for space, supplies, and in some cases funding for chapter coordinators.

ARC House

In Advocates for Battered Women, the Rape Crisis Center, and Women Reaching Women, members could hope for, but could not expect or demand, the changes they themselves would have wished for their consumers. In contrast, ARC House staff were obligated to establish desired outcomes for each of its residents and to actively assist each one in achieving specified outcomes.

> Successful completion normally means that a woman is enrolled in a vocational training program with a reliable, legal source of income or has maintained employment for a specified period of time with a satisfactory evaluation of work performance from the employer; has an acceptable independent living situation; and sufficient savings for at least one month's expenses. (Renewal grant, 1983)

Based on their own experiences with female offenders, staff shared the concerns of the Division of Corrections. As case managers and as counselors, they focused on vocational counseling, education, housing, and employment. However, ARC House also addressed personal issues.

> The residents usually have histories with chemical abuse and incest. Some have very caring families, but most of them don't. They've had tremendously hard lives. Many of them have been dependent on welfare or the criminal justice system or the drug and alcohol system for years. They haven't stood on their own and don't know how to take responsibility for their lives. . . . Feminism to me means taking a holistic approach. It's not enough to get a woman a job. You've got to deal with her family and relationships and how she feels about herself and her health. If a woman is suffering from PMS or her birth control is screwing her up, that's got to be dealt with. If you have a woman in prison because of child abuse, we need to deal with the issues that led to the abuse. And most of those women have left backgrounds of incest and abuse. I'm not saying "most" meaning more than 50%. I'm meaning just short of 100%. The statistics are overwhelming. If they want change, that person has to be dealt with in her entirety.

ARC House defined its goals as "having women improve their self-image as women, not solely looking at their capacities to go out and get jobs"; "focusing on how women can improve the quality of their relationships with men and not let themselves be taken advantage of as women in those relationships"; decreasing their dependence on men; and helping residents deal with family relationships, parenting skills, substance abuse, eating disorders, experiences with incest and other forms of abuse, and health care. Also, unlike other correctional facilities, ARC House allowed some women to have their children with them.

> It's a problem to have a woman leave not having tried to combine her new sense of herself and her new life with trying to raise a child and keep a job. We wanted the women to have the practical experience of having a child right there, in her life all along.

In describing the problems of female offenders, members of ARC House consistently highlighted women's low self-esteem, dependency, alcohol and drug abuse, and experiences of incest and other forms of abuse. Research has confirmed members' insights into the critical connections among these factors in women's lives. For example, the current literature stresses that a history of physical and sexual abuse increases the likelihood that women will abuse alcohol and other drugs (Covington and Surrey, 1998; Newmann, Greenley, Sweeney, and Van Dien, 1998; Renzetti, Edleson, and Bergen, 2001). More specifically, the current research verifies that female offenders have disproportionately high rates of victimization and substance abuse (Chesney-Lind, 1997; van Wormer, 2002).

ADVOCATING ON BEHALF OF INDIVIDUAL WOMEN

In Advocates for Battered Women, the Rape Crisis Center, ARC House, and Women Reaching Women, advocacy was an essential aspect of their work. Their consumers had difficulty obtaining appropriate assistance on their own for several reasons. First, at that time, most service providers were not aware of the problems and needs of these women, and their attitudes toward them tended to be very negative. Many were convinced that rape victims and battered women had only themselves to blame for their problems; in many circumstances, people refused to believe women's accounts of what had occurred, or they discounted their pain. Most often, people disapproved of and distrusted women offenders and women who abused alcohol and drugs.

Second, most of these consumers were inexperienced in negotiating the complex rules and roadblocks that characterize public services; some had previous demeaning experiences with the "helping professions." Many of these women were dependent economically and psychologically; many were in crisis, with little support from friends and family. Having a supportive and knowledgeable advocate was a means of ensuring that consumers would receive appropriate and respectful assistance and be able to handle the multiple issues before them.

In these four organizations, members helped consumers gain access to other agencies for counseling, legal and financial assistance, child care, medical care, help in finding housing and employment, and vocational training. When consumers requested it, they negotiated clients' complaints and requests and represented their viewpoints to family and friends, medical personnel, lawyers, social workers, landlords, employers, child care providers, and school personnel. They provided legal information and assisted women with their legal battles.

Providing advocacy for adult and child sexual assault victims and their families was the core mission of paid staff in the Rape Crisis Center, and some volunteers assumed this responsibility as well. They offered information on available options and explained how the legal system worked. They accompanied consumers through law enforcement investigatory interviews, medical examinations, interviews with social service workers, court appearances, and hearings. They maintained contact throughout the process, updating consumers on the disposition of their cases and following up to evaluate their experiences.

> Because of our belief that the criminal justice system is inherently antifemale, we take that belief and lots of experience in surviving in a system that devalues women to our clients and empower them with that knowledge and that belief. That means they don't get destroyed or eaten alive by the system in the way that they might if we weren't able to prepare them for that.
>
> Advocacy is court accompaniment, explaining procedures and answering questions; mediating disputes between the survivor and the police, courts, or the hospitals; and negotiating complaints that the survivor has about the way her case is being handled or the way she's being treated. But it's not just work with the criminal justice system. I can turn my advocacy skills to any person, agency, or institution that I'm directed to do so by the survivor. I may end up in small claims court if she's trying to get out of a lease and gets evicted. I have talked with employers if people get fired and want their jobs back. . . . We deal with the whole continuum of sexually exploitative behaviors. The basic rule of thumb is that if something happens to a person that they define as unwanted and sexual, we can probably deal with it. It could be a battery, sexual harassment at work, harassing phone calls, or an ex-boyfriend she can't get rid of. It could be helping the family of someone who's been raped and murdered. We provide advocacy in all those different arenas.

Unlike the Rape Crisis Center, where all staff and some volunteers confronted the legal and medical systems, Advocates for Battered Women identified one or two staff who assumed primary responsibility for legal advocacy for consumers and for providing legal information to police and district attorneys. In reevaluating its overall approach to assisting battered women, in the mid-1980s, the organization shifted one staff position from the shelter into its legal advocacy program. This change was in response to the fact that about 80% of the battered women who came into the shelter and about 80% of the women on the crisis line were requesting assistance with legal issues.

> We decided we could best be political at this point by giving women more information, more support, and more advocacy with their legal battles.
> Information is power, and women generally don't have access to information. Having legal information is incredibly powerful.

Serving shelter residents and nonresidents, legal advocates provided battered women with legal information and assisted them in obtaining domestic violence restraining orders and in pretrial hearings, divorce proceedings, child custody disputes, and any other difficulties they were experiencing within the legal system.

Women Reaching Women helped women gain assistance from AODA treatment centers, halfway houses, therapists, battered women's shelters, credit counselors, and career counselors. Their volunteers did "everything we possibly can do" to assist with child care problems; and they accompanied women to visits with doctors and other service-providers.

> You get into all areas. You take them to the doctor and you tell the doctor you don't want them to be on any other chemicals. You run interference for them to help get them established back in the community. We're finding people who are staying out of detox longer. We've found they've been making it 6 months and up to 14 months where before they were in detox every month.

In ARC House, emphasis was placed on providing the advocacy necessary to help women obtain employment, education, and independent living arrangements. It assisted women in obtaining and keeping jobs; in securing medical coverage; in obtaining appropriate, affordable, and well-located housing; and with custody issues.

AFFECTING SOCIAL CHANGE

Members of these organizations pursued social change through a wide range of different activities. At the broadest level, the longevity of these organizations was a form of social change, and their public-education efforts were a continuing force for social change. More directly, members of these organizations provided training and case consultations to police officers, probation and parole officers, therapists, teachers, clergy, doctors, nurses, social workers, lawyers, and district attorneys. Advocates for Battered Women and the Rape Crisis Center worked to assure that workers in the medical, legal, mental health, and social service systems were aware of the needs of victimized women and children and the ways in which they could be more helpful. Similarly, ARC House and Women Reaching Women worked to educate the correctional and AODA systems about the needs of their consumers. They spoke with individual administrators and frontline workers, and they sponsored statewide conferences in their respective fields.

In addition, these organizations worked to change public policy and social legislation. They used many reform-oriented strategies to achieve their long-range goals of radical social change (Bunch, 1974). For example, in addition to increasing women's safety by educating them about self-defense, the Rape Crisis Center advocated for improvements in street lighting and for ordinances on security measures in rental housing and public transportation. It worked with other feminists in the community to gain reform of Wisconsin's sexual assault statutes and to help victims of sexual assault obtain financial compensation for medical and psychiatric expenses through the state's Victims Compensation program, and it publicized legislative reforms of the laws regarding rape and rape trials. " There are many things that are different from 12 years ago and because of us, because we make noise."

A lot of the major changes took place in the first three years. The sexual assault law changed. Most of the agencies we were working with established policies and procedures. We could move on to some different issues, like the quality of service, and we didn't have to argue about whether or not cases could go to court. That's how we spent our first two years, trying to talk prosecutors into prosecuting cases when most said they wouldn't. All of a sudden, 99% of all of the cases reported got prosecuted if there was a suspect. The law made a big difference. More people were getting some measure of justice in that, and some measure of recognition from the community that they had, in fact, been assaulted. That hadn't happened before.

This agency has been influential in getting laws changed, in making it safer for women to report sexual assault, in raising the consciousness of the legal community and the medical community.

We've done a lot to improve the treatment of victims by the police and to get the rape shield law passed, where they're not allowed to question a victim on her past sexual conduct.

Similarly, Advocates for Battered Women joined with members of the Wisconsin Coalition Against Woman Abuse and the Wisconsin Women's Network, a statewide political advocacy group consisting of individuals and organizations concerned with women's rights, to advocate for change in domestic abuse laws. Due to their efforts, legislation was passed in April 1984 that enabled battered women to obtain temporary restraining orders and to do so without the assistance of a lawyer.

A major success was the legislation that we were involved in getting passed, domestic abuse legislation that secures state funding for shelters and a new statute that allows for domestic abuse restraining orders for battered women. The state of Wisconsin was finally acknowledging how pervasive the problem was.

Advocates for Battered Women, along with other community activists, also influenced change in policies regarding arrest and prosecution. In the 1970s, police offered little protection to battered women. No arrest would be made unless the police directly observed the violence; few cases proceeded through the legal system. By the mid-1980s, the district attorney had established new policies. An arrest could be made whether or not the police had witnessed the violence, and they would take a case to court whether or not the woman signed a complaint.

I can see the changes that have been made in police department policy. Those are things we started talking about six, seven years ago. Recently, they've finally made these changes. It took that amount of time, but they did it. I would not have wanted to see Advocates not continue to do that kind of work.

By the mid-1980s, Advocates for Battered Women had restructured its program to devote more staff time to creating change in the community: "We wanted to reach a lot more women. Some of it was because of the frustration of seeing the same things over and over and over in the shelter and wanting to work on a broader scale." It decreased time spent with individual women in the shelter; continued its public education and efforts to change the legal system; and began advocating for changes in the welfare and housing systems, trying to make those systems more responsive to the needs of battered women.

The emphasis on the shelter that was so important in the beginning is less now because we've seen we'll never be able to provide enough shelter. We've grown to see that we have to do more systems advocacy, trying to change how the community reacts to battered women, to do more public speaking and more dealing with the courts.

It's easy to get pulled into the social services, but our goals have changed more toward recognizing that we can't do that, that that's not the way to go about eliminating woman abuse.

The decisions made by Advocates for Battered Women in the mid-1980s moved them in the direction of current practice. By the mid-1990s, feminist approaches to assisting battered women emphasized developing a coordinated community response, with priorities placed on reforming the criminal justice, health care, and child welfare systems (Saunders, 1995; Schechter, 1996).

As it gained credibility in the community and within the criminal justice system, ARC House became more active in advocating for systems change. Its executive director served on the Department of Corrections' Advisory Council on Women Offenders and as the chair of the Wisconsin Women's Network's Task Force on Women in the Criminal Justice System, a statewide task force concerned with influencing changes in the women's prison. Educating the correctional system about the needs of female offenders was a consistent theme.

> What we're doing right now is something we've always wanted to do, which is to participate in looking at resources and services for the women offender in the entire correctional system. We do educational work constantly with probation officers. We've sponsored the only conferences that have happened on women offenders. We are the ones that approached the administrator of Corrections with our board to establish the Advisory Council on Women Offenders, so we are playing a very pivotal role.
>
> ARC House is a model program at this point. People within the system are always calling on ARC House to share their experiences. That's important in furthering the cause of women offenders.

In Women Reaching Women, social change goals were addressed largely through the efforts of the project director. She prepared materials for distribution throughout the state, did public speaking, provided training for AODA treatment program directors and staff, assisted chapters in developing their educational efforts, organized members to press the legislature to fund child care for women in treatment, and worked with the State Bureau of Alcohol and Other Drug Abuse in evaluating treatment programs and making recommendations for change. Also, she cochaired two advocacy groups: the Wisconsin Women's Alliance on Alcohol and Other Drug Abuse and the Women and Substance Abuse Task Force of the Wisconsin Women's Network. Members of Women Reaching Women agreed that they were having an increasing impact on service providers and on community attitudes.

> The thing that keeps us all going is that women's issues in this field each year gain a little more credibility, and we're getting a little more done. When the governor addresses the AODA field now, he remembers to bring up women's issues. Sure, he's doing it for political reasons. But at least he knows that there's enough

movement there that he'd better at least mention women. We've created enough visibility and there's enough focus that now it's politically astute.

The project director has gotten requests to submit a workshop proposal for a national conference. People from all over the states and outside the United States have started asking her what she's about. There's more awareness of women's issues in the AODA field and new programming, and Women Reaching Women has been very instrumental in this.

Through public speaking and workshops, members of Women's Transit Authority educated the public about the problems women face when they go out alone at night and addressed community issues about sexual assault and its prevention. Representatives of Women's Transit Authority served on the City-County Committee on Sexual Assault and were involved in planning No More Assaults Month activities.

Events like No More Assaults Month make people more aware. We need to keep reminding people that there is a problem out there, and there are solutions, but it requires the whole community to act. It's not enough to feel, "Okay, with our tax money, we pay for this ride service." That doesn't do it.

BALANCING SOCIAL SERVICES AND SOCIAL CHANGE

Pursuing social change while at the same time providing services to individual women was a continuing challenge in feminist service organizations (Amir and Amir, 1979; Ferraro, 1983; O'Sullivan, 1978; Withorn, 1984a, 1984b). Problems emerged due to the constraints of funding and conflicts between members' political versus service/treatment orientations. With limited resources, members had to choose between assisting more women in need versus devoting time to effecting social change. Efforts to change conventional agencies were constrained by the fact that members needed to cooperate with these very same agencies in providing services to their consumers.

Acknowledging their successes, Advocates for Battered Women, the Rape Crisis Center, ARC House, and Women Reaching Women recognized that expanding needs for direct services constantly threatened to overwhelm their ability to work for change in the community. Members agreed that providing direct services was their bottom line. Their deliberations focused on the extent to which they were devoting sufficient resources to public education and advocating for changes in legislation, social policy, and the practices of other organizations.

Expectations that Advocates for Battered Women would serve as an agent of social change were tempered by its need to address the multiple and

extensive needs of shelter residents and by the time-consuming work required
to staff and physically maintain the shelter.

> Where we've differed, where a lot of arguments and issues have come up, is
> how much time and energy should be put into work with individual battered
> women versus working toward systems change. There's always been a commit-
> ment to make sure that there is a community education component along with
> providing shelter and safety to women. We've never had to make the choice of
> whether we're just going to work with individuals and forget about social
> change. But, when it comes down to the possibility of people being laid off or
> we're overworked in some way and we cut back, it's always the first contro-
> versy. . . . Do we put our time and energy into the shelter or do we go out into
> the community and say, "Hey people, wake up. This is a problem. You're re-
> sponsible for it. Get into the courts, get into the law enforcement agencies," to
> start making people be responsible for taking care of the problem, rather than us
> just trying to work with individual women. We're feeling more relaxed because
> we have the staff and the money to do both right now.

Like Advocates for Battered Women, members of the Rape Crisis Center
were concerned about the appropriate allocation of resources to direct services versus community education and advocating for change in other systems, and the extent to which their social change efforts could impede their
ability to help individual women and maintain funding. Like Women's Transit Authority, they considered the extent to which their participation in political activities would impede their credibility and legitimacy in the community. However, unlike with Advocates for Battered Women and Women's
Transit Authority, these issues were not mentioned as sources of intra-organi-
zational tensions in the Rape Crisis Center.

From its beginning, the Rape Crisis Center maintained a culture that included an explicit commitment to social change, and members took great
pride in their advocacy efforts. While Women Reaching Women, ARC House,
and Advocates for Battered Women influenced other service providers
through a slow and incremental process, the Rape Crisis Center volunteers
began with and maintained a vocal, aggressive, and "radical" public posture:
"On occasion, it's nice to have people say, 'We'd do something, but god, we'd
have to deal with the Rape Crisis Center, and god forbid.'"

> It's very useful to have paid staff who can be worthy advocates and work face-
> to-face with the cops and the DAs. Once they learned to trust us and that they
> could work with us, we had a good working relationship. We could work coop-
> eratively. But it was useful then to have the volunteers, who were more anony-
> mous, who were more separate from that. As some people put it, they could be
> the crazies. They could come out and advocate the extreme positions, whereas

when the paid staff did it, the cops and DAs thought we were being unreasonable, and that made things tense. But it was nice if you could have these crazies from the Crisis Center going, "No. No. No. We want X, Y, Z," all these demands. They could put on a different pressure that was not only useful to the paid staff but could keep the social change focus present.

The initial and ongoing focus on changing the medical and legal systems and the primarily woman-identified membership both contributed to the apparent lack of divisiveness within the Rape Crisis Center. Nonetheless, the expanding need for its direct services constantly challenged its ability to pursue social change.

We started out with lots of energy for social change, but we also had lots of time for it. What ended up happening around four, five, six years later was that we were so busy trying to keep up with services that we didn't have the time and the luxury to think about, "Okay, what other changes do we want to bring about?" We were just running crazy. We had to make a conscious effort to set aside the time to think about those issues. It's a difficult balance.

In contrast, ARC House and Women Reaching Women acknowledged the constraints placed on their social change efforts and the limitations of direct services.

One of my frustrations in being with Arc House is, no matter which way you look at it, it's a band-aid. We need band-aids for people who are suffering. That's fine. But I worked for so long providing the band-aids that I'm tremendously frustrated, because I want social change. We are trying to provide the women with the tools to help them survive when they get out of the program. Yes, we're doing that. But, we send them back out into a society that does not support them. How are they supposed to develop a whole new support system in a world that doesn't provide that for them? People say, "Do the women change?" It's such a ludicrous question. The women who make it are remarkable people as far as I'm concerned. It's because they were so motivated that they were able to use Arc House as a catalyst. It's a tremendously frustrating thing to talk about. We're a little drop in the bucket, the larger social context not being anything that supports what we're working for.

Women Reaching Women needs to maintain some alignment with the traditional system in order to keep this project alive. That's the bottom line, because that's where our dollars come from. So, there's a part of this project that's very much tied to the traditional system, but yet, there's an expectation that somehow we will change things within that system. We always have to be careful about how far we push. It's a strange mixture of trying to stay alive within a traditional system but yet trying also to accomplish what we see as our goals.

Embedded in conservative bureaucracies and dependent on referrals from agencies within highly conservative systems, ARC House and

Women Reaching Women developed their services slowly and maintained a relatively apolitical public posture. Neither organization could deliver services without first educating and gaining the support of staff in male-dominated organizations. Yet, justifying their existence on the basis of unmet needs, they were implicitly and unavoidably critiquing the attitudes and practices of those with whom they were required to work most closely. Furthermore, members of these two organizations were females negotiating primarily with males who worked almost exclusively with other males, a highly stressful work environment for women at that time. Remarkably, both organizations were able to establish credibility within systems that have remained male-centered into the 21st century.

Of all five organizations, Advocates for Battered Women had the most difficulty in creating consensus on the nature of its services. Throughout its development, major splits existed among staff concerning self-help versus counseling, helping women and children as a family versus focusing on battered women, and pursuing social change versus providing more direct services to sheltered women. Among the three explicitly feminist organizations, this question would be most problematic in Advocates for Battered Women, for two reasons.

First, more than in the Rape Crisis Center or Women's Transit Authority, members of Advocates for Battered Women needed to choose between helping individual women versus promoting social change. Advocates for Battered Women was funded primarily for the most conventional aspects of its work, that is, for providing shelter, information, peer support, and counseling. Though they are extremely important, these services do not directly affect social change. In contrast, by funding the Rape Crisis Center staff specifically to provide advocacy for victims of sexual assault, funders were acknowledging the need for change in the medical, social service, and criminal justice systems. Through their advocacy work on behalf of individual women and children, the Rape Crisis Center worked directly to alter the sexist attitudes and practices that pervaded these systems. Similarly, a rape-prevention ride service, by definition, serves a political purpose. Unlike with Advocates for Battered Women, when members of the Rape Crisis Center and Women's Transit Authority devoted their time to the provision of direct services, they were also working directly for social change.

Also, tensions over service priorities were most likely exacerbated by the constraints placed on what Advocates for Battered Women could accomplish through direct services. Unlike ARC House, the Rape Crisis Center, and Women Reaching Women, Advocates for Battered Women had only up to 30 days to assist residents. Other agencies assumed most responsibility for providing longer-term assistance and advocacy on behalf of individual women. Also unlike the other organizations, Advocates for Battered Women was dealing with clients who would not necessarily take advantage of its services. The Rape Crisis Center and Women Reaching Women worked with consumers who sought out their services and expected support, counseling, and assistance in dealing with other organizations. ARC House residents also understood that particular services would be provided. Advocates for Battered Women was prepared to assist residents with a wide range of problems but recognized that women might want only safety and shelter. Moreover, Advocates for Battered Women was often offering assistance to women who chose to return to the homes they had fled. While understanding the economic, social, and emotional factors that would lead women to return to their abusive partners, its staff and volunteers would not necessarily see political victories in their work with battered women.

AN EXTERNAL PERSPECTIVE ON SERVICES

Interviews with 30 individuals in the Madison area who had contact with members based on their roles in funding sources, law enforcement, or health and social services provided an external perspective on the work of these five organizations. Members asserted that throughout their internal debates and divisions and with limited funding, they continued to provide high-quality direct services and worked effectively for social change in their community. The community interviews fully supported members' evaluations.

The Rape Crisis Center and Advocates for Battered Women were given considerable credit for increasing public awareness of and concern about sexual assault and battered women and organizing the community to address these problems. These were viewed as "outstanding achievements." Their community contacts agreed that members of these two organizations changed the attitudes of those in law enforcement so that victims were treated with greater sensitivity and understanding. Both organizations were mentioned as being a catalyst for the creation of sensitive crime units within law enforcement agencies.

The initial strains between the police and the Rape Crisis Center were frequently mentioned. In fact, those involved in law enforcement placed more emphasis on these problems than did the members of the Rape Crisis Center, perhaps because the Rape Crisis Center took this aspect of its history for granted. Also, being on the receiving end of activists' efforts, police and prosecutors would have a heightened awareness of the ways in which their work was disrupted and would have direct knowledge of the complaints and anger that were being expressed within their organizations. Conversely, the members of the Rape Crisis Center would view as most significant their ability to overcome distrust.

Community members reported that the Rape Crisis Center was viewed as impeding investigations by its insistence on interviewing victims before the police did, trying to dictate what questions would be allowed in police interviews with victims, and discouraging victims from maintaining contact with the police. Respondents also reported advocates' "pushing" victims into being even more angry with perpetrators, hiring attorneys, and going to court. They attributed the "horror stories" to the Rape Crisis Center's being uninformed about the criminal justice system and unrealistic in its dealings with police, given that the police, at that time, were very conservative, "the last of the old school." One person commented that early members of the Rape Crisis Center were "sometimes too fanatic. They had certain ideas and there was no toning it down. They went straight ahead and didn't know how to be diplomatic yet. They didn't know how to play the game." At the same time, community members acknowledged that strained relationships were inevitable and may have even contributed to the organization's success.

> There was a belief that people were trying to screw everything up, that police didn't care about sexual assault. You could leave meetings with them at times feeling like, these people really think that I like rape. For the most part, their preconceived notions were not true. That was a put-off. There is no doubt that the system was not working very well and needed change. I am not saying that the system was good by any means. But they showed their impatience at times. It's hard to list that as a negative because, in fact, they succeeded in doing what they set out to do. The shows of impatience and intolerance at times are maybe one of the reasons why they ended up where they are. They had to become part of the system without becoming part of it.
>
> Those early people struck a very good balance. Their militancy was needed. The system did stink in those days and, in order to change it, you had to be tough. They combined that with a very practical approach. They were able to strike that balance of working within the system and not getting bought off by it. The early people were very important in that, to set that tone.

There was consensus that, over time, the Rape Crisis Center had established positive working relationships with police and prosecutors and that it delivered high-quality services. Pressure from the Rape Crisis Center was cited as a major factor in the police having written policies regarding sexual assault investigations. Much like members of the organization, these respondents asserted that the Rape Crisis Center ensured that sexual assault cases were handled and handled properly.

> You knew with Rape Crisis around, you couldn't let a case slide because there was going to be hell to pay. They were vigilant. They made sure that sexual assault cases stayed a priority.

They have a lot of political clout based on their credibility. If Rape Crisis stands up and says that someone, a DA or police officer or whoever, is doing a lousy job, that can be devastating. People listen to it and they buy it. That is a lot of power. If somebody looks like they are soft on sexual assault, forget it.

Similar to the situation with the Rape Crisis Center, community members noted that Women's Transit Authority's strong feminist stance and ignorance of the systems within which it worked led to strained relationships in its early years. These difficulties occurred with members of the university police, with whom the organization shared equipment, and some people who were involved in its funding. Also as with the Rape Crisis Center, Women's Transit Authority's contacts believed that these early problems may have been inevitable.

Philosophically, there were some differences that perhaps could have been smoothed over to save them from unnecessary difficulties. But I am not sure, given the time period, that they could have done it too much differently. If they were starting now, the whole issue of women's rights and feminism has been assimilated into most people's lives, it wouldn't be an issue. But back then, it was something brand-new. I don't know how they could have avoided that.

The community interviews confirmed that, with more experience, Women's Transit Authority had established itself as a key resource in the community. They pointed to its expanded cab service as a major accomplishment, especially since the cab companies were initially angry over Women's Transit Authority's taking away potential customers. They mentioned the political significance of the organization, as well as its more pragmatic purposes.

We have a serious problem in the university community as well as in the larger society with sexual assault. This is a very pragmatic approach to sexual assault prevention. We know women have less access to cars and have to depend on public transportation.

It provides a service, safe rides for women, and it keeps the issue of sexual assault in the consciousness of the public simply by its existence. It keeps sending out that powerful signal to the community, "Hey, community, we have a real problem on our hands." It's that powerful signal that has been steadily beaming.

Much more so than its members, people outside of the organization were "amazed" at Women's Transit Authority's ability to attract and maintain such a large group of volunteers. The major problems identified by these respondents were that long waits for rides often discouraged riders and that the service extended only within a four-mile radius of the campus, and that there was little chance of additional funding for additional vehicles.

With respect to ARC House, Advocates for Battered Women, and Women Reaching Women, there was little mention in these interviews of confrontational or tense relationships. Instead, funders, law enforcement officers, and administrators of other agencies emphasized the value of their services, cooperative relationships, effective referral systems, and dedicated staff and volunteers.

In discussing Advocates for Battered Women, respondents stressed the high quality of its services and the positive impact of its community education efforts. Community members praised its competence in working with the police department, with mental health practitioners, and with the school system and the effectiveness of its outreach efforts in rural areas. With respect to the DA's pro-arrest and pro-prosecution policies, "A lot of that had to do with the pressure that has been put on the police department and the DAs from Advocates." They credited Advocates for Battered Women for "implementing, monitoring, and evaluating the DA's pro-arrest and pro-prosecution policies, making sure restraining orders are used and assisting women through the civil and criminal justice system."

> Advocates has continued to provide a very needed service, a very difficult service to provide, and they've made the problem visible to the community. They have taken away the real secretive kinds of things, so more people are willing to talk about it.
>
> Their goals have focused on providing the basics for the women, what to do after the shelter time, where to live, where to work, preparing them for survival. Also, they help with emotional awareness, looking at the dynamics in an abusive situation. It's helping them with their self-esteem, helping them to begin to understand that they haven't caused the battering, those initial things that are critical before anything else can happen. They do an excellent job of that. We see these women after they have left. They may not have internalized a lot of the things that they have heard about why they are in the situations they are in as battered women, but they certainly can tell you exactly what they need to do.
>
> When they first began to educate the community about domestic violence, it was a very dramatic change to have those services in existence. The community now is so aware of the problem that they don't debate the need for the shelter. It's accepted as a priority for funding.

Analysis of these interviews crystallized a major difference between the Rape Crisis Center and Advocates for Battered Women. Even more so than its members, these respondents emphasized the Rape Crisis Center's community-wide political clout, whereas both the Rape Crisis Center and Advocates for Battered Women were praised for the effectiveness of their community education efforts and direct services. Several factors may account for the Rape Crisis Center's ability to develop such clout while Advocates for Battered Women assumed a more incremental and less confrontational approach to social change. Among these factors were the conservatizing nature of shelter services and the constraints of United Way funding. Also, the Rape Crisis Center maintained some services that were provided solely by volunteers, and volunteers had more latitude than paid staff in maintaining the public, radical stance of the organization. Most important, once convinced that rape was a crime of violence, not a crime of passion, the community was prepared to address the problem. The Rape Crisis Center's mission was to shape the ways in which the problem was addressed.

> They were successful because they were right on things. The cause they were working on was not a controversial cause. Conservative men, liberal men, conservative women, liberal women don't like sexual assault.
>
> At the beginning, the police's attitude would be "get out of here" and to laugh at them. By the end, it was, "Call up so and so, get her down here." The officers wanted to know how to handle these cases.
>
> In some ways, Rape Crisis is a sacred organization. If the policy makers are going to make budget cuts, one of the last agencies they will cut is Rape Crisis. Policy makers are not going to want to be perceived as being for sexual assault by trying to cut that agency out.

The public was prepared to address male violence against women *except* when that violence took place within the family, as evidenced in the progress of legislation on woman abuse. Efforts to change the status of rape victims in Wisconsin began in the early 1970s and were successful within five years. In 1976, the Wisconsin legislature passed a comprehensive statute defining rape as a crime of assault rather than as a sex offense. The legislation identified four degrees of sexual assault, focusing on the extent of the coercion used by the assailant rather than on the resistance offered by the victim, and it severely limited the admission of evidence concerning the victim's sexual conduct. However, the law specified that a spouse could not be prosecuted under this statute unless the husband and wife were living apart and one of them had filed for an annulment, legal separation, or divorce. Over a decade later, in 1989, Wisconsin adopted a mandatory arrest law, requiring the police to arrest the primary aggressor in domestic crimes. Changing societal attitudes toward woman abuse within the family required an extended process of education and lobbying.

Interviews with people within the criminal justice system confirm that ARC House had considerable support and "broad acceptance" throughout the Corrections community and that they did "incredible work with their clients, making that transition and getting back into the flow of society and becoming self-sufficient." They supported members' views about the unique difficulties in working with female offenders.

Women offenders are harder to supervise than male offenders are. By the time a woman gets into the criminal justice system, she's usually had a number of passes from the court system. About 95% are victims of some type of sexual offense or physical abuse. Their relationships with men are horrible. You also work with the whole service system because a lot of these women are physically abusive to their children. So, people really don't want to supervise them.

The executive director of ARC House was viewed as being a "powerful" member of the Advisory Council on Women Offenders: "Her very strong ideas certainly influenced the Council's report and that report is already having an impact on the budget. For the very first time, the budget has a separate item on women offenders, and there's new money in the budget now to meet women offenders' needs."

Community members would have liked to see ARC House receive additional funding to increase its use as an alternative to incarceration; to allow more women to live with their children before being released from the system; to serve more women by having two houses; and to establish a day-treatment program "not only for parole purposes for transitional living for women coming out of institutions, but also for women in the community who are on probation who may be living from place to place." ARC House was viewed as potentially serving as an umbrella organization.

ARC House has the best show on the road. In terms of serving specific populations, whether it was for minority women or even older women or youthful offenders, I would prefer to see ARC House as the umbrella organization, assisting others in operating a halfway house like this. They have the knowledge and the expertise.

Women Reaching Women was viewed positively as well. Its strengths included "the networking that was being done, the acceptance by others, the amount of time that was donated by participants and their energy." Its volunteer base was viewed as "just incredible," its trainings as a major contribution, and its chapters as effective. Community members acknowledged the time it had taken for Women Reaching Women to obtain local funding and support and that, with turnover, "You have to go back and retrain or restimulate the chapters." That Women Reaching Women had to be developed through local programs was discussed as one major constraint.

Every locality is different. You cannot do a manual and say, "This is the way it is going to work in your community." You need local people who know what the differences are within that locality. It's a grassroots effort, and those are very difficult to organize. They take a lot of time. They take a lot of nurturing.

Respondents agreed that "they are effective in meeting minimum needs. To increase above that level requires additional funding from a governmental agency or from the locality." They envisioned more geographical locations and additional staff, including paid outreach workers or regional coordinators; greater impact on state and local decision making so that AODA programs would address women's special needs, including child care; and establishing a women-only treatment center.

Notably, community members detailed numerous ways in which ARC House and Women Reaching Women could expand their services. After the organizations proceeded in a deliberative and somewhat cautious manner within very conservative systems, it appears that their successes served to highlight how much more could be accomplished. Also, it may be that the changes effected by ARC House and Women Reaching Women created the possibilities for further change.

Most community members did not mention the feminist orientation of these organizations until they were asked at the end of their interviews, "Do you consider this to be a feminist organization?" Their generally brief responses included references to members' being committed to the rights of women and to the equality of women; helping to change attitudes toward women; being advocates for women and their needs; empowering women to help themselves; rebuilding women's self-image; being a very supportive environment for women; helping a woman be an advocate for herself; helping women be less dependent; being concerned about the best interests of women; promoting the best in the women they serve; bringing a strong sense of feminist values into their work; and being part of the women's movement.

A few of these respondents stated that an organization was feminist but were concerned about the connotations of the term.

It was started by what I consider feminist-type people. I am not saying this in a negative way.

Yes, it is a feminist organization, but that doesn't mean it is bad. I don't think that you need to use feminist as a nasty word.

I guess so. That carries excess baggage with it for a lot of people. Because it is women helping other women, I guess that sort of qualifies it to be a feminist organization.

All the word "feminist" means to me is equality for the sexes. Obviously, Women's Transit is a feminist organization in that sexual assault strikes women unequally. It is a feminist organization in that sense, it is trying to make things more equal by preventing women from becoming victims. I don't put any heavy connotations on the word "feminist."

In several interviews, organizations were not viewed as feminist.

> A feminist attitude means you don't listen as well as you verbalize. It is a kind of myopic view, "My vision is the only vision. Because I have been a victim for a long time, I need to overcompensate and make sure that women get more than their fair share now." It is definitely an attitude of aggressiveness, which means, "It is important for me to be heard regardless of what your opinion is."
>
> It serves women well, but I don't think that it is feminist in the sense that I would use the term. It's not angry. It's not to the exclusion of men at all. That is taking my definition of feminism, an angry definition, that women need to stay as far away from men as possible.
>
> I don't like the word feminist. It's a program working with women, but I do not see them as turning down other volunteers that will enhance their goal. When someone says that you are a feminist organization, that means you will only deal with the female population and you will only listen to constructive criticism or recommendations for improvements from the female population, that you would not accept any help at all from the male population.

The brief references to feminism in these interviews, including some very negative statements, suggest that most people interviewed were not strong supporters of feminist causes and did not have political investments in the success of these organizations. Their highly positive evaluations of the work of these organizations do not appear to be politically motivated or based on an in-depth understanding of the philosophical commitments of their members. Apparently, these organizations justified their goals and demonstrated their effectiveness to funders, law enforcement officials, and other service providers in terms that could be readily understood and accepted.

Given that those interviewed had ongoing relationships with these organizations, it is not surprising that their comments were generally positive, especially with respect to their current contacts. What is most significant is that these interviews strongly support the opinions offered by the members of these organizations. The community interviews confirm members' own views that they had established productive linkages with other agencies; had overcome initially tense and distrustful relationships; and had significantly altered understandings of women's problems and needs within the criminal justice, health, and social service systems and in the community at large.

The accomplishments discussed throughout this chapter illustrate that service work can be an effective means of realizing feminist principles and goals. Although assisting individual women based on feminist principles remained a priority, all of these organizations retained social change as a significant aspect of their work. Addressing the problems of individual women heightened members' awareness of the importance of changing the practices of other agencies, community attitudes, and social policies. It assured a commitment to social change goals informed by the everyday experiences of women. Conversely, direct knowledge of the political realities that constrained the magnitude of the changes they could accomplish affirmed the necessity of and informed their work with individual women.

Chapter Seven

Developing Feminist Organizational Structures

Any decision-making process can be used in a feminist way or in an antiwoman way. We have always struggled with what inequities a certain decision-making process will bring to our organization. There has always been a certain amount of self-consciousness about the effects of using one decision-making process or another. (WTA)

In each of the five organizations, women sought to *empower members through egalitarian work structures.* Their understandings of how power is used under patriarchy to dominate and control provided the standard against which members measured their progress in developing more equitable and humane workplaces. They eschewed bureaucratic organizational structures on the grounds that they encouraged competition and discouraged subjectivity and the expression of emotions. To avoid replicating patriarchal organizations, which silenced and marginalized women, they envisioned organizations that were egalitarian and nonhierarchical. They sought to develop organizational structures and patterns of communication that reflected the same values for which they were advocating in the society at large.

Sometimes, I'm not so sure that it would be bad to just say, "Let's be a hierarchy," until I think about what it is we do. If I really believe that patriarchy is at the root of the problems that allow for women to be abused in society, then why would I espouse and embrace a system that's patriarchal? That's what hierarchy is. (ABW)

Like many women who identified with the work of the early radical feminists, these feminists viewed collectivity as the organizational structure most consistent with feminist values (Ferree and Hess, 1985; Freeman, 1975; Pahl, 1985a; Riger, 1984; Rodriguez, 1988). Ideally, in a collectivist organization, authority belongs to the collective, although it may be temporarily delegated. Every member is responsible to the group, and all decisions are made by the group. Methods of operation are flexible and open to negotiation, not constrained by fixed rules or formal sanctions. There is minimal division of labor, with staff responsibilities being shared or rotated, with limited differences in benefits and rewards, and with an emphasis on personal relationships and shared values (Rothschild-Whitt, 1979; Rothschild-Whitt and Whitt, 1986).

Women Reaching Women faced the most constraints in incorporating collectivity. It was fully embedded within a hierarchical parent organization. The project director of Women Reaching Women reported to the executive director of WAAODA. The executive director of WAAODA represented the project to the WAAODA board, to other members of the AODA system in the state, and to legislative and planning bodies. In all of these organizations, the primary commitment was to the AODA field, not specifically or necessarily to Women Reaching Women.

Within Women Reaching Women, however, power was decentralized. Feminist notions of shared power fit well with the organization's focus on democratic, peer-oriented self-help groups. The project director worked closely with chapter coordinators in determining the priorities and needs she ultimately forwarded for approval. Volunteers had significant input into program planning and priority setting in their local chapters and at training events, and through regional meetings and statewide conferences.

Like Women Reaching Women, ARC House was closely tied to a bureaucratic system from its inception. However, its members had considerable leeway in defining the parameters of the internal structure. ARC House began, much as did Advocates for Battered Women, the Rape Crisis Center, and Women's Transit Authority, with an idealistic commitment to collectivity. Thus, this chapter focuses on these four organizations.

In the formative stages of Advocates for Battered Women, ARC House, the Rape Crisis Center, and Women's Transit Authority, the deliberate inclusion of all members in all decisions empowered women and increased the likelihood that traditional power relationships would not be replicated. Also, collectivity was an important factor for the dedication and cohesiveness of their early members.

People felt like Rape Crisis was their organization, and they had an investment in it, mostly because everybody could participate. You could have an influence on what happened. There was a lot we were personally getting out of it, and you wouldn't have gotten that in an organization where somebody else was telling you what to do. (RCC)

We usually tried to make decisions as a group. That's because we needed the support. ARC House was a scary program. We shared a lot, spent a lot of time

together. We did a lot of weekend retreats, which were wonderful, dealing with
what was going on with us personally and professionally. It was a real supportive atmosphere. (ARC)

Nonetheless, as among feminists in general, issues regarding power were
very difficult to address (Baker, 1982; Hartsock, 1974, 1979; Hooyman,
1978; Miner and Longino, 1987). Members recognized the oppressive nature
of power defined in terms of dominance, superiority, and control, but they
struggled in their attempts to redefine leadership, influence, and expertise in
nonoppressive terms. In an atmosphere of trust, influential and successful
women were viewed as "empowered"; others valued them as being strong,
self-confident, and skillful. However, under less positive circumstances, the
same qualities could be defined as controlling, self-serving, and coercive. The
same leadership behaviors could be seen as important for the attainment of
group goals or as evidence of an individual's need to dominate. The development of individual expertise could be seen as an invaluable resource or as evidence of the inappropriate accumulation of power by one person.

> We confuse power and responsibility. We see any display of autonomy or ini-
> tiative or responsibility as a power play. That's destructive. There's a view that
> power's not good so it shouldn't exist. But it does exist, and you need to look at
> it responsibly. (ARC)
>   The struggle around defining power differently than it's been defined for us in
> this society is always going to be an issue. I would like to see power not defined as
> "over somebody else." How you define it is a whole new frontier. (ABW)
>   Other people will perceive that you have power over them or they have power
> over you, when really, people would just empower themselves. Working for a
> feminist organization is an empowering thing. But people who might not un-
> derstand that think that you're power hungry or empire building, and that's not
> so. (WTA)

When structural changes were viewed as congruent with their principles,
women reaffirmed the feminist nature of their organizations. Contrarily, perceived abandonment of these principles was a source of distrust, alienation,
intense conflict, and emotion-ridden departures.

> It's the stress of working in an organization that there aren't models for. You're
> never quite sure how to act. People that quit sometimes are quitting just to look for
> a clearer place to work, even if it's a hierarchy. The struggle gets tiring. People can
> get caught in crunches and not know how to get out except by quitting. (ABW)

Over time, members' idealism was joined by recognition that their political visions did not necessarily or easily translate directly into workable orga-

nizational practices. Slowly, members moved away from automatic rejection of bureaucracy (Ferguson, 1984) and valorization of collectivity and instead weighed the usefulness of features from both types of structures (Martin, 1987, 1990; Reinelt, 1995). As in many other feminist organizations, members recognized that collectivity impeded efficient and effective decision making, obscured lines of responsibility, and created tense work environments (Freeman, 1973; Mansbridge, 1973, 1982, 1983; Morgen, 1994; Riger, 1984; Rodriguez, 1988). They discovered the benefits of active boards of directors, worker specialization, written policies, and standards of performance (Iannello, 1992; Perlmutter, 1994; Riger, 1994). Throughout, they worked to maintain the core element of nonoppressive structures, that is, that "the group will have the power to determine who shall exercise authority within it" (Freeman, 1973, p. 299).

DEMYSTIFICATION OF CONSENSUS DECISION MAKING

The strength of consensus decision making is that each person has the opportunity to contribute and that the overall outcome of that decision will speak more directly to broader needs. Individuals are asked to think for themselves, to sort out their alternatives, to do creative thinking, and to bravely communicate that to other people. That is hard work. The negative is that it's a very time-consuming process and people get very impatient. (ABW)

Members of these organizations envisioned workplaces where the personal concerns and feelings of each individual would be important, and all contributions would be equally valued. They looked to decisions made by consensus as the primary mechanism for ensuring equal access to information, equal participation in discussions, equal authority to shape policies and practices, and equal responsibility for the decisions made. However, over time, they found that consensus decision making was incompatible with the tasks before them and, more importantly, that it did not necessarily fulfill its political purpose. For a collectivist structure to be viable, there must be sufficient time for discussion and negotiation and an interactive process that facilitates consensus building. As these organizations increased in size, this set of conditions could not be maintained.

Going from four people to about eight, that's when the structure started to go downhill. We had to keep adding on more paid staff to do the work and the more employees we had, the less efficient the decision-making structure was. We were burning out. We were getting sick. We were all working 60 hours a week, and decisions weren't being made efficiently. We were working harder, and things were going down the drain. Information wasn't getting shared, decisions weren't being made well. (RCC)

To create new types of organizations, it was essential that feminists be willing to spend extraordinary amounts of time in discussing problems and possible solutions regarding every aspect of their work. Further, given women's long history of being ignored and discounted, it was critical that members pay close attention to task-related contributions *and* personal feelings. However, even when long discussions resulted in consensus, good decisions, and positive feelings, there was considerable tension. Members were devoting too much time to deciding what to do and not enough time to actually doing it. Their challenge was to maintain feminist principles without devoting so much time to discussing their work that they could not do their work.

> It's very, very difficult to do a good job and also to spend hour after hour in staff meetings and board meetings to struggle about what is the best structure for us, what are our goals, what direction should we be going in. All those decisions take such an incredible amount of time, and so much care is given to listening to every individual. When you insist on involving everyone's input, it takes a lot of energy, and then there's not enough energy left over to do a good job. (ABW)

In addition to issues of time and energy, a number of other dilemmas made the realities of collective decision making far from the ideal.

- Seeking consensus based on the full participation of each member not only was inefficient, but it also discouraged the very same positive relationships that it was supposed to engender and protect: "It has an effect on coworker relations. You get to a meeting that you know is going to last three hours, and at the end of that meeting, you're not going to want to see anybody for a long time." (RCC)
- Consensus decision making did not necessarily guarantee equal participation and equal influence among all group members. Consensus could emerge as a result of members' capitulating to others' assertiveness, quick thinking and verbal acuity, persistence, and forcefulness.

> When it is working, you take care of your own views and needs and you hear what the other views and needs are. Hopefully, going through this together will unite your beliefs, and you've got a foundation on which to carry out the action. But what can happen is that the person who can hold out the longest wears the other people down. The other people, who are less powerful or are less vocal or don't have the stamina, come around to agreeing for the sake of consensus. (ABW)

If one person wants something and can't convince others, they can create enough of a commotion so that eventually people will give in or make some sort of compromise, just to get rid of the irritation. (ABW)

Moreover, group members could place considerable pressure on those who disagreed with the majority and would not capitulate or compromise.

I've seen some pretty strong emotions erupt because a decision has to be made. Say we have seven people in the room that agree and we have two people that don't agree; those two people are psychologically squashed. The anxiety of not getting the decision made runs right over us... Although we give people permission to disagree, women who disagree are under a lot of pressure. It's not direct pressure. It's not, "You change your opinion or you lose your job." It's much more subtle. Some of it is even nonverbal. All of a sudden, we magically have a consensus. (RCC)

Conversely, decisions could also be too easily blocked if members were unwilling to compromise.

The people who begin a meeting with "I can't live with this any other way" tend to have more power than people who want to function more as a collective and hear from everyone first. If one woman is claiming that she can't live with something, then she's basically making the decision for us. (RCC)

- Members' explicit commitments to equality did not prevent the evolution of informal hierarchies, "which sometimes can be more insidious and a lot harder to deal with because you don't have explicit rules about how to cope with that." (ABW)

There were hidden powerholders that weren't accountable and it wasn't out front, and it could really wreck up the dynamics. (ARC)
There's been a lot of assumptions that we're all women and we're all feminists, so we're not going to have any problems making decisions. I've seen the whole power hierarchy just zip out of nowhere as soon as a conflict comes up. (WTA)

- As the memberships of these groups became larger and less homogeneous and as service provision became more complex, there was greater diversity in women's interests in collective decision making. A greater proportion of volunteers were interested only in providing services, and many staff were willing to delegate decision making: "Why should everyone be involved in every decision when it was clear that some of the staff didn't care, and why should they? Just that, since it was the 'right thing to do,' everyone should do it?" (RCC)

Fears of the abusive aspects of hierarchy led to extended periods during which shared decision making was a source of pride and value affirmation, but delegation of authority was the operational reality. If decisions had to be made and there was no consensus, the group would often shift decision making to a smaller group or to an individual.

> The positives are that, if you have a group of people who are more knowledgeable about a particular issue, they should be able to make thoughtful decisions. Good, intelligent, skillful decisions can be made in a shorter period of time. The negative is that many perspectives will be excluded and devalued in the process of others claiming a superiority by their skills or by their experiences. (ABW)

Members found that consensus decision making did not guarantee mutual respect, open and caring communications, or equal levels of influence. Ironically, the feature in which members had most confidence, consensus decision making, was very problematic, and the feature most worrisome, having to conform to the demands of funders, was more beneficial than anticipated, as discussed in chapter 5.

ESTABLISHING FORMAL POLICIES

> Until very recently, we operated in terms of verbal policies and people asserting how it was done before. Everyone has a different memory. (RCC)

Bureaucracies are characterized by formal policies designed to regularize organizational operations. Ideally, their rules are impartial and relatively stable. In collectives, operating procedures are constantly in flux, based on the particulars of specific situations (Rothschild-Whitt, 1979). In the early stages of development of these organizations, working as a collective was highly beneficial. Having formal policies would have discouraged the openness, creativity, and shared understanding of organizational history essential for the development of innovative approaches and the integration of feminist principles. Encouraging ongoing reassessment of organizational practices allowed members to respond to new situations and the unforeseen consequences of past decisions and to benefit from the perspectives of new participants. Reconsideration of issues allowed for the full involvement of each individual and increased the likelihood that personal feelings and needs would be addressed.

However, with more experience and knowledge about consumer needs, service delivery, and management, the absence of set rules became more dysfunctional than empowering. Informality and the feeling that decisions were never "final" led to anxiety and disorganization. Too often, group members were not certain what decisions had been made in the past and even what decisions they made in a meeting that had just ended. They were continually traveling the same ground.

> There's a tremendous amount of work that people do that gets ignored. It's like we have historical amnesia. We set up policies that we spend two or three weeks developing, and then we forget that they exist. There's a lot of wasted effort. (ABW)

In response, members created formal policies and procedures to govern their overall operations. Their decision-making processes benefited from members' being able to rely on well-formulated and consistent policies.

> We don't have to keep rehashing over old stuff, we don't have the constant staff meetings that we used to have, we're not changing policy every two weeks. When there's a crisis, it's usually something that has come up before in a similar way, so that people have a much firmer foundation on which to make decisions. (ARC)

At the same time, policy making needed to include mechanisms that respected the judgments of members as they changed their views with experience and that encouraged input from new members.

> When new staff members come in, we sometimes have to go back over all the old issues we've already taken care of, because you have to take into account that a new person has to feel validated and heard. But then again, those new folks shake us up and get us to rethink things that we've gotten rigid about. There's always a flip side to everything. (ARC)

Formal policies and procedures ensured that members utilized the results of their lengthy and often complicated deliberations. As long as members had the freedom to change established policies, they retained control over their organization, the core element in their viewing themselves as having a feminist structure.

MAKING JUDGMENTS ABOUT
THE QUALITY OF WORK PERFORMANCE

> It's hard to separate out how we feel about one another as people and whether or not somebody's doing a good job. Even though feedback is being given directly and honestly, there isn't a move to say, "You've got to improve or you're

going to leave by such and such a time if you haven't." It's hard to have the set
of values of mutual support and equally develop that other set of values. (ARC)

Members prided themselves in paying close attention to personal needs
within the work setting. They devoted considerable time to providing guidance, support, and assistance to each other. Valuing each person encouraged
close personal relationships, increased women's self-confidence, and reinforced women's willingness to take the risks required for the development of
alternative services and structures. From this perspective, standards of performance were seen as elitist, exclusionary, and unresponsive to women's individual needs and personal histories.

The absence of standards of performance, however, created confusion and
stress for women who were dedicated to two often contradictory goals: serving consumers effectively *and* assisting other members with their personal
problems. Their dilemma was where to draw the line. At what point have feminist principles been too readily discarded when women are criticized for poor
performance rather than being assisted and supported? At what point does the
lack of standards for performance seriously impede organizational functioning? Should women continue to deal with individual needs at the expense of
getting the work of the organization done?

> There is much more empathy with the daily requirements of life that end up tak-
> ing people away from the agency. I'm afraid, though, that the compassionate
> component of feminism, "Yes, women can empathize more with the plight of
> another working woman," is used in a very facile way sometimes to excuse a
> shoddy job that someone is doing, "She's going through hard times." To be as
> successful as the agency is, everyone can't be going through hard times too reg-
> ularly. (ABW)
>
> We let it go for so long. People couldn't make the separation that you can en-
> joy being with this person, you can like her, but that doesn't mean that she has
> the skills to do the job. Some thought that everything is workable if we will only
> be committed to each other and try to understand what's going on. "We're all
> women, we can work this out." They should have been more concerned about
> how effective the services we were providing were, but they were not able to get
> out of the personal. (WTA)
>
> It was a hard decision, the first time, to go to a woman and say, "I'm sorry,
> but right now, you can't be with us." It was grueling and it seemed somehow
> elitist, that all of a sudden we think we're so good at it and here's one person
> who is too needy right now to do it. But we did it. She did come back a few years
> later and was a wonderful counselor. (RCC)

By the mid-80s, every organization had developed written policies to clar-
ify expectations around work roles. They developed mechanisms to deal with

work-performance issues, including detailed job descriptions, probation periods, staff support groups, staff evaluations, procedures for grievances and termination, and volunteer training and evaluation committees. Still, they retained an emphasis on maintaining strong personal bonds among members.

FROM SHARED RESPONSIBILITIES
TO ROLE SPECIALIZATION

We weren't very good at delegating because we thought that everybody had to know everything. It was like, if somebody had lots of information, that's power. Well, that's true, but the point was that there are other ways of getting access to that information without everybody having to be involved in everything. (RCC)

One major difference between bureaucratic and collective organizations is the extent to which tasks are assigned by position. In bureaucratic organizations, administrative, direct service, clerical, and maintenance responsibilities are assigned to separate positions that are differentially valued. In contrast, in collectivist organizations, tasks are shared or rotated, administrative and direct service roles are combined, and responsibilities are equally valued (Rothschild-Whitt, 1979). These four organizations began with considerable overlap in roles. The absence of internal role differentiation encouraged close bonds and shared knowledge.

In their first year, members of Women's Transit Authority organized the organization's services, provided rides, and recruited new volunteers: "There were so few of us that you needed to do a lot of everything." In the following years, by separating management and direct service roles, they were able to attract many more volunteers as drivers/dispatchers. They made no distinctions among the coordinators.

All of the founders of Advocates for Battered Women participated in fundraising; community education; planning for the shelter; providing information and support to the volunteers working the crisis line; and meeting with the police, family court counselors, and other service providers. Similarly, in their beginning years, Rape Crisis Center volunteers shared all tasks and responsibilities: "We were all so overextended at that point that there was no way that anybody could get by with just doing one thing. Everybody had to do everything." Even with the addition of paid staff, there was substantial overlap in the Rape Crisis Center, with all members being involved in planning, public speaking, fund-raising, and decision making.

ARC House founders listed five different positions and titles in their grant, including a director. However, nondifferentiation of job responsibilities characterized the organization's early internal functioning. The director served more as a facilitator than a decision maker and defined her role as carrying out the decisions of the group. The staff shared responsibility for in-house therapeutic work and for helping clients find jobs and establish ties with other community services. In addition, they shared administrative tasks, including writing funding proposals and attending budget meetings to defend their requests: "We had titles basically to satisfy funding sources, but we all did everything. We saw ourselves as this great collective. It was very, very intense, to say the least."

Viewing all roles as equally important and having to share information and resources reinforced feminist notions of equality and empowerment. With experience, however, members recognized that de facto specialization was occurring. Their lack of role differentiation did not meet organizational or individual needs. Participating in a wide range of duties was very time-consuming because members had to share information about all aspects of their work. Rotating responsibilities assumed that, given sufficient levels of support and training, all participants would be able and willing to take on a full range of assignments. However, personal interests and abilities did not fit the shared-responsibilities model. Some members preferred and excelled in administration, fund-raising, and dealing with the public; others were more comfortable with and more skilled in internal programming and counseling. With expanded services and funding requirements, members realized the additional advantages in their developing expertise in specific areas. Specialization empowered women by giving them more control over their work and by allowing them to be more effective.

Specialization and establishing formal policies and procedures were the facets of bureaucracy that most members readily accepted as unavoidable consequences of the organizations' becoming larger and more influential. Members recognized that these mechanisms improved group functioning and enhanced member goal attainment. However, specialization also limited the extent to which members could share information and maintain close personal relationships and thus interfered significantly with shared power. Women in different positions accumulated different kinds of knowledge and expertise and were accountable for their performance on different tasks. Asking for approval from a larger group began to feel increasingly cumbersome, unnecessary, and a waste of valuable time. Generally, the larger group accepted the recommendations of those who were most informed about specific issues and who were most directly affected by the outcomes of decisions. Ultimately, ad hoc, situation-specific delegation was replaced with formal delegation of authority by role.

CREATING MODIFIED HIERARCHIES

I do not think that the feminist stance has changed. The circumstances through which that position can be articulated have changed. (WTA)

With specialization, formal authority was delegated to individuals (directors or coordinators), to committees, and to components (staff, volunteers, or boards). Reaching consensus continued to be the preferred mechanism for group decision making, although there was no consensus as to what was meant by "consensus." Members shared the goal of having everyone in the group agree, but a range of opinions existed as to whether agreement was based on "true" consensus or achieved by individual forcefulness, behind-the-scenes lobbying, differential willingness to block consensus, or apathy. They agreed that their evolving structures were definitely feminist in nature, although a far cry from their early commitments to collectivity.

Decision Making among Staff

In Women's Transit Authority, the coordinators shared administrative responsibilities, including grant writing, reporting to funding sources, office management, and preparing and monitoring the budget. They recruited, trained, and supervised volunteers; scheduled volunteers; did public speaking; and handled public relations. They shared power as a group, making all decisions by consensus and taking their issues to their board when they could not reach consensus.

Specialization was joined by a differential salary structure in ARC House in 1979, with the executive director being the highest paid. In the three explicitly feminist organizations, there was no formal system of seniority, and all staff received equal wages. Specialization was adopted to increase efficiency, effectiveness, and job satisfaction. Having equal salaries signaled the equal value of each position and each person.

By the mid-1980s, Advocates for Battered Women and ARC House each had an executive director who assumed responsibility for external relations and finances and a program director who focused on internal programming and coordination. Additional administrative roles were established in Advocates for Battered Women, ARC House, and the Rape Crisis Center, and there was some specialization among direct service workers in Advocates for Battered Women and ARC House (see table 1).

Still, more role sharing took place in these organizations than in conventional bureaucracies. For example, in ARC House, the program director did direct service work with residents. Staff in Advocates for Battered Women did maintenance chores in the shelter and worked shifts as receptionist "so our administrative assistant is not burdened with all of that." The business coordinator in the Rape Crisis Center did some counseling and community education.

In ARC House, hierarchical decision making developed after considerable debate.

> There was a struggle about the whole issue of decision making. We had fights and arguments and all-day discussions. We don't do that anymore. When new people come in, they expect some kind of a line of authority, so that conflict isn't there as much as it used to be. We started acknowledging who was what and who had responsibility for what decisions, and it alleviated a lot of the tension.

TABLE I. Paid Staff Positions

	Administrative Staff	Direct Service Staff
ABW	Executive Director	Advocate Counselors (2)
	Program Director	Legal Advocates (2)
	Administrative Asst./Business Manager	
	Property Manager	
	Children's Program Coordinator	
	Community Education Coordinator	
	Volunteer Coordinator	
ARC	Executive Director	Vocational Counselor
	Program Director	AODA Counselor
	Administrative Asst./Business Manager	Counselors (2)
RCC	Business Coordinator	Advocate Counselors (5)
	Administrative Asst./Bookkeeper	
	Direct Services Coordinator	
	Education Coordinator	
	Volunteer Coordinator	
WTA	Coordinators (3)	
WRW	Project Director	

Feminist decision making was maintained largely by the administrators' personal commitments to consulting with the other staff. Members reported that "people who want to be included have a way to be included in every decision." They labeled their structure a "collective hierarchy," with consensus being the preferred mode within committees and within the staff as a group.

> The collective hierarchy reflects that there is a flexibility in how things are done. It's not strictly hierarchy. Some decisions are made through committees, some are made collectively, and some are made by the director.
>
> Everybody has input into major decisions. Formally, the system is set up so that there's some way to come to a decision, if need be, in a speedy manner. However, if there were a complaint about it being done, it would be reopened. Consensus is pretty much held to.

In ARC House, decision-making processes were developed with the explicit goal being "to facilitate maximum decisiveness while considering all factors affecting both the individual and the collective welfare." For most decisions, the committee system was used to insure input and also to hold specific people responsible for decision making. Still, final authority rested with the executive director, and some members remained concerned that changes in administration easily could be accompanied by reduced commitment to shared decision making.

In Advocates for Battered Women, building consensus among the staff was complicated by two early structural decisions. The first was its board's creation of the position of executive director. When the shelter opened in April 1978, Advocates for Battered Women was administered by a steering committee consisting of a shelter coordinator, an advocacy and outreach coordinator, a fund-raiser, and a fiscal manager. By the fall of 1978, however, the board had decided that Advocates for Battered Women should have an executive director and established this position over the strenuous objections of the majority of the staff and volunteers. As discussed later in this chapter, this change marked the beginning of a three-year period of bitter disputes over structure.

The second problematic factor was the separation of shelter staff from those who did fund-raising and community work. Initially in Advocates for Battered Women, all staff devoted some time to working with battered women in the shelter or staffing the crisis line. By the fall of 1979, to increase the organization's effectiveness and efficiency and "to make jobs and services less chaotic," staff roles became more specialized. Advocate counselors worked with women and children in the shelter. Other staff, working out of the downtown office, focused on fund-raising, training workers in other agencies, and community education. Staff were divided by function and by location.

Working in two different locations interfered with staff communication and cohesiveness. Moreover, having some staff associated with the shelter program and other staff associated with community work created, in some people's minds, an implicit hierarchy. Those who worked downtown had "nice offices" and were performing functions most directly associated with social change. Those who worked in the shelter performed more conventional and emotionally draining roles: they assisted individual women and children in crisis over a 24-hour period, helped with house maintenance, and dealt with the often strained relationships among the women and children in the shelter. They had "no desks, no drawers, no private space." Assuming very different roles made different staff members likely to be most familiar with different problems and needs. Thus, debates over program priorities could easily place shelter staff in opposition to the "out-house" staff, with the priorities of one group being defined as more "political."

> When it comes down to having to prioritize, that's where people's different philosophies surface. It's when we have to choose. Unfortunately, people have felt like, "If you support the kids' program over community organization or a community education program, you are less politically radical than the person who's into community organizing." Those were very nerve-wracking times to be asked what your opinions were, "Do you support this program or this program? What is your philosophy on it?"

By the mid-1980s, Advocates for Battered Women had purchased two adjacent buildings, and all of the staff were housed in one location. The director retained more authority than other staff. However, committees (shelter and services to battered women, children's program, legal advocacy, community education) had decision-making authority over their specific components of the program. Most decisions were made within programs and by consensus. Decisions that affected the entire organization were considered by all staff members and made by consensus or majority rule and needed to be approved by the board, although "our history has been that, by and large, the board has been relatively open to us doing our thing in regards to programming."

The Rape Crisis Center was unique in that specialization was not formalized until 1980, and segmented authority did not develop until 1983. For many years, all Rape Crisis Center staff worked as advocate counselors and shared administrative tasks. For example, all staff helped write funding proposals and attended budget meetings to defend their requests: "Fourteen-hour days weren't at all unusual. No one thought of only attending to the funding matters."

Although staff maintained the philosophy that they all did the same tasks, in fact, over time, one advocate counselor assumed most administrative responsibilities. Working 60 to 80 hours per week, she also maintained a direct services caseload comparable to other advocates and conducted workshops. It was only when they prepared to write a job description for her replacement that the staff fully recognized that she had performed two full-time jobs. After considerable deliberation, they decided her replacement, hired in 1980, would be their "business coordinator." Two years later, they created the position of volunteer coordinator and, over the next two years, the positions of direct services coordinator and education coordinator. In 1983, the Rape Crisis Center staff delegated very limited decision-making authority to a coordinating committee, consisting of the full-time coordinators (business, direct services, and education).

They are responsible for making decisions that don't affect in a major way our current programs or aren't dealing with new program elements. It's just the on-going types of decisions. However, anybody who reads the notes of those meetings and is not happy with the decision has a route to get involved and the decision can be remade or, if it's too late, a grievance can be heard so the same thing won't happen again.

The three coordinators were allowed to make minor monetary decisions (under $100) and to make decisions in emergencies. Major changes continued to be considered by all of the staff. Staff retained sole authority over matters that affected only the staff, and their decisions were made by consensus.

Decision Making among Staff and Volunteers

ARC House volunteers held auxiliary service roles, and there was never an expectation that they would be involved in decision making. In contrast, the three explicitly feminist organizations were founded by volunteers who expected that the addition of paid staff would not interrupt commitments to equality and shared power. Only in Women's Transit Authority did circumstances permit these expectations to be realized.

Throughout, all Women's Transit Authority volunteers could choose to participate in policy making through the organization's Voluntary Advisory Board (VAB). During the first six years, coordinators and active volunteers made policy and budgetary decisions at weekly VAB meetings. By the mid-1980s, the VAB met monthly and primarily dealt with issues related to the ride service, including rider eligibility, no-shows, problem riders, and abusive callers. It continued to serve as an effective mechanism for volunteer involvement in decision making, making decisions by consensus when possible and by majority rule when consensus could not be achieved: "Transit's basically a volunteer organization. The coordinators never saw themselves in the position of making the decisions for the organization."

There was no evidence of tensions between volunteers and staff around shared power in this organization. Their distinctly different roles eased delegation of authority; it was clear which group had the most expertise and investment in specific decisions. Also, as discussed later, staff and volunteers in Women's Transit Authority had equivalent levels of involvement and influence in board decisions.

In contrast, having differences in power paired with overlapping roles contributed to stresses between staff and volunteers in Advocates for Battered Women and the Rape Crisis Center. In these two organizations, volunteers shared many tasks with staff. However, staff maintained formal responsibility for the effective delivery of services, were likely to remain with their organizations for longer periods than volunteers, and developed expertise and contacts not generally shared by volunteers, and their salaries were directly affected by their work performance and the success of their organizations.

In Advocates for Battered Women, the founding volunteers worked collectively, and they expected that paid staff would "share equally in decision making with all other members." However, the two part-time staff hired in March 1977 soon engaged in "hot debates" with the volunteers, asserting that decisions needed to be made in between the general bimonthly meetings. They also believed that, since they were devoting more time to the organization, they were in the best position to make most decisions. By that summer, the founding volunteers had left the organization, largely because their goal of obtaining money for paid staff had been met and their energy was depleted. "People were burned out; they were glad somebody was getting paid to do the work."

After the training of new volunteers in August 1977, the two part-time staff and 10 volunteers continued to work collectively, but only with respect to the overall direction of the program: "Now, the paid staff had the expertise and the volunteers were the newcomers. This changed the collective decision-making pattern forever. Paid staff now had more control." By January 1978, Advocates for Battered Women had funding for eight full-time staff positions and one part-time position as well as funding for the shelter. The staff focused their energies on hiring and training the new staff and on locating and preparing a facility for the shelter. Some of the volunteers were hired as staff; the others moved on. Volunteer involvement in decision making ended without much notice.

By the time the shelter opened in April 1978, the volunteers consisted of women who had no previous experience in Advocates for Battered Women. Staff were preoccupied with establishing staff and volunteer roles; developing and providing services; and, as discussed later, struggling over the hierarchical structure that had been imposed by their board. With the ongoing battles among Advocates' board and staff and the accompanying high levels of turnover among staff and volunteers, attempts over the next three years to formalize volunteer involvement in decision making were neither successful nor a great source of dissension.

By the mid-1980s, Advocates for Battered Women had developed a structure more consistent with feminist principles, and for the first time a cohort of volunteers had been part of the organization for extended periods. With structural stability and member continuity, volunteers became increasingly concerned about their lack of involvement in decision making. The established avenues for volunteer input, both direct and through the volunteer coordinator who had responsibility for communicating volunteer concerns to the staff, were far too limited.

To effect any change in the most simple procedures at the shelter, it's been very frustrating to be just a volunteer. Though we are told we can consider ourselves as having as much authority in certain realms as paid staff, we've been too much on the margins of decision making. Channels have been there for volunteers, although they were informal. If you were persistent, ways were made for you to influence decision making.

At the time of these interviews, the volunteers at Advocates for Battered Women were beginning to meet among themselves and with staff to push the organization toward increasing their involvement in decision making. This process both highlighted a nonfeminist aspect of the structure of Advocates for Battered Women and confirmed its feminist foundations. Volunteer concerns were based on the discontinuities between principle and practice, not on the absence of feminist values.

We're feeling isolated from the paid staff, but we have some hope of having some effect. I guess that's why we're even bothering to do it at all, because we have some faith that our collective voice will be heard and will make a difference.

Unlike in Advocates for Battered Women, the addition of paid staff in the Rape Crisis Center was not joined by either a dramatic shift in group membership or dramatic differences between the levels of staff and volunteer expertise. In fact, all four staff had worked as volunteer counselors before they were hired. Staff and volunteers knew one another and had similar experiences with police and in-court accompaniment. They continued to make decisions collectively in weekly meetings: "Nobody knew that much about the legal process, so everybody could feel equal in terms of the amount of information they had. Nobody changed the structure. They just assumed it would work out okay, that there really weren't any distinctions."

However, physical separation and increasing differences between the experiences of the Rape Crisis Center staff and volunteers strained commitments to worker equality and consensus decision making. As noted in chapter 1, volunteers were housed separately from paid staff to underscore that confidentiality would be maintained for those who called the crisis line. With paid staff working primarily in the daytime and volunteers working largely at night, contact between these two groups would be limited under any conditions. Still, having separate offices eliminated interaction and "psychologically, as much as anything, created a split." In addition, assuming most responsibility for public relations, education, funding, and ongoing client contact, staff became much more knowledgeable than the volunteers about the operations of the organization. With their increasing caseloads, they found sharing information with volunteers to be burdensome.

When you start seeing several hundred clients and you've dealt with district attorneys and cops and hospital people on a daily basis, your experience is very
different than a volunteer's. So even when we wanted to share information or
share what our experiences were like, it got massive.

It wasn't so much whether somebody's paid or not, but that paid staff would
put in 40-plus hours a week, and most volunteers were there maybe two times a
month. So the level of involvement, what they knew about, was necessarily different . . . You're tired from working all week, and then you're supposed to go
to a meeting on Sunday. People didn't want to.

Acknowledging that staff were no longer attending regularly, by the late
1970s, the organization replaced weekly meetings with monthly potlucks that
both staff and volunteers were expected to attend for purposes of information
sharing and decision making. Decisions affecting the volunteer component
were handled at this monthly meeting, with volunteers and staff having to
reach consensus. As with all decision-making groups in the Rape Crisis Center, using majority rule was an option, but only when agreed upon by the entire group: "The body involved would have to reach consensus to suspend
consensus and use another model." Only committees had moved into majority rule, and this occurred only "a few times."

In 1979, regular monthly meetings of the full collective were discontinued:
"There weren't enough people who were interested in doing that." Instead, as
discussed in the following section, the Rape Crisis Center established a steering committee to improve communications and minimize distinctions between volunteers and staff. Every volunteer could choose to become a member. This model increased volunteers' knowledge about the organization and
participation in decision making, and it decreased the administrative burden
on staff. However, the authority of the steering committee with respect to staff
activities remained a subject of debate, and consternation over the appropriate roles of volunteers and staff in decision making persisted.

The tensions between volunteers and staff reached a level in 1982 that
"could not be ignored any longer. It was affecting the work of the agency. We
realized that we had to change, either by acknowledging that we must be separate organizations with separate functions or by tightening the bond." By the
end of 1982, the volunteers and staff had decided to merge; both groups
moved into a new facility, one that had more space for offices, counseling,
large meetings, and the public library of resource materials.

When we merged into shared space, we became more unified, and there was a
lot more trust in each other . . . It provided the volunteers with access to more
resources and information, which empowered them in a way they had not been
empowered before. Materials in our library and updated referral resources were

now available to volunteers as well as staff. Services were improved because the volunteers had greater access to resources for themselves and greater access to the staff as resources.

Efforts to equalize the status of volunteers and paid staff in the Rape Crisis Center were also evident in the terms used to describe their positions. Volunteers were referred to as "night staff" and "volunteer staff," and paid staff were referred to as "day staff." (To maintain consistency throughout the book, only the terms "volunteer(s)" and "staff" are used, including in the quotations from the Rape Crisis Center.)

Coming to Terms with the Power of Boards

As another form of specialization, members of ARC House, Advocates for Battered Women, the Rape Crisis Center, and Women's Transit Authority requested that their boards take on increased responsibilities and assume more formal decision-making power, and only partially in response to increased pressures from funders. With their increased workloads, members looked to their boards to handle legal matters and legislative issues, to assume responsibility for guiding them on fiscal matters and difficult personnel issues, to deal with external demands for accountability and fiscal responsibility, to concentrate on community relations and fund-raising, to develop policies, and to engage in program evaluation and long-range planning Having an active board also legitimized the organizations' efforts and increased their credibility in the community.

ARC House

The ARC House board initially consisted of members of Ananda Marga, "well-meaning people who weren't quite sure what they were supposed to do." Within a year, in response to the concerns of ARC House's primary funder, the Wisconsin Council on Criminal Justice, the composition of the board included members of Ananda Marga and other members of the community. Over time, there was heightened understanding of the benefits of a board and a broadening of board responsibilities. In addition to interest, commitment, and "being good-hearted," board members' qualifications were expanded to include having the ability to help garner community support and funding.

> To survive in that outside world, a strong board is important. What has helped is having more people on the board who have had long-standing involvements in the community, rather than just being a very tight-knit internal board. It's made connections in the community that have led to more recognition. In a

grassroots program, one of your lifelines is your board of directors. If you're not connected in your community, when trouble starts, the community has no investment in whether you stay or go.

The board of ARC House assumed major responsibility for dealing with the agency's image in the community, especially with respect to its affiliation with Ananda Marga, public relations with funding sources, and legal matters and legislative issues. The board advised the executive director with respect to program directions and growth, difficult personnel issues, fiscal matters, and policy making. There were no internal debates in ARC House over its board's decision-making authority. Strong bonds existed between board and staff members affiliated with Ananda Marga, and the board functioned primarily to support ARC House in ways requested by the executive director: "Now, the board has been given more authority, but the board is supportive of what the staff wants to do internally. The internal part of the program isn't so influenced by the board."

In Advocates for Battered Women, the Rape Crisis Center, and Women's Transit Authority, the externally sanctioned authority of their boards was a focal point for tensions around shared power. Members recognized that, as nonprofit corporations, they were legally required to have boards of directors, and they understood the benefits of having active boards. Their debates centered on the internal impact of board members. Their challenge was to reconcile the power-laden legal and fiscal responsibilities of a board with feminist investments in equality.

> There's a continual struggle about whether we want a board to be our rubber-stamper or actually do work. We want them to rubber-stamp the decisions that we make and make the decisions we don't want to. (ABW)
>
> There was a tug-of-war because, while they needed some of the workload taken off of them, the staff didn't feel comfortable giving that power to an inexperienced group who had the power to fire them. That was difficult, giving up power and tasks that they had done and took pride in doing, but they also needed help doing it. (WTA)

Staff and board members saw themselves as potentially at risk under different circumstances. Board members felt pressure from their oversight role; they felt personally accountable to funders and for being responsive to community views of organizational activities. Principled commitments to collectivity among board members were tempered by their legal obligations.

> The staff places a higher value on process, and the board, being more aware of our corporate responsibilities, is feeling like sometimes we have to sacrifice process. (ABW)

We try to keep equality as strong as possible by not exercising a lot of power as a board over the staff. It's something that we do admittedly struggle with because my perspective as a board person is that I have the ultimate responsibility should a mistake be made or something major happen. (WTA)

Correspondingly, staff were nervous about their board's authority to set salaries and hire and fire staff and questioned the appropriateness of board members' setting policy when they were detached from the everyday operations of the organization. Staff felt directly accountable for the effectiveness of their services. They wanted their boards to focus on long-range planning and fund-raising, not on the day-to-day operation of their organizations.

Shared values and goals were joined by confusion and mistrust as members confronted the dilemmas involved in maintaining shared decision making in organizations governed by policy-making boards. Problems were exacerbated when staff, volunteers, and board members did not share common values and goals.

Advocates for Battered Women

In August 1977, the staff of Advocates for Battered Women created an advisory board to facilitate fund-raising for the shelter. Based on criteria traditionally used for selecting board members, they recruited people with financial expertise and "pull and power" in the community. Within a few months, again to facilitate fund-raising, the staff member who handled fund-raising recommended that Advocates for Battered Women become a nonprofit corporation and that the advisory board become the organization's board of directors. The other staff member and some of the volunteers objected strongly, but the board approved the change, reserving two seats on the board for staff. Policy-making responsibilities shifted from the staff and volunteers to the board. This marked the beginning of highly strained relationships within the staff and between the staff and board.

Early in 1978, Advocates for Battered Women obtained funding for the shelter from United Way, a funder that required a policy-making board and an executive director. Staff believed that they had no other options: "There weren't a lot of other places to get that kind of money." That fall, the fund-raiser proposed that she be formally assigned the title of executive director. She was frustrated that United Way was requiring her to sign as director when neither the board nor the organization viewed her as actually having that position. She also proposed that staff not serve on the board, asserting that their presence was a threat to continued funding. In response, the board established the position of executive director, appointed the fund-raiser to this position, and created a four-tiered salary structure (director, coordinators, other staff, secretary).

"Pandemonium ensued. The majority of the staff were outraged." They objected strenuously to the removal of staff from the board and "rejected the leadership of the fund-raiser." Two of the three coordinators refused to accept a higher salary than other staff. Some feminist staff did not object to having a director, but most did. By the end of the year, the director had left the organization. The community education coordinator became the acting director until the new director was hired in May 1979. Staff representation on the board continued, as did the position of director, and "all efforts at consensus decision making came to a bitter halt."

Efforts to create feminist processes within this structure continued in an atmosphere of personal animosities, dissension, and turnover. Some staff and most board members did not view Advocates for Battered Women as a social movement organization. Feminist staff and board members continued to struggle to return Advocates for Battered Women to "our original political and philosophical roots, which is social change as opposed to social service." In January 1981, the director and half of the staff quit, primarily due to conflicts over goals and services: "They were the people who were trying to develop programs that would appeal to funders, wanting there to be a more therapeutic emphasis." Their resignations allowed the remaining staff to make progress on reinstating equal salaries.

> By then, it was a two-tiered structure. Staff had kept pushing whenever salaries got brought up. When the director was leaving, they saw that as their opportunity. There were some people on the board who were in agreement, so it wasn't like a board-staff split. Staff was pretty united at that point, too. The board agreed that they would advertise at an equal salary for the director. If they couldn't find anyone, then they'd readvertise with a higher salary.

When the new director was hired in the spring of 1981, equal salaries had been reinstituted. However, the organization had been decimated by the turnover and staff-board dissension. In the following months, a small number of staff and board members "carried us through a time of organizational disaster."

> Half the staff left, and left with information. There was no history, no anything to rely on for new people coming in to fill those shoes. The next six months, at least, were spent not only filling the positions, but trying to get ahold of information that made it possible to function. People came in and had no one to train them. There was no administrative staff for three months. Staff morale was just nothing. The board and the staff refused to talk to each other. The staff acted as though the board didn't exist. The board acted as though it could continue to govern an organization without having any contact with what was going on.
>
> We had a horrible one-day retreat, and it was very painful. Even new people already considered the board the enemy. But what came out of the retreat was

some energy for staff and a little bit of hope. It took a few board people saying, "It's clear that not only do these members of the board need to leave, but we need to look at alternatives for a board structure." That started the ball rolling.

The new director worked successfully with the now more cohesive staff and with feminist board members to reconstitute the board. There was consensus among board members, staff, and United Way that the membership of the board needed to change and that "the structure that was in existence admittedly was not working."

Many members attributed these years of internal turmoil to personality conflicts, poor communication, and women's problems dealing with leadership and the accumulation of power by one individual. However, a number of overlapping circumstances certainly contributed significantly to their struggles.

- Given the importance of member empowerment, it was critical that the power of the board and executive director evolve out of a process of shared decision making. Even as feminist organizations incorporated aspects of bureaucracy, they sought to maintain the principle that "the group will have the power to determine who shall exercise authority within it" (Freeman, 1973, p. 299). Bypassing this basic principle was a recipe for conflict.
- A conventional structure was imposed on a collective that had yet to confront the everyday realities of management and service provision; members had no time to develop an understanding of the usefulness of a board or having administrative staff. Understanding through their own experience the productive roles of a board and executive director within a feminist organization could have mediated staff's unwavering resistance. Conversely, having the board unilaterally appointing an executive director and imposing unequal salaries reinforced members' fears.
- Early staff and volunteers had little reason to anticipate that their advisory board would act in such an autocratic fashion. Correspondingly, early board members did not foresee that they would become enmeshed in lengthy discussions of women's rights, collectivity, and social change. These were issues that many board members viewed as irrelevant to meeting the needs of battered women. The rapid growth of this organization provided little time for members to build consensus on the criteria for selecting board members. A board that shared values with staff and volunteers would have been more likely to broaden their contacts with members rather than adopt a conventional reliance on communication with a director.
- No alternative structure was in place to serve as a contravening force to the imposition of a conventional hierarchical structure. The early imposition of a policy-making board and a director precluded experiential development

of an alternative model. Moreover, when its board exerted its power, unlike the Rape Crisis Center and Women's Transit Authority, Advocates for Battered Women did not have an experienced group of volunteers and established mechanisms for volunteer involvement in collective decision making. Volunteer energy, knowledge, and commitment to collectivity could have lent additional voices to help maintain a nonconventional structure.

• The high turnover among volunteers and staff intensified the organization's turmoil. Shared information and experience most likely would have enhanced their problem-solving efforts: "Part of the problem in the past was that the turnover was so rapid that nobody had any history to call on."

By March 1982, the board of Advocates for Battered Women consisted of community people who "shared a feminist orientation towards domestic violence and saw domestic violence as caused by sexism, and who'd had some experience with collective decision making." After establishing a new board, Advocates for Battered Women proceeded to establish a decision-making structure that would increase the communication and trust among staff and board members. Board members shared information with and obtained input from staff by consulting with the administrative director, but now, it was explicitly understood that the director would "make sure that major decisions are not made without consulting staff." Staff were no longer members of the board. However, board committees now consisted of both staff and board members, "so that staff's really 'on board,' participating where the work's getting done." Staff were required to attend all board meetings, and board members were required to have more direct knowledge of the organization's services.

> Staff has an incredible amount of decision-making power in terms of the entire organization and how it runs. We make recommendations to the board about personnel policies, about how the programs are going to run, what kinds of programs we're going to have, what our philosophy and goals are going to be . . . We don't get to vote on the major issues, but since we are actively involved in every committee of the board, we have a tremendous amount of input in deciding what comes out of those committees. Most of the board work is done in committees.

Advocates for Battered Women returned to a more collective structure, with consensus decision making being the preferred method within the staff and within the board. Their goal was to reach agreement among staff and board members. If this were not possible, ultimately, the board would make the decision.

The history of Advocates for Battered Women provides a vivid example of how members of feminist service organizations struggled with difficult organizational issues and, at the same time, not only did not abandon their mission but increased their commitment to it. Given the circumstances, becoming a conventional social service agency may have been Advocates for Battered Women's only option for avoiding these tumultuous years. What is most compelling about this story is not the animosities and disruptions but that Advocates for Battered Women maintained its feminist mission and developed effective services throughout this period.

In sharp contrast to Advocates for Battered Women, both the Rape Crisis Center and Women's Transit Authority had considerable time to develop member roles and services before having to deal with an active board. The Rape Crisis Center's Project on Rape consisted of four paid staff for its first five years, and Women's Transit Authority operated for five years before acquiring funding for three part-time coordinators. In both cases, members worked with "paper boards" for over five years. With substantial additional funding and greatly expanded services, both organizations wanted their boards to assume more responsibility, and board members wanted to take their roles more seriously. Although their organizations had better planning and more member control than Advocates for Battered Women, members of the Rape Crisis Center and Women's Transit Authority also could not have anticipated the disruptions this shift would entail.

Women's Transit Authority

In 1974, Women's Transit Authority created a four-person board that had no authority or major responsibilities. Each of the four women worked separately to assist the coordinators in writing funding proposals, and they signed contracts. In 1980, a formal eight-person board was created in response to pressure from funders, but this board merely rubber-stamped decisions made by members. In 1981, due to tighter fiscal controls and more accountability being required by funders, the staff asked the board to become more active: "The coordinators alone could not provide the direction and did not want to." The board began to consider its legal obligations and its internal responsibilities, which included fund-raising, examining Transit's political role in the community, developing personnel policies, approving budgets, and long-range planning. However, major conflicts over personnel issues and Transit's sponsorship of an all-women march stalled its progress.

In mid-1981, conflict among the three coordinators involved the staff and board in extended discussions over worker responsibilities. The specific conflict was eventually resolved by the resignation of one coordinator. However, significant tensions remained over what personnel policies should be adopted and what authority the board should assume. A conflict over sponsoring an all-women "Take Back the Night" march exacerbated these divisions: "This issue in particular made it clear that our structure didn't fit the needs of the organization."

Feminist activists have organized "Take Back the Night" rallies and marches across the country to remind communities that public places are not safe for women at night and to demand community action to ensure women's safety. The events symbolically represent women's joining together to assert their power. They present sexual assault as a community problem, not exclusively a problem for women (Aiello, 1984). In Wisconsin, annual "Take Back the Night" rallies began in 1979, after a series of brutal rapes and murders in Milwaukee.

In November 1981, a group of Women's Transit Authority staff and volunteers began organizing "No More Assaults Day" and a women-only "Take Back the Night" rally and march. This planning group had held three meetings by the time the board met in February 1982 to consider Women's Transit Authority's annual budget, which included funds for the march. Much to their surprise, a board member announced that she would not approve any of the budget until men were allowed to be part of the march. After much discussion, the board ruled that Women's Transit Authority's sponsorship and funding were dependent upon men being allowed in the march.

> I was shocked at this "Take Back the Night" thing. I always thought everyone in that organization would want an all-women's march. I was way off base. They thought having men in the march would not impinge upon the purpose of the march. There were others of us who thought it would. It really became explosive. The politics really rocketed at that time.
>
> Get any 20 Transiters in a room, and I could never predict how they would vote on where, if anywhere, men should be positioned at the march. It's something that, with Transit's history of women-only activity, one would think would be a fairly easy decision to make, but it wasn't. There were always people on both sides of the issue.

The board focused on the potential loss of funding and community support: "The march was funded by separate donations that we had raised, but they felt even the publicity could be viewed as so negative that it could impinge upon our future funding." Also, the board felt that it was important to allow the participation of anyone who supported the theme of the march.

> One of the rationalizations that the board used for its move in withdrawing funding for "Take Back the Night" was that they felt that our women-only stand was alienating to the community and that we should modify that stand wherever it was marginally possible for us to do so. It was their perceptions of the force of public opinion that were influencing how they expressed themselves. God knows if those perceptions were accurate or not.

The planners were furious, believing that "the board had ample opportunity to influence the decision, that the planning meetings had been open and on-going, and that they had no right to come in at this late date and seize control." They asserted that it was inappropriate for the board to question Women's Transit Authority's role "in a social activity." In addition, the planners were committed to the symbolic importance of a women-only activity and were personally invested in marching only with women.

> Having an all-women's march, that wasn't strictly lesbian versus straight. There were clearly a number of women who wanted a woman-identified march and felt that it was very important to make that statement, the need for women having space, the need for women marching together without men.

Additional meetings between board members and the organizers were held to try to resolve this dispute, but without success. Antagonism between the board and the staff and volunteers grew. Finally, board members met with all of the staff and volunteers to explain their decision and to see if, with the help of outside facilitators, they could work out a decision that everyone could support.

> Everybody was really, really pissed. Everybody was brought up short because their understanding of how power was distributed in Transit, assumptions that had never been tested, was being tested real fast and real hard. It was a really unpleasant meeting.

Ultimately, with no consensus emerging, the decision of the board was not altered. However, a compromise evolved wherein the front of the march would be reserved for people wearing banners saying, "I survived rape," thereby emphasizing who would be leading the march rather than who would not. At the march, men were asked to move back if they came to the front, but "very few men came to the front."

Although this conflict lowered morale and "the members of the board left as quickly as they could," members believed that organizing these events also had positive effects. Approximately 2,000 people participated in the all-day and -night event. Workshops on street assertiveness, incest, self-defense, lesbian- and gay-directed assault, and coalition work were offered. The evening rally featured six speakers, and many women joined the march as it moved through central Madison. Sponsoring the march, rally, and "No More Assaults Day" activities energized the volunteers, increased publicity about Women's Transit Authority, and helped its public relations, volunteer recruitment, and fund-raising efforts. Staff, volunteers, and community members became closer, and volunteers developed a variety of skills.

The debate over the "Take Back the Night" march illustrates well how assumptions of shared beliefs in feminist groups can be severely disrupted when a specific decision requires choosing among different and competing priorities. The majority of the board represented maintaining good community standing; not alienating men or women with men; concern over loss of funding; and the importance of including all people who supported sexual assault awareness, the theme of the march. In general, the volunteers and staff represented empowering women; providing women with the opportunity to express their solidarity with other women; symbolizing women's right to be out at night without the protection and support of men; and the importance of collective decision making. Although a compromise was eventually fashioned, it became apparent that members who identified with the values of the early radical feminists could not achieve their goals when their board adopted positions that were more closely associated with liberal feminism.

Women's Transit Authority was able to integrate a formal policy-making board within a feminist structure but, like Advocates for Battered Women, only after electing a new board that uniformly supported shared power among board members, staff, and volunteers.

> Because the new board members were all in the organization or close to the organization when all this mess was going on, and they saw everything that happened, they're that much more committed to not letting it happen again. The board is much more united, much more harmonious, and much more able to work effectively as part of the organization. The past board got so bogged down in all this other shit for so long, they couldn't get any work done . . . People on the new board want to make sure that decisions are made with a clear conscience by all, are talked about by everyone and, as much as possible, are agreed on by everyone. They make a strong attempt to include all three segments—the volunteers, the staff and the board—in any decisions which affect the organization overall, which is a difference from the old board.
>
> The major change in the board is that we all acknowledge that what we're doing may not be right, and we're all open to seeing that it was wrong and making changes.

Like Advocates for Battered Women, the organization's goal was to change its structure to increase communication and trust. Instead of the board selecting its new members, the board was elected by staff, board members, and volunteers. Board committees consisted of staff, volunteers, and board members. On a rotating basis, one staff member participated, but did not vote, in every board meeting and reported back to the other staff. One seat on the board was designated to be held by an active volunteer who would serve as the liaison with the VAB. Volunteers could also be elected for other seats on the board. Like the VAB, the board worked for consensus but would use majority rule if necessary.

All of our volunteers have direct input into the board through the volunteer advisory board. We actually refer a lot of issues to them because we, as a feminist board, say, "We have our feelings on this issue, but if we make this decision, it's going to ultimately be something that our volunteers deal with," so we ask for their input first. We create a lot of extra work for ourselves as a board to make sure that everyone's heard and has a voice.

In reality, only the staff has the consensus decision-making component. It's unrealistic with the volunteers because the volunteer pool is so large that consensus is not likely to happen. The board strives hard and long at making decisions by consensus, but we need decisions to be made. If they aren't going to be made by consensus, they need to be made anyway. Because the staff has to live daily with the decisions that they make, because it absorbs so much of their lives, it's nice that the staff work so hard to agree.

In Women's Transit Authority, each component determined its own decision-making process and had responsibility for certain types of decisions. A recourse process was developed so that any component could object to decisions made by another component and call for reconsideration. The board retained final authority. Nonetheless, the level of involvement of staff and volunteers in decision making was viewed as maintaining the collective spirit of Women's Transit Authority: "All the women have a say. There's the coordinators, who also answer to the board of directors, who also answer to the volunteer advisory board, which is made up of any volunteers who happen to show up at the meeting. So everybody has a voice."

The Rape Crisis Center

In 1974, the Rape Crisis Center established a "paper board" consisting of staff and volunteers to sign contracts. By the late 1970s, all three components of the organization saw the benefits in having an active board. Although the de facto director had regularly informed volunteers about administrative issues at weekly and then monthly Rape Crisis Center meetings, no group of volunteers consistently attended those meetings. The funding crisis with the county over its requiring the reporting of consumer names, which was described in chapter 5, served to highlight this problem. Volunteers became more concerned about their lack of involvement in funding decisions.

At the same time, the board "expressed their discomfort with not knowing enough about what they were signing." They began to raise questions about what their role was and should be. Similarly, the de facto director wanted volunteers to share the decision-making burden. She did not believe that it was appropriate or useful for the staff to possess so much more knowledge about the center than the volunteers. Also, members recognized that, in meetings of the full collective, "decision making was such a lengthy process, so unwieldy because of the growth in the numbers of both volunteers and staff, that the agency was paralyzed half the time."

In 1979, the de facto director and "some very assertive volunteer board members" provided the leadership for establishing a steering committee to serve as the Rape Crisis Center board and assume responsibility for policy approval and financial matters. The steering committee model assigned decision-making responsibility to identified members of the organization but extended participation and voting power to all members of the collective. It was designed to guarantee continuity, reliability, and accountability without restricting member involvement.

> The steering committee is the seven people who have to be responsible, who have to show up and run the business. We needed to know that there were people who would provide that kind of continuity, who we knew were going to be there. Then, anybody else who wanted to take part in the business end of the operation could participate.

The five elected volunteers on the steering committee constituted the volunteer board required of nonprofits, but the entire steering committee functioned as the board of the Rape Crisis Center. Unlike most boards, the steering committee consisted of current volunteers and representatives of the staff, and every member of the organization could attend steering committee meetings and vote. Decisions were made by consensus. By the mid-1980s, the steering committee had expanded to include six volunteers and three staff. Major issues could still be taken to the collective as a whole.

The steering committee was responsible for advising members on issues that significantly involved the Rape Crisis Center's public image and the future directions of the organization, drafting policies that pertained to the work of the volunteers, and approving policies drafted by paid staff when the proposed change involved volunteers or funding. The steering committee increasingly assumed responsibility for budgetary matters, fundraising, volunteer and staff evaluations, and grievances. The full staff and the steering committee needed to reach consensus on major budgetary issues.

Only after it was forced to deal with a difficult personnel issue in 1983 did the steering committee begin to expand its authority in ways that were perceived as significantly altering established power relationships in the Rape Crisis Center.

We had a termination situation that was very chaotic. That was the issue that made the steering committee realize that they had some more work to do on their role. They were being asked to hear about firing issues, and they didn't feel at all prepared to deal with that. Even who could fire and who could make the recommendation to fire was very cloudy. There was no maliciousness directed at the person, but it was a very hard issue to go through because the process was so unclear . . . The staff could not reach any consensus about firing this person. Not knowing what else to do, they turned to the steering committee. That was the only thing they could reach consensus on. The paid staff couldn't vote because of conflict of interest, so the volunteers on the steering committee ended up dealing with the decision. They had to act like a traditional board of directors, and they weren't prepared for it. It was a very stressful time.

Nothing like that had ever happened before. The steering committee doesn't make decisions about the staff, except on that one occasion. It brought up all kinds of issues. What is the role of the steering committee overall, and what is its relationship to the staff? It shook up our whole decision-making process and brought up lots of issues about the interrelationship of the parts of the organization that we still are thrashing out now.

At the time of these interviews, many of the volunteers on the steering committee wanted to expand their authority over staff decision making. The staff believed that they should maintain autonomy over their day-to-day operations and that the demands of the volunteers were unrealistic and inappropriate.

There's the overall youngness of the volunteers, and the fact that's a transient population. But they have equal voting power. Their age, their place in their lives, their transiency makes them think that some things are possible that I don't think really are. There's an energy that comes from naivete and a commitment that comes out of that spirit. But it also gets in the way of getting some realistic things done and causes some problems.

We, as paid staff, have more time. We get paid to look at issues and to respond to them. Oftentimes, the steering committee feels like we shouldn't have responded, that they should have responded. Then, we feel like we're the ones who are going to get the shit for it if we don't respond right away. We are responsible. We are the ones who are answerable. Sometimes, we have to make decisions quickly, and they don't understand that or get pissed off about that.

Creating the steering committee and delegating minor authority to the coordinators made decision making in the Rape Crisis Center more efficient, more effective, and in some ways less stressful. Still, allowing any member to vote in steering committee meetings was problematic, and members were considering ways to insure that those voting were well-informed. Unavoidably, the full empowerment of all members would be restricted by concerns about matching power with responsibility, involvement with accountability.

We're going to have to set some limits. How much of the time are we going to allow people who are only half-informed about an issue to drop in and then vote at a steering committee meeting? How much commitment are we going to require from people in order to be part of that group? That's a sticky issue, because you're talking about excluding people who haven't been there before but who are collective members. But it's getting in the way of the decision-making process to have people who hear something about an issue, get upset, come in, and want to be part of the process. We have to go back and explain everything to any woman who chooses to come in. It can go on forever.

The women who are taking on most of the responsibility are resentful because people who take almost no responsibility have the power to come in at the last minute and stick their hands in the air and say, "No, I block consensus." "Well, how much information do you have?" "Well, so-and-so told me . . ." She can't be allowed to do that. We're letting someone who hasn't put in work and hasn't put in think-time take away all the work we've done. I don't want to take away that one woman's power either, but I want to make it proportionate to how much work she's willing to put in.

At the time of these interviews, a subgroup of the steering committee was trying to design mechanisms to address this problem. Implementing any changes would require approval by the full collective.

We will still use a consensus process to come up with what we will finally do. The consensus process has worked well. It's taken a lot of time and energy, but we've felt good about the decisions that have come out with that. Even when people start out on different sides of an issue, we've been able to come up with something that's acceptable to everybody. I'm pretty optimistic that, even though people feel differently about the importance of the involvement in decision making, we'll come up with something that will be a good compromise.

AN EXTERNAL PERSPECTIVE
ON ORGANIZATIONAL STRUCTURE

The community members who had contact with these organizations based on their roles in funding agencies, law enforcement, and social services identified three structural issues. Not surprisingly, these included the absence of a single spokesperson, the time devoted to decision making, and internal conflicts. However, these problems were generally framed in terms of their negative impact on the organizations' members, not in terms of their jeopardizing community support and funding. In no case were internal conflicts discussed as being detrimental to clients or as interfering with the delivery of services.

For example, with respect to Advocates for Battered Women, the central message was that the organization had been successful programmatically and, if it addressed its internal problems, "then their future would be even stronger." In terms of past administrative problems, Advocates for Battered Women was viewed as very interested in and open to correcting them but enmeshed in interminable discussions that often did not generate solutions: "They make their struggle a lot harder by not allowing staff to take leadership in making decisions." Currently, Advocates for Battered Women was viewed as having "more of a healthy process in dealing with problems."

Of all the organizations, community members were most aware of and concerned about Advocates for Battered Women's internal difficulties. That organization's problems were most visible due to high levels of turnover over many years. Also, the turnover in the director's position and the conflicts between board and staff had interfered with its ability to develop sound business practices. Several funders had assisted the organization in improving fiscal management of its program and in preparing funding proposals.

"Personality conflicts" and "power struggles" were also mentioned with respect to ARC House, the Rape Crisis Center, and Women's Transit Authority. Community members were aware of such problems but seemed to know little about them and expressed little concern: "There are some knotty internal politics. I don't follow all the ins and outs."

> I have a stronger knowledge base about their funding operations and what services they provide and what we use them for. I have gotten no complaints about their services. I am aware that they have had some organizational problems. I think they have reorganized recently.
>
> I know that internal staff conflicts have come up again. I can only go by what I have heard, that there were some personality conflicts. My understanding now is that a lot of those problems have been alleviated by some staff changes.

It appears that internal strains in ARC House, the Rape Crisis Center, and Women's Transit Authority did not rise to a level that engaged much external scrutiny. Internal conflicts did not significantly affect external relations.

The fact that the Rape Crisis Center worked collectively was a problem for some people in law enforcement who wanted one person in charge: "We were getting transferred from one person to another saying, 'Well, that is not really my responsibility.'" At the time of these interviews, one member of the Rape Crisis Center had been identified as a contact person for the police department. Others found the Rape Crisis Center's decision making cumbersome but saw this as an internal pressure primarily.

It got to be very difficult to get stuff done at various times because everything
had to be taken back to the group. They wanted to reach a consensus. Their decision making would get bogged down in that kind of process. I guess that
would be one of the problems, but I wouldn't call it a very serious problem.
Things got done. People worked very hard. They had the advantage of having
people who were totally committed to what they were doing. They put in long
hours, and if it took them longer to reach a decision than the other places, then
it took them longer to do it. The work got done.

For every organization, community members spoke highly of particular administrative staff with whom they had worked. For example, one individual
described the directors of Advocates for Battered Women as being "extremely
talented women" who were caught up in battles over collectivity. Another
mentioned coordinators of Women's Transit Authority who were "particularly
effective" in working with different groups on campus. The project director
of Women Reaching Women was described as a "major strength." Administrators of ARC House were "impressive in terms of how they have commu-
nicated with us, how we have been able to share ideas." In other instances, respondents referred positively to the overall administration of an organization.

> Their process is to me the most interesting part of ARC House. They run things
> in a very participatory fashion. I'd like to know more about how they do it, be-
> cause it seems to work beautifully.
>
> The survey work that they do is great, and also their ability to prepare budg-
> ets. In fact, when we went down to the City Council on this backup cab program,
> I couldn't believe the slick job Transit did with their presentation.

Ironically, the organization that received the most praise, and in glowing
terms, was the one that operated most like a collective. The Rape Crisis Center was frequently cited as a group that had people with strong administrative
skills and the ability to relate well to traditional bureaucracies and funding
sources. Those who represented the Rape Crisis Center were described as
having "a level of professionalism," "strong administrative talent," and "business savvy"; as being "the cream of the crop." Perhaps these qualities received so much attention because they were so unexpected from members of
a radical feminist organization.

> Their record was perfect. They have the ability to communicate well with the
> funding source and to provide information in a timely way, in an articulate way,
> too. Their proposals were models of the way proposals should be presented and
> the way services should be described.
>
> They were working on a collective model, and yet they were able to relate to
> a bureaucracy, which is so important if you're funded by a bureaucracy. They

were very, very good at that. I know they were true to the consensus model, but they were somehow able to manage that and to still have someone responsible for decision making on a day-to-day basis. They somehow did that.

Operating internally as a collective and sharing many administrative responsibilities, members of the Rape Crisis Center formalized a business manager position in 1980 and had a de facto business manager prior to 1980. These individuals were valued members of the collective. At the same time, funding sources viewed these "administrators" as highly effective. Apparently, having individual members of a collective accumulating specialized knowledge and external influence is not in ánd of itself anathema to radical feminists.

MERGING COLLECTIVITY AND BUREAUCRACY: APPROPRIATING THE BEST OF BOTH

We're allowed to participate in making decisions that will affect our work. Everyone has that power. It doesn't mean everyone takes that power, but because you have that right, you can participate as much as you so choose. I can be right up there with policy making, or I can just come in and do my night shift and let other people make those decisions. But the fact that I have that right means that I can make that choice. (RCC)

Being pioneers in the creation of feminist service organizations, understanding what they did not wish to emulate and replicate was the essential first step in members' moving toward the more difficult task of developing new models and methods. Women in Advocates for Battered Women, ARC House, the Rape Crisis Center, and Women's Transit Authority were establishing unique workplaces, with goals and processes antithetical to commonly accepted approaches. Under these conditions, perhaps only their intense commitment to *women helping women* can explain their willingness to endure endless self-examination, meetings that could easily go on for four to five hours, decisions that could take weeks to make, and continual organizational change.

With respect to every aspect of their internal operations, members assessed the external requirements and internal pressures that conflicted with their ideals to determine the appropriate mix of the ideological and the practical. Members created specialized roles and formal policies; they identified lines of responsibility and avenues for addressing grievances, eliminating some of the more negative aspects of relying solely on interpersonal influence. Specialization was defined in terms of expertise, not elitism; it was used to increase accountability and effectiveness, not to oppress or silence. Standards of performance were applied in the context of caring, taking into account the unique circumstances of individual members.

In the three explicitly feminist organizations, members began with very different board structures but moved toward models that had much in common. Board members had specialized expertise and authority but, unlike conventional nonprofits, they also had considerable knowledge about the internal operations of their organizations and ongoing, direct communication with administrative staff *and* frontline workers. In all three organizations, board members and administrative staff exerted less power than they would have in conventional service organizations. Direct communication and shared experiences among different groups and different positions increased levels of familiarity and trust.

Substantial autonomy among individuals and small groups was maintained, promoting the exercise of personal initiative, the expression of individual talent, and the realization of personal fulfillment. With the exception of volunteers in Advocates for Battered Women, members had control over those decisions that directly affected their work unless their decisions had major implications for the organization as a whole. Unlike in traditional bureaucracies, members sought the highest levels of involvement and the broadest support for decisions that were central to the overall mission of their organization. As in Iannello's (1992) study, their goal was to have the most significant decisions made by the largest number of people, distributing authority as widely and as equally as possible.

Consensus decision making remained an essential component. In the absence of consensus, members strived to maintain the core elements of consensus building. They encouraged openness to diverse opinions, respect for differences, and broad participation. Decision making was considered to be consistent with feminist principles when members had *access* to information, *input* on specific issues, and *influence* on major decisions. Acknowledging the formal authority of individuals who held administrative positions and the legal responsibilities of their boards, members remained enthusiastic about and confident in their own power when they believed that they were well-informed and that their views were valued and taken into account. By sharing information, influence, and responsibility throughout their organizations, women increased the personal power of every member. All components most effectively exercised power when they were also able to share power.

The shared yet different interests of board members, staff, and volunteers illustrate the paradox of empowerment in feminist organizations. Women were empowered by having autonomy in their work, as individuals and as members of small groups with similar responsibilities. At the same time, maintaining authority within the organization as a whole, women were empowered through their equal participation in and shared responsibility for organization-wide decision making. Member empowerment required delegating authority and then empowering those delegated to make decisions *and* ensuring that those with delegated power established channels for input from other sectors of the organization and were responsive to the opinions and priorities of others in the organization.

Given the multiple interpretations of feminist beliefs, the intense personal meanings of active participation, and the pioneering nature of their efforts, it is not surprising that conflict permeated organizational development, especially in the three explicitly feminist organizations. Their survival as feminist organizations was dependent on members' willingness to confront and productively address the incongruities of principle and pragmatism. Rather than being ideologically bound to specific methods, they created new structures through an incremental process that applied experience and feminist values to both external and internal circumstances, all the while balancing individual empowerment and organizational survival. Given the tasks before them, it may be that only conflict joined with high levels of commitment could break through traditional assumptions and idealistic visions to create viable structures.

In their early years, members of these organizations equated a feminist structure with a collective structure. Over the years, they had moved from their central question being "How do we function as a collective?" to "How do we organize ourselves in ways consistent with our feminist principles?" Through this process, members developed new understandings of what constitutes a "feminist" organization. They incorporated features of bureaucracy and collectivity in innovative ways that built on the positive aspects of both types of organizations, were consistent with feminist principles, and were responsive to their specific missions and organizational ties with established bureaucracies.

Conclusion

Advocates for Battered Women, ARC House, the Rape Crisis Center, Women's Transit Authority, and Women Reaching Women were established in the 1970s as part of feminists' early efforts to translate their principles and beliefs into concrete strategies. Through service work, members sought to alter their own experiences as women while contributing to social change. These organizations were created to meet unrecognized needs of women, to provide alternatives to existing services that reinforced the status quo for women, and to alter women's sociopolitical circumstances. Their members educated their community about the debilitating effects of conventional gender roles and gender inequality on women's lives. To benefit women as a group in their community and the users of their services, they advocated successfully for changes within law enforcement and health and social services, affected changes in legislation and social policies, and assisted individual women in improving the conditions of their own lives. These organizations exemplified feminist efforts to promote social change and, at the same time, stood as evidence of the success of such efforts.

Building on the tenets of the early radical feminists, members of these service organizations developed new knowledge about women's problems and new methods for addressing these problems. Except for those involved in Women Reaching Women, the founders and early staff of these organizations were inexperienced in creating and delivering social services. Their early services were based on understandings derived from their own experiences as women and from the experiences of their consumers, and their services changed over time as they learned more about consumer needs. Similarly, in Advocates for Battered Women, ARC House, the Rape Crisis Center, and Women's Transit Authority, members began with feminist ideals of collectivity and antipathy toward bureaucracy. Again, through their own experiences, they derived organizational models that incorporated feminist principles with the aspects of collectivity and bureaucracy that would enhance their internal functioning and the effectiveness of their service delivery. They successfully obtained funding for efforts that were inherently challenging established services and social norms.

Members identified five core principles as characterizing their organizations as feminist: *women helping women*; *understanding gender inequality as a source of women's problems*; *promoting both individual and social change for women*; *empowering consumers through consciousness-raising, self-help, and sisterhood*; and *empowering members through service work and egalitarian work structures*. Members applied these overarching principles in different ways, based on their client populations and the organizational context within which they worked.

These organizations were controlled by women, although men delivered services to children in Advocates for Battered Women and to women in ARC House; served on the boards of Advocates for Battered Women, ARC House, and Women Reaching Women; and provided some assistance with building maintenance, office work, and financial matters in every organization but the Rape Crisis Center. Every organization focused primarily on women's issues, although Advocates for Battered Women provided some services for children, and the Rape Crisis Center assisted children and men who were victims of sexual assault. Members of every organization asserted the benefits of *women helping women* for members and consumers. Having women working with women on behalf of women was viewed as personally meaningful and politically significant. Members in every organization were confident that there were practical advantages in women's providing services to women and working in woman-centered organizations.

The dictum *the personal is political* guided members' efforts in helping women deal with the personal problems and psychological distresses associated with the inequitable distribution of power and material resources in society at large. Gender inequality was viewed as the cause of woman abuse, creating the problems of battered women and victims of sexual assault and contributing significantly to women's criminal behavior and substance abuse. Understanding that *the personal is political* meant that members' efforts were directed toward assisting individual women and also eliminating the social, economic, and legal barriers that limited women's opportunities and contributed to their victimization. Their community education and systems advocacy efforts were designed to improve the treatment women received and to broaden their options.

Furthermore, these organizations embodied feminism's focus on female empowerment. Women's Transit Authority offered women autonomy and self-assurance. In the other four organizations, services were designed to empower consumers by helping them to discover and act upon their own strengths, to achieve a sense of self-sufficiency, to view themselves as equals in interpersonal relationships, and to work toward goals that they themselves identified as desirable rather than toward goals set on the basis of socially prescribed roles. Female empowerment included consumers' understanding through consciousness-raising how their ability to influence the conditions of their own lives was tied to the power women have in society as a group. This understanding was a critical aspect of consumers' identifying meaningful directions for change and not blaming themselves for not being able to accomplish all of their goals. Consumers were also empowered through supportive relationships with members of the organization and by understanding the commonalities and "sisterhood" between themselves and other women, including members of the organization. Although necessarily limited with female offenders, self-help was an important aspect of empowering consumers.

In general, active members of these organizations shared an identification with the women's movement and viewed their work as a form of feminist activism. They were empowered by having the opportunity to work in a concerted manner with others who shared their visions. Also, they created organizational structures that reflected the same values they were applying in their work with consumers. Members exerted substantial influence over organizational goals and practices, emphasizing shared power and mutual support. Furthermore, female empowerment was evidenced by the very existence and survival of these organizations since they were developed by women to promote change in the lives of women, individually and collectively, in direct opposition to established social norms and institutions.

Delivering direct services and promoting social change reliably empowered both staff and volunteers. In reference to their work, members exuded confidence and enthusiasm. In every organization, members were initially inexperienced in building the type of organization they were creating. In each case, members became highly knowledgeable about the needs and concerns of their consumer group and skilled in gaining the acceptance and cooperation of other service providers. Experiencing high levels of autonomy and success in their work with individual women, in their community education efforts, and in their training of other practitioners was extremely rewarding. Having their organization survive was in and of itself viewed as a major accomplishment.

Internally, member empowerment was also a consistent goal, but with mixed success. Having control over decisions regarding their services and the internal operations of their organizations was personally reaffirming. Members felt empowered when their interactions with one another were characterized by the expression of shared convictions, by shared responsibilities, and by mutual support and caring. They felt empowered as they became increasingly politically adept in dealing with funders and policy makers. However, member empowerment was an illusion when power was not effectively shared, that is, when decisions could not be made, when consensus was based on intimidation or apathy, when the views of some were imposed on others, and when conflicts could not be resolved amicably. Collectivity did not guarantee member empowerment, and increased bureaucratization did not preclude it.

As in other studies of feminist organizations (Morgen, 1995; Taylor, 1995), members' accounts included frequent references to strong bonds, high levels of trust, and passionate commitments as well as bitter disappointments and debilitating conflicts. Formalization of rules and policies mediated some sources of strain. However, increased bureaucratization did not eliminate intense interpersonal relationships, fervent allegiance to feminist ideology, and unwavering determination to pursue social change. The expression of strong feelings characterized members' interactions with one another, their views of their work with consumers, and their responses to external victories and opposition.

Radical feminism encompassed a range of theories and goals that members incorporated into their work selectively and differently, merging principle and pragmatism. At the same time that members of Advocates for Battered Women, the Rape Crisis Center, and Women's Transit Authority were publicly denouncing male violence against women and labeling such violence as a manifestation of female oppression, feminists in ARC House and Women Reaching Women were explaining how established services were failing to recognize and address the unique needs of female clients. By their actions, however, members of ARC House and Women Reaching Women were making significant inroads into male-dominated and male-centered domains. Much like the other three organizations, their work was confronting the patriarchal structures that restricted the lives of the women who were dependent on these structures. The different methods that evolved in these five organizations support the view that many feminists in the 1970s and early 1980s held similar radical beliefs but pursued different political strategies (Freeman, 1975; Ryan, 1992). More generally, these five organizations confirm that similar values and goals characterized feminist organizations with different structures and practices (Ferree and Martin, 1995; Martin, 1990; Riger, 1994). Their work reveals that as early as the 1970s, the tenets of the early radical feminists were being incorporated into feminist service organizations situated outside of conventional agencies and into service organizations embedded within conservative, mainstream bureaucracies.

Members in every organization began with an allegiance to collectivity, and they maintained aspects of collectivity within structures that contained features of bureaucracy. However, they did not uniformly begin as small feminist collectives. Only Women's Transit Authority and the Rape Crisis Center began as feminist collectives that maintained a separatist stance. Women Reaching Women was established within a conservative, hierarchical parent organization. However, in its local chapters and statewide meetings, mutual support and shared power were emphasized. ARC House began with a commitment to collectivity based on the value systems of feminism and Ananda Marga, although it had an external board and an executive director. When Advocates for Battered Women began its shelter work, it had a conventional hierarchical structure; aspects of collectivity were incorporated over time. The differences among these five organizations, beginning with their creation, suggest that collectivity was an important force in feminist service organizations, but the incorporation of collectivity did not follow a single path.

The range of motivations, interests, and involvements represented among members of these organizations illustrate that "being feminist" did not constitute rigid adherence to pre-existing dictums or represent one particular "type" of woman or social group. Members integrated radical feminist principles into their own interests and goals in a variety of ways. Some women had been actively involved in feminist grassroots activities prior to their service work. Others were engaged based on their personal experiences with woman abuse or their growing interest in the women's movement, and they developed a feminist identity through their participation in the work of their organizations. For some, feminism was incorporated into personal commitments to spirituality and "bringing about a new social order where all men and women can be assured of the necessities of life" (Ananda Marga Yoga Society job listing in *Vocations for Social Change*, January 1972). Others were involved in the AODA treatment system and were integrating feminist goals and methods with their professional interests or personal circumstances. Some members were young students; others were in their 30s and 40s. Some were professionals, but most were not. Some volunteered, with *helping women* being their primary concern. Others became deeply involved in organizational life, with developing a feminist organization being a major and long-term investment.

Moreover, "being feminist" was not a static state. To the contrary, members' accounts reveal that "being feminist" was a synergistic process based on the dynamic interplay of ideology and experience. Within the boundaries of overarching principles, what constituted "being feminist" in these organizations was responsive to new information and changing circumstances and took into account different organizational contexts. Similarly, within each organization, knowing that a woman identified herself as a feminist did not provide a firm basis for predicting her perceptions, attitudes, and behaviors in any one specific situation. At best, it predicted commitment to broad feminist principles and gender equality and excluded conscious acts that reinforced female subordination and victimization. Members with similar beliefs argued for very different actions, and members with dissimilar beliefs unified around specific strategies. Their views were continually refined and revised based on new experiences and their desires to take into account differences among women.

In every organization, members engaged in ongoing evaluation and reevaluation of their policies and practices. Throughout this process, they explicitly and consistently worked to exert power defined "not as domination, but as ability to act and capacity to perform ... as energy, strength, and effective interaction" (Hartsock, 1998, p. 63). Perhaps most important, the members of these organizations were committed to devoting considerable time and energy to problem solving and to creating and employing decision-making processes that incorporated feminist principles. Several quotations capture the essence of their commitments:

> We just have to do more communicating to work on it . . . Despite the differing opinions and personal conflicts, there is this spirit of always working things through. We will work it through. (RCC)
> Those arguments and discussions have always been healthy. They've always kept us striking a healthy balance. (ABW)
> If a decision is made, it's almost always that we've hassled it out together. We try to give one another equal power as much as possible. (ARC)
> We have always struggled with what inequities a certain decision-making process will bring to our organization. There has always been a certain amount of self-consciousness about the effects of using one decision-making process or another. (WTA)
> Differences are actually healthy, because it means that we have to seriously think about what we're doing. It means that there has to be a lot of time and energy devoted to wrestling with the differences. (RCC)

It was not that rigid standards and polarities did not characterize members' thinking at various points. Certainly, many members retained their own criteria for what constituted a feminist organization. However, the tasks required in developing effective services pushed members to move beyond their own definitions, to adopt an organizational perspective rather than only an individual one. Their successes were ultimately accompanied by members' acknowledging differences and identifying points of agreement that could form the basis of unified efforts toward the accomplishment of agreed-upon goals.

As foremothers in the development of feminist service organizations, members had few models to help them focus their deliberations, to define and narrow their options, and to predict the consequences of their decisions. Conflict appeared to be inevitable as members translated politics into practice, especially when decisions were viewed as operational representations of feminist principles. They were confronted with the multiplicities of female experience and highly charged personal investments in feminism. Yet, members' willingness to engage in conflict and their fortitude in addressing conflicts were certainly among the keys to their success. Resolution of major conflicts required intense and time-consuming debates. Many of these conflicts were painful and divisive, and their resolutions were sometimes dependent on individuals' leaving the organizations. As difficult and discouraging as these conflicts were, it was through such lengthy debates that members developed the terms of their survival as feminist organizations.

Women's difficulties in dealing with conflict have destroyed many feminist groups, especially over the period of history when these five organizations were established (Riger, 1984; Ryan, 1989). The fact that members of these organizations were able to persevere effectively through times of conflict in the 1970s and early 1980s is worthy of praise. Their achievements are even more remarkable in light of the fact that conflict in feminist organizations remains a major concern: "Developing... an 'etiquette of conflict,' which permits differences to be negotiated while retaining connections among women, is a formidable task facing women's organizations today" (Riger, 1994, p. 295).

Through their long and often torturous deliberations, members moved beyond the dichotomous thinking that has characterized most discussions of feminist organizations. They developed models of feminist practice that did not choose between being separatist organizations or integrated into mainstream agencies; pursuing radical change or incremental reform; being collective or hierarchical; providing social services or promoting social change; pursuing equality or accentuating gender differences. Combining aspects from both sides of these polarities often created anxiety and confusion. Nonetheless, it is likely that these organizations' long-term survival as effective feminist service organizations can be attributed in large measure to members' establishing services and structures based on thoughtful applications of feminist principles to specific circumstances rather than remaining within the confines of preestablished binary oppositions.

Members pursued a mix of goals and methods within their organizations. They retained their dual focus on promoting social change through education and advocacy and providing direct services for which understandings of gender inequality provided the foundation. They challenged the status quo by radically altering understandings of women's problems and by creating separate, woman-centered alternatives for ameliorating these problems. They utilized reformist strategies to obtain stable funding, to build linkages with conventional agencies, and to alter the laws and policies that directly impeded their goals. Members maintained their commitments to feminist values while working closely and effectively with politically conservative consumers; funders and policy makers; doctors and nurses; police, prosecutors, and probation and parole officers; child care workers and school personnel; therapists; and providers of social services. Members promoted gender equality as a rationale for their services, demanding equal access to community resources and services for women and men. At the same time, they asserted women's unique needs and pressed for the provision of different services than those provided for men. Their successes support the view that placing equality in opposition to difference does not reflect and is not particularly useful for the complex realities of feminist practice (Jaggar, 1990; Scott, 1990; Young, 1990).

In the debate over whether or not a unified group called "women" exists, many feminists have asserted that referring to "women" promotes essentialist and universalistic views of female experience, ignoring differences based on, for example, race, culture, locale, and time in history. Others have argued that stressing the uniqueness of each woman's experience eliminates the basis for joint political action (Butler and Scott, 1992). The stance taken in these organizations supports the view that feminists can develop a politics on behalf of women without postulating an essential female identity or a constant and inevitable solidarity among women (Alcoff, 1989; de Lauretis, 1990). As such, these organizations can be seen as one of the "multiple forms of unity and common action" envisioned by Chantal Mouffe:

> Feminism, for me, is the struggle for the equality of women. But this should not be understood as a struggle for realizing the equality of a definable empirical group with a common essence and identity, women, but rather as a struggle against the multiple forms in which the category "woman" is constructed in subordination . . . The absence of a female essential identity and of a pregiven unity, however, does not preclude the construction of multiple forms of unity and common action. As the result of the construction of nodal points, partial fixations can take place and precarious forms of identification can be established around the category "women" that provide the basis for a feminist identity and a feminist struggle. (1992, pp. 381, 382)

For their particular projects, it was crucial that members cast their missions in terms of specific problems experienced by "women." Obtaining funding and community support was necessarily based on articulating the common problems of women as an oppressed group and then the specific needs of women with certain types of problems. As a form of identity politics within a particular form of feminist practice, members' uses of the concept "women" were politically necessary, pragmatic, and effective.

While members' commitment was clearly to the unified category of "women," they understood this category to be multifaceted and with significant tensions among its various parts. Members were particularly concerned about divisions among conservative women and feminists, lesbians and non-lesbians, and women of color and white women. They were aware that having culturally diverse organizations required dramatic and difficult shifts in their understandings of women's lives. Given the time period when these interviews were conducted and the community in which these organizations were located, it is not surprising that issues around lesbianism had been more successfully resolved than those concerning race. Still, assertions that white radical feminists ignored racial differences among women throughout the 1970s and early 1980s are not supported.

All of these organizations benefited from government funding and had financial ties with other mainstream institutions. The organizations began with funding from LEAA, CETA, and other federal grants for innovative programs. They expanded through purchase of service contracts with the city and county; block grants from the State of Wisconsin Bureau of Alcohol and Other Drug Abuse; and funds allocated by the state legislature and City Council, United Way, the University of Wisconsin-Madison, the State Division of Corrections, and local AODA service providers and councils. All of these sources of funding placed constraints on members' activities, but they did not consign these organizations to co-optation.

Women Reaching Women had no control over the structure of its parent organization, but the project director shared decision-making power with chapter coordinators and other volunteers. Advocates for Battered Women, ARC House, the Rape Crisis Center, and Women's Transit Authority formed "hybrid" organizations (Bordt, 1997). Rejecting conventional bureaucratic structures and ideals of collectivity, members developed organizational practices that took advantage of the desirable aspects of both types of organizations, were consistent with feminist principles, and would assist them in achieving their goals. Their functioning was enhanced by incorporating modified hierarchies, but they maintained the nonelitism and sense of community associated with collectives. Like bureaucracies, they developed areas of specialization and high degrees of division of labor, and decisions were governed by rules and policies. Like collectives, they maintained high levels of face-to-face communication, shared information, and caring. Only the members of the Rape Crisis Center continued to make all decisions by consensus. The coordinators of Women's Transit Authority and the staff within programs of Advocates for Battered Women also relied on consensus decision making. In general, in Advocates for Battered Women, ARC House, and Women's Transit Authority, consensus was not required as in collectivist organizations, but unlike in bureaucracies, attaining agreement throughout the organization was explicitly valued and actively pursued. The decisions that would have the greatest impact on the organization were influenced by the largest number of people. Decision making was considered to be consistent with feminist principles when members had *access* to information, *input* on specific issues, and *influence* on major decisions.

To understand the magnitude of what these five organizations had accomplished, we can look to the recent scholarship on feminist organizations, which often contrasts its analyses with the thinking of the early radical feminists. For example, Patricia Yancey Martin (1990) states, "Few scholars claim that an organization must have a collectivist structure to qualify as feminist, although activists committed to collectivist organizations have tended to make such claims" (p. 184). Claire Reinelt (1995) notes that in the early years of the battered women's movement, "If a shelter or a movement organization was organized collectively to empower people at the grassroots level by engaging in political confrontation against patriarchal institutions, then it could be considered feminist. If it worked with mainstream institutions, developing hierarchical or bureaucratic organizational structures, then it was co-opted" (p. 91). She concludes that engaging with the state and other mainstream institutions can be viewed as feminist, that feminism does not require a particular organizational form or strategy, and that "many feminists in the 1990s accept this as the condition of their activism" (p. 101).

Similarly, Stephanie Riger (1994) observes, "Many [women's movement] organizations began with a preference for collective structures and a desire for unity among women. The experience of the last two decades has tested those values against the realities of organizational growth and has deepened our understanding of organizational dynamics" (p. 295). She concludes, "To condemn organizations as nonfeminist because they adopt bureaucratic features is to deny some of the realities of life in a growing organization. To adopt bureaucracy without recognizing its tension with feminist values, however, is to reduce the potential of our organizations to act as vehicles for social change" (p. 296).

Obviously, the preceding descriptions of feminist organizations in the early years of the movement do not represent the characteristics of Advocates for Battered Women, ARC House, the Rape Crisis Center, Women's Transit Authority, or Women Reaching Women. Their work in the 1970s and early 1980s exemplifies approaches that scholars in the 1990s have praised as important for the long-range viability and effectiveness of feminist organizations. With maintaining feminist principles as a consistent standard against which they judged the merit of their decisions, members of these five organizations incorporated positive aspects of collectivist and bureaucratic structures as they changed in response to increasing numbers of staff and volunteers, expanding services, the requirements of funders, and their own desires for efficient and effective decision-making processes. They worked effectively with policy makers and other service providers at the same time that they confronted mainstream practices and policies. Their accomplishments provide additional evidence that feminist service organizations can be agents of social change with diverse sources of outside funding and organizational arrangements (Koss and Harvey, 1991).

All of these organizations were affected by the conservative shift in public attitudes marked by the election of Ronald Reagan as president of the United States in 1980. As one woman remarked: "These times that we're living in, it's a very oppressive environment for women in general in the United States. We have an administration that doesn't seem to give one whit for women's problems." Reductions in federal support for social services in general and the growing political strength of the New Right jeopardized feminist services throughout the country (Whittier, 1995). Some did not survive. Others responded by actively resisting external pressures, by diversifying their sources of funding, by emphasizing their work as human service agencies, by presenting a more professional image, by increasing their ties with conventional agencies, by increasing their social change efforts and building coalitions with other feminist groups in their community to oppose attacks from the New Right, or by a combination of these (Hyde, 1995). The backlash against feminism continued into the new millennium, with legislation and court decisions eroding many of the gains of the 1970s (Jarvis, 1998).

Although the backlash against feminism made their work more difficult, Advocates for Battered Women, ARC House, the Rape Crisis Center, and Women's Transit Authority continue as feminist service organizations at this writing. Women Reaching Women survived for almost two decades; it lost its funding in 1997. As in the study conducted by Hyde (1995), these organizations benefited from being in an environment with many proactive feminist organizations and coalitions working to preserve past victories and to increase equality for women. In Madison and throughout the state of Wisconsin feminist activism increased in response to the backlash. For example, in 1993, the Women's Candidate Development Coalition was founded to "increase the participation of progressive women at all decision-making levels of government" (*The Stateswoman*, a publication of the Wisconsin Women's Network, July-September 1995). Founding members of the organization included Wisconsin chapters of the American Association of University Women, the League of Women Voters, the National Women's Political Caucus, Republicans for Choice, the Federation of Business and Professional Women, the Minority Women's Network, and the National Organization for Women.

The Wisconsin Women's Network, a statewide coalition of organizations and individuals "dedicated to promoting equal rights in Wisconsin through advocacy and education on public policy issues," was mentioned throughout the interviews as a source of support and shared efforts. This statewide coalition sponsored a Wisconsin Women's Summit in September 1995 to "devise state and local strategies for dealing with the antiwoman backlash and reenergize and revitalize the Wisconsin Women's Movement." Skill sessions included lobbying, coalition building, and "dealing with extremists."

In 1998, the Madison Chapter of NOW began its "'F' Word" campaign. Its newsletter explained that NOW and other women's rights organizations had suffered a backlash as a result of negative and incorrect perceptions of what it means to be a feminist and asserted, "It is impossible for women to achieve the equality we deserve until the stigmas behind feminism and feminists are eliminated" (*Equality NOW*, Spring 1998, p. 4). In response, NOW organized a campaign that included selling bumper stickers and T-shirts printed with the most simple dictionary definitions of feminism and feminist: "Feminism *n.* the policy, practice, or advocacy of political, economic, and social equality for women" and "Feminist *adj.* or *n.* a person who advocates feminism."

Also, Madison NOW cosponsored the 1998 Feminist of the Year banquet honoring Tammy Baldwin, elected that year as the first woman from Wisconsin and the first out lesbian elected to the House of Representatives. The regional conference announcement read, "The women's movement is not dead, we were just catching our breath. Activists will not stop until women have guaranteed rights in the United States Constitution!"

Feminists in Wisconsin continue to educate the public to counter the backlash. For example, on May 26, 2002, George Will's widely distributed newspaper column, titled "Facts Get in the Way of Modern Feminism," referred to the Independent Women's Forum (IWF) as "indispensable" and asserted that there is no gender pay gap. A member of Wisconsin NOW wrote a lengthy letter to the *Wisconsin State Journal* on June 1, 2002, in response:

> First, I would like to educate the public about the so-called "indispensable" "Independent" Women's Forum. The Washington Feminist FaxNet states that the IWF "is made up of mostly affluent lawyers and other professionals who benefited from gains forged by the very women's movement they seek to destroy" *The Wall Street Journal*, October 13, 1995. Trish Wilson Antonucci states "The conservative Olin, Coors, Bradley, and Carthage Foundations provide 90% of

(IWF's) funding." National Advisory Board Members of IWF include Lynne Cheney, Wade Horn (endorses mandatory marriage for welfare recipients), Christina Hoff Sommers (author of *Who Stole Feminism*), and other conservative ideologues (Source http//www.wlo.org/iwf/iwf2.html).

She informed readers that "contrary to Will's unsupported assertion that feminists disparage women who chose the 'mommy track,' most feminists strongly support the choice to work within the home, and have long advocated for compensation for female or male homemakers (i.e. with Social Security benefits reform), midwifery and breastfeeding." After presenting information on gender bias in the workforce, medicine, and academia, she concluded: "George Will, the IWF, and others who lead the backlash against feminism are further proof that we still have a long way to go to achieve equality."

With respect to the backlash, two of the five organizations were objects of direct attacks: Women's Transit Authority and Advocates for Battered Women. In both, funding was jeopardized by New Right accusations that *women helping women* was a form of reverse discrimination. In 1992, the University of Wisconsin-Madison cut off all funding for Women's Transit Authority because it provided rides only for women and by women: "WTA flatly refuses to give men rides or to hire [sic] men as drivers or dispatchers. UW lawyers believe that the university, as a publicly financed institution, simply cannot support an organization that publicly discriminates against men" (*Madison Newspapers*, 5/8/92). This was no small matter in that the university provided approximately 40% of its funding. Women's Transit Authority survived with funding from the city, employee payroll-deduction campaigns, fund-raising events, and private donations. Its ability to maintain a sufficient level of funding without the support of the university confirms the confidence members expressed in the mid-1980s with respect to the strength of their organization.

Women's Transit Authority continues as a volunteer program for women by women that offers free nighttime rape-prevention rides in Madison and Dane County. From 7:00 p.m. to 1:00 a.m. seven days of the week, its ride service prevents the sexual assault and harassment of women and children and increases their mobility.

Women's Transit Authority's daytime community assistance ride service provides free transportation to medical and mental health appointments; to food resources, including grocery stores, food pantries, and free meal sites; and to organizations such as the battered women's shelter and the Salvation Army for emergency assistance. It provides transportation for the elderly to local senior centers, where they are provided with meals and opportunities to socialize with others. It provides rides for Spanish-speaking, Hmong, and Cambodian families to medical appointments, support groups, and other needed services. It provides rides to battered women and their children and to runaway teens to safe havens. Women's Transit Authority also contracts with the Well Woman's Program to ensure that low-income women have access to routine medical care, including mammograms. As it stated in its brochure, "When folks are isolated by poverty, age, disability, neighborhood, or language barriers, a free ride is more than just a free ride." Women continue to provide Women's Transit Authority's nighttime rape-prevention ride service. Male volunteers may drive for its daytime community assistance ride service.

Women's Transit Authority sponsors an annual Clothesline Project, which is an audiovisual display of T-shirts created by women who have suffered from and survived some form of violence or made by others to commemorate women who have been murdered. T-shirts and art supplies are made available for women wanting to add to the display. Its Clothesline Project is part of an annual nationwide T-shirt display that is organized to acknowledge the effects of sexual assault. Women's Transit Authority provides speakers to clubs, churches, and businesses and works with other organizations to end sexual assault, for example, during Sexual Assault Awareness Month.

In 1997, due to pressures similar to those encountered by Women's Transit Authority, Advocates for Battered Women changed its name to Domestic Abuse Intervention Services. Members viewed this change as a small price to pay to avoid larger problems, and in fact it had substantially increased the scope of its services: "We chose a name that connotes the umbrella connecting the many different programs that comprise our agency" (Advocates newsletter, February 1997). The organization offered services to all victims of domestic violence, while it retained its explicit emphasis on feminist goals, services, and organizational structure. Its current mission statement reads:

> Domestic Abuse Intervention Services (DAIS) is a community-based, feminist organization in Dane County committed to ending domestic abuse. The purpose of our work is twofold: to empower those who have been affected by violence, and to transform societal attitudes and institutional barriers that perpetuate violence and the abuse of power and control in our society.

Its statement of principles reads, in part:

> . . . Because our society has valued male over female, it has perpetuated the institutional oppression of women, including woman abuse in families. This dynamic is mirrored in the batterer's use of violence or abuse to gain power and control on an individual level. Therefore, any form of societal oppression of women supports and intensifies relationship abuse . . .
> DAIS does not condone any form of violence on the part of anyone, male or female. Our goal is to empower everyone to find non-violent methods of self-defense and conflict resolution. We believe it is important to recognize that the

majority of violence on the part of women in heterosexual relationships is in self-defense or in response to the abuse of power and control in the relationship. When abuse is present in any relationship, we believe it is important to evaluate the motivation for the abuse and the degree of fear instilled by the partner . . .

Domestic Abuse Intervention Services continues to provide support and safety in its 25-bed shelter for women and their children who are experiencing violence at home. Its shelter services include housing, food, and clothing for up to 30 days. Advocates work with residents on issues related to income and employment, physical and mental health services, parenting skills, education, and day care. The organization provides housing advocacy to help women locate safe and affordable housing and legal assistance for dealing with the courts, filing for a restraining order, going through legal procedures, and obtaining a lawyer. It offers support, counseling, and positive social experiences for children staying at the shelter.

Domestic Abuse Intervention Services staffs a 24-hour crisis/help line and offers support groups for people dealing with the effects of emotional, physical, and verbal abuse by a partner or ex-partner; and groups are offered for children from the community whose parents are attending support groups. Its Crisis Response Program enables victims of domestic violence who are in immediate abuse-related crisis to schedule a face-to-face meeting with an advocate at a community partner site where they can be provided with safety planning, restraining order assistance, 911 cell phones, alarms, and internal and external referrals for additional services.

The community awareness, prevention, and education efforts of Domestic Abuse Intervention Services include the education of individuals, training of professionals and paraprofessionals, and outreach to community groups and faith communities in order to increase awareness of domestic violence and its effects. Its programming for children includes a 10-week structured prevention curriculum, "Healthy Relationships," a group for area middle-school students that focuses on making and maintaining healthy relationships in all aspects of life.

ARC House continues to offer comprehensive services to 15 women offenders and up to three of their children by providing an alternative to jail or prison and by assisting women in returning successfully to the community following incarceration, and it remains a licensed AODA facility. Its services include counseling; chemical dependency assessment, education, counseling, and referral; vocational assessment and counseling; employment and educational placement; money management and housing issues; independent living and parenting skills; and development of community support networks for its residents. It addresses past physical and sexual abuse, dependent and abusive relationships, health problems, and child custody and other mother/child reunification issues. In addition, it offers a transitional program wherein women participate in the full ARC House program on a nonresidential basis. In 1992, the National Institute of Corrections recognized ARC House's pioneering work, naming it one of the nation's 10 "Promising Female Offender Programs" (National Institute of Corrections, *Female Offenders in the Community: An Analysis of Innovative Strategies and Programs*, 1992).

ARC House is now one of 11 projects sponsored by ARC Community Services, Inc. (ACS). Developed by members of ARC House, this private, nonprofit umbrella agency specializes in women-specific, family-focused, community-based services for women at risk for criminal activity or substance abuse or both on a residential, day treatment, and outpatient basis in the state of Wisconsin. Its mission statement reads:

> ARC provides integrated, multi-disciplinary services provided within the family context particularly the mother/child bond, in order to foster healthy family functioning and family intactness and reduce out-of-home placements of young children and to assist in stopping the cycle of family violence, abuse and neglect as well as to provide for the development of safe, economically viable, constructive lifestyles . . . ARC promotes women responsive services that are designed to empower women to make responsible and healthy life choices and focuses on addressing a woman's recovery within the context of her relationship with her children.

In addition to ARC House, ARC Community Services, Inc. includes (1) ARC–Dayton St., a residential facility for female offenders that serves as a bridge from institutional living to parole status in the community; (2) RESPECT Project on Prostitution, which provides diversion services and HIV/AIDS education for women involved in prostitution and assists women in leaving prostitution; (3) ARC TAP Case Management Unit for Women, which provides case management services for female substance-abusing offenders enrolled in a diversion project for drug-dependent individuals; (4) ARC Center for Women & Children, which is an AODA day treatment program with services specifically for the children of the mothers served; (5) ARC Maternal & Infant Program, which is a residential program for adult pregnant female offenders or mothers who have infants up to one year of age; (6) ARC Healthy Beginnings, which provides day treatment AODA services for pregnant and postpartum women; (7) ARC Fond du Lac, located in Fond du Lac, Wisconsin, which is a facility for adult female offenders that serves as a diversion alternative for women at risk of incarceration as well as a transitional living placement to assist women with community reintegration; (8) ARC Drug Treatment Court, which provides case management services for women enrolled in Dane County Drug Treatment Court, a diversion program for offenders with AODA issues; (9) ARC Integrated AODA Work Services for Women & their Families, which addresses the needs of AODA-affected women on welfare and their families; and (10) Fond du Lac Women & Children Day Treatment Services, which provides day treatment substance abuse services for poor women and their children in Fond du Lac, Wisconsin.

The Rape Crisis Center continues to serve women, children, and men, providing services to the survivors (and their family and friends) of all forms of sexual violence, including sexual assault, incest, sexual harassment, and sexual exploitation. Its current mission statement reads: "To work with the Dane County community to eliminate sexual violence and victimization, and to enhance self-determination by providing a supportive, healing environment for those affected by the issue of sexual violence." Its objectives include "(1) Promote a community standard which includes education, awareness, and sensitivity concerning the characteristics, frequency, and impacts of sexual assault; (2) Increase the ability of educational institutions, health care providers, and the criminal justice system to respond to sexual assault issues, victim behavior, and victim needs; and (3) Promote and expand prevention-oriented activities, including self-defense instruction, public discussion forums, and education through the media and the Internet" (Rape Crisis Center Strategic Plan 2000-2003).

The Rape Crisis Center offers crisis intervention and support through its 24-hour crisis line and on-call advocate/counselors. It provides counseling for assault survivors ages 5 to 18, for adult survivors, and for family members and friends; support groups for adults healing from sexual assault, for adult survivors of incest, and for teen survivors; and legal and medical advocacy and accompaniment, all at no charge. It opened a satellite office on the University of Wisconsin-Madison campus to better serve students at the University of Wisconsin and other colleges located in Madison. The Rape Crisis Center instituted a support group program at the Dane County Jail, responding to the increase in the female offender population in Wisconsin and to the knowledge that many female offenders have histories of traumatic abuse.

The community education efforts of the Rape Crisis Center include trainings and presentations on topics such as sexual assault, sexual harassment, and gender stereotyping. It places a priority on helping middle and high schools provide sexual violence prevention and education. In two area high schools, they support the IMAGINE program, a peer-based sexual assault education group created by the Rape Crisis Center. Students who participate in the IMAGINE program increase their own awareness about sexual violence and gender issues and they, in turn, educate their peers about the issue of sexualized violence. Its outreach efforts extend to communities of faith: "We hope that churches, synagogues and mosques will recognize the impact of sexual violence on their members, and will make a point of reaching out to survivors and providing an atmosphere of healing" (Rape Crisis Center newsletter, Spring 2003, p. 6).

Consistent with its focus on prevention, the Rape Crisis Center expanded its program to include Chimera self-defense training for girls and women. Chimera self-defense focuses on psychological skills as well as verbal assertiveness and physical techniques to prevent and stop harassment and assault. It teaches women and girls that they have the right and ability to protect themselves. This aspect of the organization's prevention programming "is a practical means for a woman to gain confidence and control of her life and prevent sexual assault. Women do not have true equality unless they are able to live, work, attend school, travel, and conduct their lives as they choose" (Rape Crisis Center newsletter, Spring 2003, p. 3).

Each April, the Rape Crisis Center coordinates the community's observance of Sexual Assault Awareness Month. Through weekly editorials in the newspaper and a wide range of community events, including the annual "Take Back the Night" rally and march, Sexual Assault Awareness Month focuses on educating the community about sexual violence and encouraging involvement.

As noted previously, the only organization that no longer exists is Women Reaching Women. The Bureau of Substance Abuse Services discontinued its funding as of January 1997. Until that time, the organization had retained its focus on empowering women to maintain healthy lifestyles. In its all-women support groups, members had continued to discuss a wide range of women's issues. Speaking to civic groups and in schools, members had increased public understanding of the gender differences in alcohol use, abuse, and treatment effectiveness. Still, a 1996 newspaper article on Women Reaching Women reads as if it had been written in 1986, affirming members' beliefs in the mid-1980s that creating change in the AODA field would be very difficult. The article reiterated, for example, that between 75% and 90% of women with AODA problems have been sexually abused, victims of domestic violence, or both, and that women alcoholics face greater social stigma than their male counterparts. With respect to treatment programs, in 1996, Women Reaching Women was urging that issues such as eating disorders be addressed and that programs "deal with issues of child care, transportation and access to social services because women typically come into treatment with less education and less employment skills than men" (interview with project director of WRW, *Capital Times*, May 16, 1996). In the mid-1980s, members of Women Reaching Women understood their organization to be underfunded and vulnerable. They were discouraged that it remained largely dependent on funds from the Bureau of Substance Abuse Services and staffed only by one full-time person. Under these conditions, it is remarkable that this organization survived through 1996.

Advocates for Battered Women (now Domestic Abuse Intervention Services), ARC House, the Rape Crisis Center, and Women's Transit Authority entered into the new millennium with expanded services and their core missions intact. Their emphasis on *women helping women* and on the development of services that meet the unique needs of women have remained the foundation of their work. All have remained private nonprofits that stand independent of conventional service organizations. All four have retained their commitments to social change.

In 1980, Alix Kates Shulman recounted how the early gains of the women's movement were rapidly taken for granted and feminism's emphasis on female subordination was rendered insignificant.

> Co-optation and tokenism have made it easier for people to deny that anything is still drastically wrong between the sexes. . . A new generation does not know that ten years ago what are now our basic demands were unspoken, many even unmentionable. The ideas of women's liberation that were so recently shocking, thrilling, and liberating are already put down by many of the young as old hat and boring and by the old as a fad that is passe . . . The presentation of feminism in the mass media has trivialized the movement's goals . . . The renewed search for personal solutions to collective problems is as arid today as it was a decade ago. (p. 603)

Shulman's words could just as easily be describing the complacency regarding women's issues and the misconceptions of feminism that characterize the present time. The efforts of feminists since the mid-1960s have dramatically improved women's economic and social circumstances (Rosen, 2000). Yet, there is little recognition of the linkages between earlier feminist activism and the broad-based social changes in women's lives that are now widely valued.

To the contrary, feminists are credited with destroying "the family," forcing women into the workforce, destabilizing their communities, and undermining the moral fabric of society. Mothers who work outside of their homes have been accused of promoting their own interests at the expense of their children's, and affirmative action has been redefined as demeaning to those it has assisted and as unfair to those it has not. Accusations of "political correctness" serve to trivialize the concerns of those who continued to push for social change on behalf of oppressed groups. Building on the antifeminist efforts of the 1980s, "the word 'feminist' has fallen (and been pushed) into a place beyond disrepute—a nadir, even when people responded to issues feminism raised or agreed with some feminist demands" (DuPlessis and Snitow, 1998a, p. 15).

The backlash against feminism has been reinforced by widespread misconceptions about feminist efforts in the 1970s and 1980s. Negative stereotypes of feminists have been deliberately propagated by those with a conservative political agenda (Bashevkin, 1998; Faludi, 1991; Melich, 1996). Also, conservative, antifeminist women writers such as Rene Denfield, Laurel Doyle, Camille Paglia, Katie Roiphe, Christina Hoff Sommers, and Naomi Wolf have appropriated the label "feminist" and captured the attention of major publishing houses and the media (Hammer, 2002). However, for others, misconceptions about feminism in the 1970s and 1980s are based on the lack of information necessary to dispute the myths. These people believe in gender equality but do not see the similarities between themselves and the feminists who brought their beliefs into mainstream culture, hence the common disclaimer "I'm not a feminist but..." Under these conditions, it is essential that we document all forms of feminist activism and raise public awareness of the connections between the rights, opportunities, and protections women now enjoy and earlier feminist efforts (see Baxandall and Gordon, 2000; Brownmiller, 1999; DuPlessis and Snitow, 1998b; Kahn, 1995). *Tales from the Trenches* is intended to be a part of this larger project, one that "stands against historical forgetting" (DuPlessis and Snitow, 1998a, p. 23).

The detailed and heartfelt accounts of the members of these five service organizations confront current misconceptions in several ways. First, although only a small part of a much larger picture, the voices of these women contradict current misrepresentations of early radical feminism as fiercely dogmatic and inflexible. Their experiences provide models of early radical feminist activism that are more adaptive, more complex, and more effective than generally acknowledged. Similarly, members' portrayals of their own experience illustrate that feminism does not constitute a system of beliefs that is imposed onto people's lives. Instead, feminism serves as a lens through which women (and men) view their worlds, integrating feminist beliefs and values with their own individual concerns, priorities, and histories. In addition, accounts of members' efforts provide numerous examples of the social attitudes about and practices toward women that prevailed prior to feminist change efforts. This information enhances understanding of the significance of feminist activism in the past, and it encourages us to consider the ways in which gender inequality continues to increase women's vulnerability, restrict their options, and impede their personal growth and sense of well-being (Landrine and Klonoff, 1997).

The members of Advocates for Battered Women, the Rape Crisis Center, and Women's Transit Authority provide an in-depth view of grassroots efforts that were part of the emerging antirape and battered women's movements, two movements that have had a pervasive impact on social attitudes and beliefs and on public policy (Bevacqua, 2000; Crowell and Burgess, 1996; Dobash and Dobash, 1992; Koss, Goodman, Browne, Fitzgerald, Keita, and Russo, 1994; Matthews, 1994; Roberts, 2002). There is now significantly less public tolerance of gender-linked violence and some degree of reform in the laws and policies regarding rape, domestic violence, and sexual harassment. Still, in the 2000s, the activities of rape crisis centers and shelters for battered women remain much the same as those developed in the 1970s and early 1980s by the members of Advocates for Battered Women and the Rape Crisis Center. The need for services far exceeds what is available, and legal reforms have been only partially successful. For example, it has been found that mandatory arrest policies and temporary restraining orders, designed to protect battered women, often serve to increase their vulnerability and abuse. Similarly, rape victims still experience inadequate and victim-blaming treatment in the legal and medical systems. Most rapists are not caught, many who are caught are not prosecuted, and many who are prosecuted are not convicted or punished (Riger, Bennett, Wasco, Schewe, Frohmann, Camacho, and Campbell, 2002). Batterers "take advantage of the fragmentation, misunderstanding, and bias of the criminal justice system to avoid prosecution and subsequent consequences for their acts of violence" (Thelen, 2000).

Victimization of women by men remains a major social problem. More than half of all working women are sexually harassed on the job (Britton, 1997). Approximately 1.9 million women are physically assaulted and approximately 302,100 women are forcibly raped each year. Furthermore, most violence against women is partner violence. Approximately 1.5 million women are raped, physically assaulted, or both each year by an intimate partner. Almost one-third of murdered women are killed by an intimate partner, compared to about 4% of men. More than one million women are stalked each year; about half of these women are stalked by an intimate (U.S. Department of Justice, May 2000, November 2000, July 2000). Feminists in this study believed that woman abuse would be significantly reduced only when society directly addressed the relationships between male dominance and male violence against women. The persistence of female victimization by men certainly gives considerable credence to their analyses.

Compared to the legal reforms and extensive services that have been developed to serve rape victims and battered women, there has been little progress for women in the criminal justice and AODA systems. Men continue to dominate these two fields, as administrators, as counselors, as probation and parole officers, and as clients. In both of these systems, funding to establish equity for women has led primarily to programs that are "gender-neutral" (Covington, 2002; van Wormer, 2002). The problem here is not simply that women's unique experiences and treatment needs are ignored in "gender-neutral" approaches.

More insidious, "gender-neutral" generally means "male-centered." As explained by Alison Jaggar:

> Throughout the battle for sexual equality, it is necessary to remain critical of the standards by which that equality is measured. In particular, feminists should be ready constantly to challenge norms that may be stated in gender-neutral language but that are established on the basis of male experience, and so likely to be biased in favor of men. (1990, p. 253)

Many current articles begin by reminding readers that, for example, women "are treated according to a male model of justice... their treatment tends to follow a one-size-fits-all model. Yet a woman's substance abuse, like her criminality, is different from that of a typical man" (van Wormer, 2002, p. 475). The interpretations of women's problems, criticisms of conventional services, and ideas about appropriate goals and services that were developed by ARC House and Women Reaching Women continue to be central themes in current discussions of effective programs and treatments for female offenders and substance-abusing women (Abbott, 1995; Chesney-Lind, 1997; Chesney-Lind and Shelden, 1992; Covington, 1999; Straussner and Brown, 2002; van Wormer, 2001; Wilson and Anderson, 1997).

The experiences recounted throughout *Tales from the Trenches: Politics and Practice in Feminist Service Organizations* illustrate how feminist activists in feminist service organizations effectively empowered themselves and other women. Their passionate commitment to feminism was accompanied by a combination of goals and strategies that moved them well beyond abstract theory and prescriptive politics. Certainly, their work does not provide a definitive guide for today's challenges. Still, we can recognize their courage, learn from their struggles, and celebrate their achievements. They have demonstrated that feminist service organizations can serve as powerful avenues for pursuing both personal and social change for particular populations of women. Members' critiques of society, analyses of needed changes, and development of organizations and services designed to make a contribution to social change offer inspiring models of feminist practice.

Bibliography

Abbott, A. (1995). Substance abuse and the feminist perspective. In N. Van Den Bergh (Ed.), *Feminist practice in the 21st century* (pp. 258-277). Washington, D.C.: NASW Press.

Abbott, S. and Love, B. (1971). Is women's liberation a lesbian plot? In V. Gornick and B. K. Moran (Eds.), *Woman in sexist society: Studies in power and powerlessness* (pp. 601-621). New York: Basic Books.

Acker, J., Barry, K., and Esseveld, J. (1991). Objectivity and truth: Problems in doing feminist research. In M. M. Fonow and J. A. Cook (Eds.), *Beyond methodology: Feminist scholarship as lived research* (pp. 133-153). Bloomington, IN: Indiana University Press.

Ahrens, L. (1980). Battered women's refuges: Feminist cooperatives vs. social service institutions. *Radical America*, 14(3), 41-47.

Aiello, A. (1984). Take back the night. In J. Ecklein (Ed.), *Community organizers* (pp. 210-213). New York: John Wiley and Sons.

Alcoff, L. (1989). Cultural feminism versus post-structuralism: The identity crisis in feminist theory. In M. Malson, J. O'Barr, S. Westphal-Wihl, and M. Wyer (Eds.), *Feminist theory in practice and process* (pp. 295-326). Chicago: University of Chicago Press.

Allen, P. (1970). *Free space: A perspective on the small group in women's liberation.* Washington, N.J.: Times Change Press.

Altheide, D. L. and Johnson, J. M. (1994). Criteria for assessing interpretive validity in qualitative research. In N. K. Denzin and Y. S. Lincoln (Eds.), *Handbook of qualitative research* (pp. 485-499). Thousand Oaks, CA: Sage.

Amir, D. and Amir, M. (1979). Rape crisis centers: An arena for ideological conflicts. *Victimology: An International Journal*, 4(2), 247-257.

Amott, T. L., and Matthaei, J. A. (1991). *Race, gender, and work: A multicultural economic history of women in the United States.* Boston: South End Press.

Apuzzo, G. and Powell, B. (1981). Confrontation: Black/White. In The *Quest* staff (Eds.), *Building feminist theory: Essays from Quest* (pp. 212-222). New York: Longman.

Arnold, G. (1995). Dilemmas of feminist coalitions: Collective identity and strategic effectiveness in the battered women's movement. In M. M. Ferree and P. Y. Martin (Eds.), *Feminist organizations: Harvest of the new women's movement* (pp. 276-290). Philadelphia: Temple University Press.

Babcox, D. and Belkin, M. (1971). *Liberation now! Writings from the women's liberation movement*. New York: Dell Publishing.

Baker, A. (1982). The problem of authority in radical movement groups: A case study of lesbian-feminist organization. *Journal of Applied Behavioral Science*, 18(3), 323-341.

Barry, K. (1979). *Female sexual slavery*. Englewood Cliffs, N.J.: Prentice Hall.

Bashevkin, S. (1998). *Women on the defensive: Living through conservative times*. Chicago: University of Chicago Press.

Baxandall, R. and Gordon, L. (Eds.). (2000). *Dear sisters: Dispatches from the women's liberation movement*. New York: Basic Books.

Beal, F. (1970). Double jeopardy: To be black and female. In R. Morgan (Ed.), *Sisterhood is powerful* (pp. 340-353). New York: Vintage Books..

Beck, E. T. (1983). No more masks: Anti-Semitism as Jew hating. *Women's Studies Quarterly*, 3, 11-14.

Beck, E. T. (Ed.). (1984). *Nice Jewish girls: A lesbian anthology*. Freedom, CA: The Crossing Press.

Bell, I. P. (1975). The double standard: Age. In J. Freeman (Ed.), *Women: A feminist perspective* (pp. 145-155). Palo Alto, CA: Mayfield.

Bevacqua, M. (2000). *Rape on the public agenda: Feminism and the politics of sexual assault*. Boston: Northeastern University Press.

Bookman, A. and Morgen, S. (Eds.). (1988). *Women and the politics of empowerment*. Philadelphia: Temple University Press.

Bordt, R. L. (1997). *The structure of women's nonprofit organizations*. Bloomington: Indiana University Press.

Boston Lesbian Psychologies Collective. (Eds.). (1987). *Lesbian psychologies*. Chicago: University of Illinois Press.

Boston Women's Health Book Collective. (1973). *Our bodies, ourselves: A book by and for women*. New York: Simon and Schuster.

Bowker, L. (Ed.). (1981). *Women and crime in America*. New York: Macmillian.

Bricker-Jenkins, M. and Hooyman, N. R. (1986). A feminist world view: Ideological themes from the feminist movement. In M. Bricker-Jenkins and N. R. Hooyman, (Eds.), *Not for women only: Social work practice for a feminist future* (pp. 7-22). Washington, DC: NASW Press.

Britton, B. M. (1997). Sexual harassment. In S. Ruzek, V. Olesen, and A. Clarke (Eds.), *Women's health: Complexities and differences* (pp. 510-519). Columbus: Ohio State University Press.

Browne, S., Connors, D., and Stern, N. (Eds.). (1985). *With the power of each breath: A disabled women's anthology*. Pittsburgh, PA: Cleis Press.

Brownmiller, S. (1999). *In our time: Memoir of a revolution*. New York: Dell Publishing.

Buechler, S. (1990). *Women's movements in the United States: Woman suffrage, equal rights, and beyond*. New Brunswick: Rutgers University Press.

Bulkin, E., Pratt, M., and Smith, B. (1988). *Yours in struggle: Three feminist perspectives on anti-semitism and racism*. Ithaca, NY: Firebrand Books.

Bunch, C. (1974). The reform tool kit. *Quest*, 1(1), 37-51.

Bunch, C. (1975). Not for lesbians only. *Quest*, 2(2), 50-56.

Bunch, C. (1981). Introduction to *Building feminist theory: Essays from Quest*. In The Quest staff (Eds.), *Building feminist theory: Essays from Quest* (pp.xv-xxiii). New York: Longman.

Burtle, V. (Ed.). (1979). *Women who drink: Alcoholic experience and psychotherapy*. Springfield, IL: Charles C. Thomas.

Butler, J. and Scott, J. W. (Eds.). (1992). *Feminists theorize the political*. New York: Routledge.

Cade, T. (Ed.). (1970). *The black woman: An anthology*. New York: New American Library.

Campbell, J., Levine, I., and Page, J. (1980). Women in midstream. In N. Gottlieb (Ed.), *Alternative social services for women* (pp. 310-319). New York: Columbia University Press.

Carabillo, T., Meuli, J., and Csida, J. B. (1993). *Feminist chronicles 1953-1993*. Los Angeles: Women's Graphics.

Carden, M. L. (1974). *The new feminist movement*. New York: Russell Sage Foundation.

Cassell, J. (1977). *A group called women: Sisterhood and symbolism in the feminist movement*. New York: David McKay.

Chesney-Lind, M. (1977). Judicial paternalism and the female status offender: Training women to know their place. *Crime and Delinquency*, 23(2), 121-130.

Chesney-Lind, M. (1997). *The female offender: Girls, women, and crime*. Thousand Oaks: Sage.

Chesney-Lind, M. and Shelden, R. G. (1992). *Girls, delinquency, and juvenile justice*. Pacific Grove, CA: Broooks/Cole.

Chisholm, S. (1970). Racism and anti-feminism. *Black Scholar*, 1, 40-45.

Combahee River Collective. (1983). A black feminist statement. In C. Moraga and G. Anzaldua (Eds.), *This bridge called my back: Writings by radical women of color* (pp. 210-218). New York: Kitchen Table: Women of Color Press.

Connell, N. and Wilson, C. (Eds.). (1974). *Rape: The first sourcebook for women by New York Radical Feminists*. New York: New American Library.

Conover, P. and Gray, V. (1983). *Feminism and the New Right: Conflict over the American family*. New York: Praeger.

Corrigan, E. (1980). *Alcoholic women in treatment*. New York: Oxford University Press.

Covington, S. (1999). *Helping women recover: A program for treating addiction*. San Francisco: Jossey-Bass.

Covington, S. (2002). Helping women recover: Creating gender-responsive treatment. In S. Straussner and S. Brown (Eds.), *The handbook of addiction treatment for women* (pp. 52-72). San Francisco: Jossey-Bass.

Covington, S. and Surrey, J. (1998). The relational model of women's psychological development: Implications for substance abuse. In S. Wilsnack and R. Wilsnack (Eds.), *Gender and alcohol: Individual and social perspectives* (pp. 335-351). New Brunswick, N.J.: Rutgers University Press.

Crowell, N.A. and Burgess, A. W. (Eds.). (1996). *Understanding violence against women*. Washington D.C.: National Academy Press.

Crites, L. (Ed.). (1976). *The female offender*. Lexington, MA.: D.C. Heath and Company.

Davis, A. (1981). *Women, race and class*. New York: Random House.

Davis, F. (1991). *Moving the mountain: The women's movement in America since 1960*. New York: Simon & Schuster.

de Lauretis, T. (1990). Upping the anti (sic) in feminist theory. In M. Hirsch and E. F. Keller (Eds.), *Conflicts in feminism* (pp. 255-270). New York: Routledge.

Dehart-Mathews, J. and Mathews, D. (1989). The cultural politics of the ERA's defeat. In L. Richardson and V. Taylor (Eds.), *Feminist frontiers II: Rethinking sex, gender, and society* (pp. 458-463). New York: McGraw Hill.

Delacoste, F. and Newman, F. (Eds.) (1981). *Fight back! Feminist resistance to male violence*. Minneapolis, MN: Cleis Press.

Denzin, N. (1978). *The research act: A theoretical introduction to sociological methods*. New York: McGraw-Hill.

Dill, B.T. (1983). Race, class and gender: Prospects for an all-inclusive sisterhood. *Feminist Studies*, 9(1), 131-150.

Dobash, R. E. and Dobash, R. (1979). *Violence against wives: A case against the patriarchy*. New York: Free Press.

Dobash, R. E. and Dobash, R. (1992). *Women, violence, and social change*. London: Routlege.

Donovan, J. (2000). *Feminist theory: The intellectual traditions of American feminism*. New York: The Continuum Publishing Company.

Dreifus, C. (1973). *Woman's fate: Raps from a feminist consciousness-raising group*. New York: Bantam Books.

Dreifus, C. (Ed.). (1977). *Seizing our bodies: The politics of women's health*. New York: Vintage Books.

DuPlessis, R. B. and Snitow, A. (1998a). A feminist memoir project. In R. B. DuPlessis and A. Snitow (Eds.), *The feminist memoir project: Voices from women's liberation* (pp. 3-24). New York: Three Rivers Press.

DuPlessis, R. B. and Snitow, A. (Eds.). (1998b). *The feminist memoir project: Voices from women's liberation*. New York: Three Rivers Press.

Eastman, P. (1973). Consciousness-raising as a resocialization process for women. *Smith College Studies in Social Work*, 43(3), 153-183.

Echols, A. (1989). *Daring to be bad: Radical feminism in America 1967-1975*. Minn: University of Minnesota Press.

Eddy, C. and Ford, J. (Eds.). (1980). *Alcoholism in women*. Dubuque, Iowa: Kendall/Hunt.

Eisenstein, H. (1983). *Contemporary feminist thought*. Boston: G.K. Hall & Company.

Eisenstein, H. (1991). *Gender shock: Practicing feminism on two continents*. Boston: Beacon Press.

Eisenstein, H. (1995). The Australian femocratic experiment: A feminist case for bureaucracy. In M. M. Ferree and P. Y. Martin (Eds.), *Feminist organizations: Harvest of the new women's movement* (pp. 69-83). Philadelphia: Temple University Press.

Eisenstein, Z. (1981a). *The radical future of liberal feminism*. Boston: Northeastern University Press.

Eisenstein, Z. (1981b). Antifeminism in the politics and election of 1980. *Feminist Studies*, 7(2), 187-205.

Elias, M. (1975). Sisterhood therapy. *Human Behavior*, April, 56-61.

Evans, S. (1979). *Personal politics: The roots of women's liberation in the civil rights movement and the New Left*. New York: Knopf.

Faludi, S. (1991). *Backlash: The undeclared war against American women*. New York: Crown.

Faulkner, A. (1980). Aging and old age: The last sexist rip-off. In E. Norman and A. Mancuso (Eds.), *Women's issues and social work practice* (pp. 57-89). Itasca, IL: F.E. Peacock Publishers.

Feminist Counseling Collective. (1975). Feminist psychotherapy. *Social Policy*, 6(2), 54-62.

Ferguson, K. (1984). *The feminist case against bureaucracy*. Philadelphia: Temple University Press.

Ferraro, K. (1983). Negotiating trouble in a battered women's shelter. *Urban Life*, 12(3), 287-306.

Ferree, M. M. (1987). Equality and autonomy: Feminist politics in the United States and West Germany. In M. F. Katzenstein and C. M. Mueller (Eds.), *The women's movements of the United States and Western Europe: Consciousness, political opportunity, and public policy* (pp. 172-195). Philadelphia: Temple University Press.

Ferree, M. M. and Hess, B. B. (1985). *Controversy and coalition: The new feminist movement*. Boston: Twayne Publishers.

Ferree, M. M. and Martin, P. Y. (Eds.). (1995). *Feminist organizations: Harvest of the new women's movement*. Philadelphia: Temple University Press.

Fine, M. and Asch, A. (Eds.). (1988). *Women with disabilities: Essays in psychology, culture, and politics*. Philadelphia: Temple University Press.

Firestone, S. (1970). *The dialectic of sex*. New York: William Morrow.

Flynn, M. (1981). Women, Inc. In D. Masi (Ed.), *Organizing for women: Issues, strategies, and services* (pp. 169-176). Lexington, Mass.: Lexington Books.

Freedman, E. (1979). Separatism as strategy: Female institution building and American feminism, 1870-1930. *Feminist Studies*, 5(3), 512-529.

Freeman, A. and MacMillan, J. (1976). Building feminist organizations. *Quest*, 3(3), 73-80.

Freeman, J. (1973). The tyranny of structurelessness. In A. Koedt, E. Levine and A. Rapone (Eds.), *Radical feminism* (pp. 285-299). New York: Quadrangle.

Freeman, J. (1975). *The politics of women's liberation*. New York: David McKay.

Frye, M. (1978). Some reflections on separatism and power. *Sinister Wisdom*, 6, 30-39.

Frye, M. (1983). *The politics of reality: Essays in feminist theory*. Trumansburg, NY: The Crossing Press.

Fuss, D. (1989). *Essentially speaking: Feminism, nature and difference*. London: Routledge.

Gager, N. and Schurr, C. (Eds.). (1976). *Sexual assault: Confronting rape in America*. New York: Grosset and Dunlap.

Galper, M. and Washburne, C. K. (1976). A women's self-help program in action. *Social Policy*, 6(5), 46-52.

Garcia, A. M. (1989). The development of Chicana feminist discourse, 1970-1980. *Gender & Society*, 3(2), pp. 217-238.

Garcia, A. M. (Ed.). (1997). *Chicana feminist thought: The basic historical writings*. New York: Routledge.

Glaser, B. and Strauss, A. (1967). *The discovery of grounded theory: Strategies for qualitative research*. Chicago: Aldine.

GlenMaye, L. (1998). Empowerment of women. In L. M. Gutierrez, R. J. Parsons, and E. O. Cox (Eds.), *Empowerment in social work practice: A sourcebook* (pp. 29-51). Pacific Grove, CA.: Brooks/Cole Publishing.

Gluck, S. and Patai, D. (Eds.). (1991). *Women's words: The feminist practice of oral history*. New York: Routledge.

Glucksmann, M. (1994). The work of knowledge and the knowledge of women's work. In M. Maynard and J. Purvis (Eds.), *Researching women's lives from a feminist perspective* (pp. 149-165). Bristol, PA: Taylor & Francis Inc.

Gomberg, E. (1974). Women and alcoholism. In V. Franks and V. Burtle (Eds.), *Women in therapy: New psychotherapies for a changing society* (pp. 169-190). New York: Bruner/Mazel.

Gomberg, E. (1979). Problems with alcohol and other drugs. In E. Gomberg and V. Franks (Eds.), *Gender and disordered behavior* (pp. 204-240). New York: Brunner/ Mazel.

Gorelick, S. (1996). Contradictions of feminist methodology. In H. Gottfried (Ed.), *Feminism and social change: Bridging theory and practice* (pp. 23-45). Urbana: University of Illinois Press.

Gornick, J., Burt, M., and Pittman, K. (1985). Structure and activities of rape crisis centers in the early 1980s. *Crime and Delinquency*, 31(2), 247-268.

Gornick, V. and Moran, B. (Eds.). (1971). *Woman in sexist society: Studies in power and powerlessness*. New York: Basic Books.

Gottlieb, N. (Ed.). (1980). *Alternative social services for women*. New York: Columbia University Press.

Greer, G. (1970). *The female eunuch*. London: MacGibbon and Kee.

Gutierrez, L. (1991). Empowering women of color: A feminist model. In M. Bricker-Jenkins, N. R. Hooyman, and N. Gottlieb (Eds.), *Feminist social work practice in clinical settings*. (pp. 199-214). Newbury Park, CA: Sage.

Haden, P., Middleton, D., and Robinson, P. (1970). A historical and critical essay for black women. In L. B. Tanner (Ed.), *Voices from women's liberation* (pp. 316-324). New York: New American Library.

Hammer, R. (2002). *Antifeminism and family terrorism: A critical feminist perspective*. Lanham, MD.: Rowman & Littlefield Publishers.

Hanisch, C. (1970). The personal is political. In S. Firestone and A. Koedt (Eds.), *Notes from the second year: Major writings of the radical feminists* (pp. 76-78).

Hartsock, N. (1974). Political change: Two perspectives on power. *Quest*, 1(1), pp. 10-25.

Hartsock, N. (1976). Staying alive: Work in feminist organizations. *Quest*, 3(3), 2-14.

Hartsock, N. (1979). Feminism, power, and change: A theoretical analysis. In B. Cummings and V. Schuck (Eds.), *Women organizing: An anthology* (pp. 2-24). Metuchen, N.J.: Scarecrow Press.

Hartsock, N. (1998). Difference and domination in the women's movement: The dialectic of theory and practice. In N. Hartsock, *The feminist standpoint revisited and other essays* (pp. 56-72). Boulder, CO.: Westview Press.

Hawxhurst, D. and Morrow, S. (1984). *Living our visions: Building feminist community*. Tempe, AZ: Fourth World.

Hirsch, M. and Keller, E. F. (Eds.). (1990). *Conflicts in feminism*. New York: Routledge.

Hole, J. and Levine, E. (1971). *Rebirth of feminism*. New York: Quadrangle Books.

hooks, b. (1981). *Ain't I a woman: Black women and feminism*. Boston: South End Press.

hooks, b. (1990). *Yearning: Race, gender, and cultural politics*. Boston: South End Press.

Hooyman, N. (1978). Redefining models of power and administration styles. *Social Development Issues*, 2, 46-54.

Hull, G., Scott, P., and Smith, B. (Eds.). (1982). *All the women are white, all the blacks are men, but some of us are brave: Black women's studies*. Old Westbury, NY: Feminist Press.

Hyde, C. (1992). The ideational system of social movement agencies: An examination of feminist health centers. In Y. Hasenfeld (Ed.), *Human services as complex organizations* (pp. 121-144). Newbury Park, CA: Sage.

Hyde, C. (1995). Feminist social movement organizations survive the New Right. In M. M. Ferree and P. Y. Martin (Eds.), *Feminist organizations: Harvest of the new women's movement* (pp. 306-322). Philadelphia: Temple University Press.

Iannello, K. (1992). *Decisions without hierarchy: Feminist interventions in organization theory and practice*. New York: Routledge.

Jaggar, A. M. (1990). Sexual difference and sexual equality. In D. L. Rhode (Ed.), *Theoretical perspectives on sexual difference* (pp. 239-254). New Haven: Yale University Press.

Jaggar, A. M. and Rothenberg, P. S. (1984). *Feminist frameworks: Alternative theoretical accounts of the relations between women and men*. New York: McGraw-Hill.

Jaggar, A. M. and Rothenberg, P. S. (Eds.). (1993). *Feminist frameworks: Alternative theoretical accounts of the relations between women and men*. New York: McGraw-Hill.

Jarvis, S. (1998). Women and the law: Learning from the past to protect the future. In C. Costello, S. Miles, and A. Stone (Eds.), *The American woman 1999-2000: A century of change – what's next?* (pp. 151-175). New York: W. W. Norton & Company.

Johnson, J. (1981). Program enterprise and official co-optation in the battered women's shelter movement. *American Behavioral Scientist*, 24(6), 827-842.

Joseph, G. and Lewis, J. (1981). *Common differences: Conflicts in black and white feminist perspectives*. New York: Anchor Press.

Kahn, K. (Ed.). (1995). *Frontline feminism 1975-1995: Essays from Sojourner's first 20 years*. San Francisco, CA: aunt lute books.

Kaplan, L. (1995). *The story of Jane: The legendary underground feminist abortion service*. New York: Pantheon Books.

Kaplow, S. (1973). Getting angry. In A. Koedt, E. Levine and A. Rapone (Eds.), *Radical feminism* (pp. 36-41). New York: Quadrangle.

Kearon, P. (1973). Man-hating. In A. Koedt, E. Levine and A. Rapone (Eds.), *Radical feminism* (pp. 78-80). New York: Quadrangle.

Kelly, L., Burton, S., and Regan, L. (1994). Researching women's lives or studying women's oppression? Reflections on what constitutes feminist research. In M. Maynard and J. Purvis (Eds.), *Researching women's lives from a feminist perspective* (pp. 27-48). Bristol, PA: Taylor & Francis.

Kessler-Harris, A. (2001). *In pursuit of equity: Women, men, and the quest for economic citizenship in 20th-century America*. New York: Oxford University Press.

Kirk, G. and Okazawa-Rey, M. (Eds.). (2001). *Women's lives: Multicultural perspectives*. Mountain View, CA: Mayfield Publishing.

Kirkpatrick, J. (1980). Women and alcohol. In C. Eddy and J. Ford (Eds.), *Alcoholism in women* (pp. 171-181). Dubuque, Iowa: Kendall/Hunt.

Kirkpatrick, J. (1986). *Goodbye hangovers, Hello life: Self-help for women*. New York: Atheneum.

Kitzinger, C. (1987). *The social construction of lesbianism*. Beverly Hills, CA: Sage.

Kitzinger, C. (1991). Feminism, psychology, and the paradox of power. *Feminism and Psychology*, 1, 111-129.

Klein, D. and Kress, J. (1976). Any woman's blues: A critical overview of women, crime and the criminal justice system. *Crime and Social Justice*, 5, 34-49.

Klein, E. (1984). *Gender politics: From consciousness to mass politics*. Cambridge, MA: Harvard University Press.

Koedt, A. (1973). Lesbianism and feminism. In A. Koedt, E. Levine and A. Rapone (Eds.), *Radical feminism* (pp. 246-258). New York: Quadrangle.

Koedt, A., Levine, E., and Rapone, A. (Eds.). (1973). *Radical feminism*. New York: Quadrangle.

Koss, M., Goodman, L., Browne, A., Fitzgerald, L., Keita, G. and Russo, N. (1994). *No safe haven: Male violence against women at home, at work, and in the community*. Washington, D.C.: American Psychological Association.

Koss, M. and Harvey, M. (1991). The rape crisis center. In M. Koss and M. Harvey, *The rape victim: Clinical and community interventions* (pp. 118-154). Newbury Park, CA.: Sage Publications.

Kurz, D. (1989). Social science perspectives on wife abuse: Current debates and future directions. *Gender & Society*, 3(4), 489-505.

La Rue, L. (1970). Black liberation and women's lib. *TransAction*, 8(1/2), 59-64.

Landrine, H. and Klonoff, E. A. (1997). *Discrimination against women: Prevalence, consequences, remedies.* Thousand Oaks, CA.: Sage Publications.

Lefkowitz, R. and Withorn, A. (Eds.). (1986). *For crying out loud: Women and poverty in the United States.* New York: Pilgrim Press.

Lewis, D. (1977). A response to inequality: Black women, racism, and sexism. *Signs,* 3(2), 339-361.

Lincoln, Y. S. and Guba, E. G. (1985). *Naturalistic inquiry.* Beverly Hills, CA: Sage.

Lorde, A. (1984). *Sister/outsider.* Trumansburg, NH: The Crossing Press.

Luker, K. (1984). *Abortion and the politics of motherhood.* Berkeley: University of California Press.

Macdonald, B. (1983). *Look me in the eye: Old women, aging, and ageism.* San Francisco: Spinsters, Ink.

MacDonald, N. (1976). The feminist workplace. *Quest,* 3(3), 65-73.

MacKinnon, C. A. (1982). Feminism, marxism, method, and the state: An agenda for theory. *Signs,* 7(3), 515-544.

Mansbridge, J. J. (1973). Time, emotion, and inequality: Three problems of participatory groups. *Journal of Applied Behavioral Science,* 9(2/3), 351-368.

Mansbridge, J. J. (1982). Fears of conflict in face-to-face democracies. In F. Lindenfeld and J. Rothschild-Whitt (Eds.), *Workplace democracy and social change* (pp. 125-137). Boston: Porter Sargent.

Mansbridge, J. J. (1983). *Beyond adversary democracy.* Chicago: University of Chicago Press.

Mansbridge, J. J. (1986). *Why we lost the ERA.* Chicago: University of Chicago Press.

Marieskind, H. (1980). *Women in the health system: Patients, providers, and programs.* St. Louis: Mosby.

Marieskind, H. and Ehrenreich, B. (1975). Toward socialist medicine: The women's health movement. *Social Policy,* 6(2), 34-42.

Martin, D. (1976). *Battered wives.* New York: Simon and Schuster.

Martin, D. and Lyon, P. (1977). *Lesbian/Woman.* New York: Bantam.

Martin, P.Y. (1987). A commentary on *The feminist case against bureaucracy* by Kathy Ferguson. *Women's Studies International Forum,* 10(5), 543-548.

Martin, P. Y. (1990). Rethinking feminist organizations. *Gender & Society,* 4(2), 182-206.

Martin, P.Y., DiNitto, D., Byington, D. and Maxwell, M.S. (1992). Organizational and community transformation: The case of a rape crisis center. *Administration in Social Work,* 16, 123-145.

Masi, D. (Ed). (1981). *Organizing for women: Issues, strategies, and services.* Lexington, Mass.: Lexington Books.

Mathison, S. (1988). Why triangulate? *Educational Researcher,* 17, 13-17.

Matthews, N. (1989). Surmounting a legacy: The expansion of racial diversity in a local anti-rape movement. *Gender & Society,* 3(4), 518-532.

Matthews, N. (1994). *Confronting rape: The feminist anti-rape movement and the state.* London: Routledge.

Matthews, N. (1995). Feminist clashes with the state: Tactical choices by state-funded rape crisis centers. In M. M. Ferree and P. Y. Martin (Eds.), *Feminist organizations: Harvest of the new women's movement* (pp. 291-305). Philadelphia: Temple University Press.

Maynard, M. (1994). Methods, practice and epistemology: The debate about feminism and research. In M. Maynard and J. Purvis (Eds.), *Researching women's lives from a feminist perspective* (pp. 10-26). Bristol, PA: Taylor & Francis Inc.

McNeely, R. and Jones, J. (1980). Refuge from violence: Establishing shelter services for battered women. *Administration in Social Work*, 4(4), 71-82.

Melich, T. (1996). *The Republican war against women: An insider's report from behind the lines*. New York: Bantam Books.

Millett, K. (1970). *Sexual politics*. New York: Doubleday.

Miner, V. and Longino, H. E. (Eds.). (1987). *Competition: A feminist taboo?* New York: The Feminist Press.

Minow, M. (1990). Adjudicating differences: Conflicts among feminist lawyers. In M. Hirsch and E. F. Keller (Eds.), *Conflicts in feminism* (pp. 149-163). New York: Routledge.

Moraga, C. and Anzaldua, G. (Eds.). (1983). *This bridge called my back: Writings by radical women of color*. New York: Kitchen Table: Women of Color Press.

Morgan, R. (Ed.). (1970). *Sisterhood is powerful: An anthology of writings from the women's liberation movement*. New York: Vintage Books.

Morgen, S. (1986). The dynamics of cooptation in a feminist health clinic. *Social Science and Medicine*, 23(2), 201-210.

Morgen, S. (1994). Personalizing personnel decisions in feminist organizational theory and practice. *Human Relations*, 47(6), 665-684.

Morgen, S. (1995). "It was the best of times, It was the worst of times": Emotional discourse in the work cultures of feminist health clinics. In M. M. Ferree and P. Y. Martin (Eds.), *Feminist organizations: Harvest of the new women's movement* (pp. 234-247). Philadelphia: Temple University Press.

Morgenbesser, M., Notkin, S., McCall, N., Grossman, B, and Nachreiner-Cory, E. (1981). The evolution of three alternative social service agencies. *Catalyst*, 11, 71-83.

Mouffe, C. (1992). Feminism, citizenship and radical democratic politics. In J. Butler and J. W. Scott (Eds.), *Feminists theorize the political* (pp. 369-384). New York: Routledge.

Murray, P. (1975). The liberation of Black women. In J. Freeman (Ed.), *Women: A feminist perspective* (pp. 351-363). Palo Alto, CA: Mayfield.

Newmann, J. P., Greenley, D., Sweeney, K., and Van Dien, G. (1998). Abuse histories, severe mental illness, and the cost of care. In B. Levin, A. Blanch, and A. Jennings (Eds.), *Women's mental health services: A public health perspective* (pp. 279-308). Newbury Park, CA: Sage Publications.

O'Sullivan, E. (1978). What has happened to rape crisis centers? A look at their structures, members, and funding. *Victimology*, 3(1-2), 45-62.

Oakley, A. (1981). Interviewing women: A contradiction in terms. In H. Roberts (Ed.), *Doing feminist research* (pp. 30-61). London: Routledge and Kegan Paul.

Padgett, D. (1998). *Qualitative methods in social work research: Challenges and rewards.* Thousand Oaks, CA.: Sage.

Pahl, J. (1985a). Refuges for battered women: Ideology and action. *Feminist Review,* 19, 25-43.

Pahl, J. (Ed.). (1985b). *Private violence and public policy.* London: Routledge and Kegan Paul.

Pendergrass, V. E. (1975). Innovative programs for women in jail and prisons: Trick or treatment. In A. M. Brodsky (Ed.), *The female offender* (pp. 67-76). Beverly Hills: Sage.

Perl, H. and Abarbanell, G. (1976). *Guidelines to feminist consciousness raising.* Los Angeles, CA.

Perlmutter, F. D. (1994). A feminist health organization. In F. D. Perlmutter (Ed.), *Women & social change: Nonprofits and social policy* (pp. 158-175). Washington, DC: NASW Press.

Pizzey, E. (1974). *Scream quietly or the neighbours will hear.* Middlesex: Penguin.

Pleck, E. (1987). *Domestic tyranny: The making of social policy against family violence from colonial times to the present.* New York: Oxford University Press.

Pride, A. (1981). To respectability and back: A ten year view of the anti-rape movement. In F. Delacoste and F. Newman (Eds.), *Fight back! Feminist resistance to male violence* (pp. 114-118). Minneapolis, MN: Cleis Press.

Pogrebin, L. C. (1973). Rap groups: The feminist connection. *Ms Magazine,* March.

Radicalesbians. (1973). The woman identified woman. In A. Koedt, E. Levine and A. Rapone (Eds.), *Radical feminism* (pp. 240-245). New York: Quadrangle.

Rape Crisis Center of Washington, D.C. (1971). *How to start a rape crisis center.* Washington D.C.: Rape Crisis Center.

Reinelt, C. (1994). Fostering empowerment, building community: The challenge for state-funded feminist organizations. *Human Relations,* 47(6), 685-705.

Reinelt, C. (1995). Moving onto the terrain of the state: The battered women's movement and the politics of engagement. In M. M. Ferree and P. Y. Martin (Eds.), *Feminist organizations: Harvest of the new women's movement* (pp. 84-104). Philadelphia: Temple University Press.

Reinharz, S. (1992). *Feminist methods in social research.* New York: Oxford University Press.

Renzetti, C., Edleson, J. and Bergen, R. (Eds.). (2001). *Sourcebook on violence against women.* Thousand Oaks, CA: Sage.

Rich, A. (1980). Compulsory heterosexuality and lesbian existence. *Signs,* 5(4), 631-660.

Riddle, D. (1978). Integrating process and product. *Quest,* 4(4), 23-32.

Riger, S. (1984). Vehicles for empowerment: The case of feminist movement organizations. In J. Rappaport, C. Smith, and R. Hess (Eds.), *Studies in empowerment: Steps toward understanding and action* (pp. 99-117). New York: Haworth Press.

Riger, S. (1994). Challenges of success: Stages of growth in feminist organizations. *Feminist Studies,* 20(2), 275-300.

Riger, S., Bennett, L., Wasco, S. M., Schewe, P. A., Frohmann, L., Camacho, J. M., and Campbell, R. (2002). *Evaluating services for survivors of domestic violence and sexual assault.* Thousand Oaks, CA.: Sage Publications.

Ristock, J. L. (1990). Canadian feminist social service collectives: Caring and contradictions. In L. Albrecht and R. M. Brewer (Eds.), *Bridges of power: Women's multicultural alliances* (pp. 172-181). Philadelphia, PA: New Society Publishers.

Roberts, A. R. (Ed.). (2002). *Handbook of domestic violence intervention strategies: Policies, programs, and legal remedies*. New York: Oxford University Press.

Rodriguez, N. M. (1988). Transcending bureaucracy: Feminist politics at a shelter for battered women. *Gender & Society*, 2(2), 214-227.

Rosen, R. (2000). *The world split open: How the modern women's movement changed America*. New York: Viking Press.

Rothschild-Whitt, J. (1979). The collectivist organization: An alternative to rational-bureaucratic models. *American Sociological Review*, 44(4), 509-527.

Rothschild-Whitt, J. and Whitt, J. (1986). *The cooperative workplace*. Cambridge, MA: Cambridge University Press.

Rubin, H. J. and Rubin, I. S. (1995). *Qualitative interviewing: The art of hearing data*. Thousand Oaks, CA: Sage.

Rupp, L. and Taylor, V. (1987). *Survival in the doldrums: The American women's rights movement, 1945 to the 1960s*. New York: Oxford University Press.

Ruzek, S. B. (1978). *The women's health movement: Feminist alternatives to medical control*. New York: Praeger.

Ryan, B. (1989). Ideological purity and feminism: The U.S. women's movement from 1966 to 1975. *Gender & Society*, 3(2), 239-257.

Ryan, B. (1992). *Feminism and the women's movement: Dynamics of change in social movement ideology and activism*. New York: Routledge.

Sandmaier, M. (1980a). *The invisible alcoholics: Women and alcohol abuse in America*. New York: McGrawHill.

Sandmaier, M. (1980b). Women helping women: Opening the door to treatment. In C. C. Eddy and J. L. Ford (Eds.), *Alcoholism in women* (pp. 161-170). Dubuque, Iowa: Kendall/Hunt.

Sapiro, V. (1986). The women's movement, politics, and policy in the Reagan era. In D. Dahlerup (Ed.), *The new women's movement* (pp. 122-139). Newbury Park, CA: Sage Publications.

Sapiro, V. (1999). *Women in American society: An introduction to women's studies*. Mountain View, CA: Mayfield Publishing.

Sarachild, K. (1970). A program for feminist consciousness raising. In S. Firestone (Ed.), *Notes from the second year: Major writings of the radical feminists* (pp. 78-80).

Saunders, D. (1995). Domestic violence: Legal issues. In R. Edwards (Ed.), *Encyclopedia of Social Work, 19th edition* (pp. 789-795). Washington, D.C.: NASW Press.

Schechter, S. (1982). *Women and male violence: The visions and struggles of the battered women's movement*. Boston: South End Press.

Schechter, S. (1996). The battered women's movement in the United States: New directions for institutional reform. In J. L. Edleson and Z. C. Eisikovits (Eds.), *Future interventions with battered women and their families* (pp. 53-66). Thousand Oaks, CA.: Sage Publications.

Schlesinger, M. B. and Bart, P. B. (1982). Collective work and self-identity: Working in a feminist illegal abortion collective. In F. Lindenfeld and J. Rothschild-Whitt

(Eds.), *Workplace democracy and social change* (pp. 139-153). Boston: Porter Sargent.

Scott, J.W. (1990). Deconstructing equality-versus-difference: Or, the uses of post-structuralist theory for feminism. In M. Hirsch and E. F. Keller (Eds.), *Conflicts in feminism* (pp. 134-148). New York: Routledge.

Sealander, J. and Smith, D. (1986). The rise and fall of feminist organizations in the 1970s: Dayton as a case study. *Feminist Studies*, 12(2), 320-341.

Seifer, N. (1976). *Nobody speaks for me: Self-portraits of American working class women*. New York: Simon and Schuster.

Shulman, A. K. (1980). Sex and power: Sexual bases of radical feminism, *Signs*, 5(4), 590-604.

Shulman, A. K. (1998). A marriage disagreement, or marriage by other means. In R. B. DuPlessis and A. Snitow (Eds.), *The feminist memoir project: Voices from women's liberation* (pp. 284-303). New York: Three Rivers Press.

Simmons, R., Kay, B., and Regan, C. (1984). Women's health groups: Alternatives to the health care system. *International Journal of Health Services*, 14(4), 619-634.

Simon, B.L. (1982). In defense of institutionalization: A rape crisis center as a case study. *Journal of Sociology and Social Welfare*, 9(3), 485-502.

Simonds, W. (1995). Feminism on the job: Confronting opposition in abortion work. In M. M. Ferree and P. Y. Martin (Eds.), *Feminist organizations: Harvest of the new women's movement* (pp. 248-260). Philadelphia: Temple University Press.

Simonds, W. (1996). *Abortion at work: Ideology and practice in a feminist clinic*. New Brunswick, N.J.: Rutgers University Press.

Simons, M. A. (1979). Racism and feminism: A schism in the sisterhood. *Feminist Studies*, 5(2), 384-401.

Slack, E. N. (1975). Remedies for wrongs: Updating programs for delinquent girls. In A. M. Brodsky (Ed.), *The female offender* (pp. 89-95). Beverly Hills: Sage.

Smart, C. (1976). *Women, crime and criminology: A feminist critique*. London: Routledge and Kegan Paul.

Smith, B. (Ed.). (1983). *Home girls: A black feminist anthology*. New York: Kitchen Table Women of Color Press.

Solomon, B. B. (1976). *Black empowerment: Social work in oppressed communities*. New York: Columbia University Press.

Spain, D. and Bianchi, S. M. (1996). *Balancing act: Motherhood, marriage, and employment among American women*. New York: Russell Sage Foundation.

Srinivasan, M. and Davis, L. (1991). A shelter: An organization like any other? *Affilia: Journal of women and social work*, 6(1), 38-57.

Staggenborg, S. (1991). *The pro-choice movement: Organization and activism in the abortion conflict*. New York: Oxford University Press.

Stambler, S. (Ed.). (1970). *Women's liberation: Blueprint for the future*. New York: Ace Books.

Stetson, D. M. (1997). *Women's rights in the U.S.A.:Policy debates and gender roles*. New York: Garland Publishing.

Strauss, A. and Corbin, J. (1990). *Basics of qualitative research*. Newbury Park, CA: Sage.

Straussner, S. L. A. and Brown, S. (Eds.). (2002). *The handbook of addiction treatment for women*. San Francisco: Jossey-Bass.

Sullivan, G. (1982). Cooptation of alternative services: The battered women's movement as a case study. *Catalyst*, 14, 39-56.

Susan, B. (1970). About my consciousness raising. In L. B. Tanner (Ed.), *Voices from women's liberation* (pp. 238-243). New York: New American Library.

Tanner, L. (Ed.). (1970). *Voices from women's liberation*. New York: New American Library.

Taylor, V. (1989). The future of feminism: A social movement analysis. In L. Richardson and V. Taylor (Eds.), *Feminist frontiers II* (pp. 473-490). New York: McGraw-Hill.

Taylor, V. (1995). Watching for vibes: Bringing emotions into the study of feminist organizations. In M. M. Ferree and P. Y. Martin (Eds.), *Feminist organizations: Harvest of the new women's movement* (pp. 223-233). Philadelphia: Temple University Press.

Taylor, V. and Rupp, L. J. (1993). Women's culture and lesbian feminist activism: A reconsideration of cultural feminism. *Signs*, 19(1), 32-61.

Thelen, R. (2000). Advocacy in a coordinated community response: Overview and highlights of three programs. *Violence Against Women Online Resources*. www.vaw.umn.edu.

Tierney, K. J. (1982). The battered women's movement and the creation of the wife beating problem. *Social Problems*, 29(3), 207-220.

Tong, R. (1998). *Feminist thought: A more comprehensive introduction*. Boulder, CO: Westview Press.

U.S. Department of Justice (May 2000). *Intimate Partner Violence*. Bureau of Justice Statistics, NCJ 178247. Washington, DC: National Institute of Justice.

U.S. Department of Justice (November 2000). *Full Report of the Prevalence, Incidence, and Consequences of Violence Against Women: Findings from the National Violence Against Women Survey*. NCJ 183781. Washington, DC: National Institute of Justice.

U.S. Department of Justice (July 2000). *Extent, Nature, and Consequences of Intimate Partner Violence: Findings from the National Violence Against Women Survey*. NCJ 181867. Washington, DC: National Institute of Justice.

Valeska, L. (1975). The future of female separatism. *Quest*, 2(2), 2-16.

van Wormer, K. (2001). *Counseling female offenders and victims: A strengths-restorative approach*. New York: Springer Publishing.

van Wormer, K. (2002). Addictions and women in the criminal justice system. In S. Straussner and S. Brown (Eds.), *The handbook of addiction treatment for women* (pp. 470-486). San Francisco: Jossey-Bass.

Vaughan, S. R. (1979). The last refuge: Shelter for battered women. *Victimology: An International Journal*, 4(1), 113-119.

Vida, G. (1978). *Our right to love*. Englewood Cliffs, N.J.: Prentice Hall.

Walker, M. and Brodsky, S. (Eds.). (1976). *Sexual assault*. Lexington, Mass.: Heath and Company.

Wandersee, W. D. (1988). *American women in the 1970s: On the move*. Boston: Twayne Publishers.

Ware, C. (1970). *Woman power: The movement for women's liberation.* New York: Tower Publications.

Weathers, B. (1980). Alcoholism and the lesbian community. In N. Gottlieb (Ed.), *Alternative social services for women* (pp. 158-169). New York: Columbia University Press.

Weitz, R. (1984). What price independence? Social reactions to lesbians, spinsters, widows, and nuns. In J. Freeman (Ed.), *Women: A feminist perspective* (pp. 454-464). Palo Alto, CA: Mayfield Publishing.

Whittier, N. (1995). *Feminist generations: The persistence of the radical women's movement.* Philadelphia: Temple University Press.

Wilson, M. and Anderson, S. (1997). Empowering female offenders: Removing barriers to community-based practice. *Affilia: Journal of women and social work,* 12(3), 342-358.

Withorn, A. (1980). Helping ourselves: The limits and potential of self help. *Radical America,* 14(3), 25-39.

Withorn, A. (1984a). *Serving the people: Social services and social change.* New York: Columbia University Press.

Withorn, A. (1984b). For better and for worse: Social relations among women in the welfare state. *Radical America,* 18(4), 37-47.

Women and Mental Health Project. (1976). Women-to-women services. *Social Policy,* 7(2), 21-27.

Young, I. M. (1990). *Justice and the politics of difference.* Princeton, N.J.: Princeton University Press.

Index

AA. *See* Alcoholics Anonymous
abortion rights, 11
Advisory Council on Women Offenders, 130, 140
Advocates for Battered Women: founding of, 27–28, 35–38; funding, 36–37, 47, 110, 111, 115; men, roles of, 35–36, 50, 119, 184; mission statement, 38; organizational structure, 64, 145, 153, 155–56, 157–58, 160–61, 164–69, 177, 178; overview of organization, 3, 48, 54; services, 59, 118–20, 127, 134–35; social change efforts, 128–30, 131–32, 135, 138–39; status as of 1997. *See* Domestic Abuse Intervention Services
affirmative action, 80
Alanon, 4, 77, 122, 124
Alateen, 4, 122
Alcoff, Linda, 103
Alcoholics Anonymous (AA), 4, 12, 77, 122–24
American Association of University Women, Wisconsin chapter, 194
Ananda Marga, 39, 41, 44, 78, 106–7, 163–64, 187;
Ananda Marga Resource Center, 40

anger, sources of: for consumers, 54, 57; for members, 31, 32–33, 35, 79, 83–85, 106, 108, 114. *See also* conflict; emotions, impact of
antifeminist backlash, 6, 193–95, 201–2; and the New Right, 11, 12, 193, 195
antirape movement, 10, 202–3
anti-Semitism, 87
ARC Community Services, 198–99
ARC House: founding of, 28, 39–42; funding, 40–41, 47, 106–7, 110, 111–13, 115; men, roles of, 41, 50, 78, 184; organizational structure, 64–65, 145–46, 153–54, 155–57, 159, 163–64, 177, 178; overview of organization, 3, 48, 55, 70–71, 197–98; services, 61–62, 111–13, 124–25, 127; social change efforts, 128, 130, 133, 139–40. *See also* Ananda Marga; ARC Community Services
Association of Faculty Women (AFW), 23
authority of personal experience, feminist principle of the, 30–31, 46, 58, 73, 89

backlash. *See* antifeminist backlash
Baldwin, Tammy, 194

Barry, Kathleen, 83
battered women's movement, 10, 202–3
bisexual women, 51, 93, 94
black women. *See* women of color
Bunch, Charlotte, 27, 104
bureaucracy, incorporating elements of,
    5, 147, 179–81; formal policies,
    150–51; modified hierarchies,
    156–76; specialization, 153–56;
    standards of performance, 151–53

Carden, Maren Lockwood, 58, 62,
    90–91
CETA. *See* Comprehensive
    Employment Training Act
chemically dependent women, women's
    issues and, 2, 11–12, 53, 72–73, 123,
    184, 203–4
Chimera self-defense training, 200
Chisholm, Shirley, 96
City-County Committee on Sexual
    Assault, 131
class privilege, 89
classism, 38, 56
Clothesline Project, 196
Coalition of Labor Union Women, 8
collective structures, 10, 63, 64, 144–46,
    147, 187; consensus decision
    making, 7, 65, 88, 147–50, 180
Combahee River Collective, 102
commissions on the status of women, 5
community development block grant
    funding, 47
community health movement, 10
community members' views: of
    organizational structures, 176–79; of
    services, 135–42
Comprehensive Employment Training
    Act (CETA), 12, 37, 45, 82, 191
conflict, 9, 16, 19, 165–69, 170–73,
    176–77, 181, 189; gay/straight split,
    90–92. *See also* anger, sources of;
    emotions, impact of
consciousness-raising: among
    consumers, 49, 57–58, 61, 117–18,

185; among members, 93, 96, 101;
    as feminist method, 7, 46, 57, 89–90;
    in CR groups, 7–8, 58
co-optation, 33, 66–67, 191, 201
councils on alcohol and drug abuse, 43,
    47, 114, 124, 191
cultural feminists, 85

Dane County Board of Public Welfare, 47
Dane County Community Mental
    Health Board, 47
Dane County Department of Social
    Services, 35
Dane County Jail, 199
Division of Corrections. *See* State
    Division of Corrections
Domestic Abuse Intervention Services,
    196–97. *See also* Advocates for
    Battered Women
DuPlessis, Rachel, 201, 202

Echols, Alice, 69
EEOC. *See* Equal Employment
    Opportunities Commission
egalitarian work structures, 49, 63–65,
    144
emotions, impact of, 16–18, 46, 75–76,
    145–46, 148–49, 151–52, 177, 181,
    186. *See also* anger, sources of;
    conflict
empowering women, feminist principle
    of, 55–56; as consumers; 49, 57–63,
    117, 126, 184–85; as members, 49,
    63–65, 144–47, 154, 180–81, 185–86
Equal Credit Opportunity Act (1974), 6
Equal Employment Opportunities
    Commission (EEOC), 6
Equal Rights Amendment (ERA), 6, 11

Family Services, 36, 45
family systems approach, 118–19
Federation of Business and Professional
    Women, Wisconsin chapter, 194
female offenders, women's issues and,
    2, 11, 12, 53, 71, 124–25, 184, 203–4

feminism, diverse meanings among
feminists, 18–20, 187–88
feminist organizational structures,
members' definitions of, 179–81,
189–90, 191–93
feminist therapy collectives, 10
feminists, antagonism
toward/stereotypes of, 13–16, 41,
43–44, 141–42, 202. *See also*
homophobia; man-hating,
accusations of
femocrats, 45
Freeman, Jo, 92, 147, 167

gender equality/difference debate,
68–70, 73–76, 85–86, 190
gender inequality: as cause of woman
abuse, 27, 31, 52, 184; as source of
women's personal problems, 9, 49,
52–53, 189, 202. *See also* male
domination
"gender neutral" programs, 203–4
gender stereotypes, 14–15, 50, 53, 71

Hanisch, Carol, 7
Hartsock, Nancy, 56, 188
Hernandez, Aileen, 96
heterophobia, 94
heterosexism, 56, 91. *See also*
homophobia
heterosexual women, traditional, 89
Hole, Judith, 84, 90
homophobia, 15–16, 87, 91;
organizational responses to, 92–96,
191. *See also* heterosexism; man-
hating, accusations of
homosexuals. *See* homophobia; lesbian
feminists
hooks, bell, 97–98
hybrid organizations, 191
Hyde Amendment, 11

identity politics, 102–3, 190–91
Independent Women's Forum (IWF),
194–95

intimate partner violence, 203
IWF. *See* Independent Women's Forum

Jaggar, Alison, 204
"Jane," an underground abortion
collective, 11
Johnson, Lyndon, 6

Kirkpatrick, Jean, 123

Law Enforcement Assistance
Administration (LEAA), 12, 31–32,
33, 40, 45, 191
LEAA. *See* Law Enforcement
Assistance Administration
League of Women Voters, Wisconsin
chapter, 194
lesbian feminists, 15, 79, 90–92, 191
lesbian-specific practices, 92
Levine, Ellen, 84, 90
liberal feminism, 68–69, 172. *See also*
women's rights branch/organizations

MacKinnon, Catherine, 7
Madison Wisconsin: characteristics of,
12–13, 23, 33, 92, 100, 108, 193;
city as source of funding, 31, 34–35,
47, 81, 107, 191
male domination: as cause of woman
abuse, 52, 203; as source of women's
problems, 7, 9, 98; resisting and
challenging, 51, 60, 97. *See also*
gender inequality
male privilege, 7, 10, 15, 97, 101
male-dominated systems, working
within, 2, 28, 39, 44, 70, 133–34,
186, 203
male-identified women, 83, 94
MANA. *See* Mexican-American
Women's National Association
mandatory presence, 90
man-hating, accusations of, 83–85, 94.
See also feminists, antagonism
toward/stereotypes of; homophobia
Martin, Patricia Yancey, 192

media, influence of, 9, 14, 108, 201, 202
Mexican-American Women's National
Association (MANA), 96
Midwest Medical Center, 30
Milwaukee Task Force on Battered
Women, 35
Minority Women's Network, Wisconsin
chapter, 194
Mouffe, Chantal, 190
Murray, Pauli, 96

NARAL. *See* National Association for
the Repeal of Abortion Laws
National Alliance of Black Feminists,
96
National Association for the Repeal of
Abortion Laws (NARAL), 11
National Association of Black
Professional Women, 8, 96
National Black Feminist Organization,
96
National Institute of Alcohol Abuse and
Alcoholism, 43
National Institute of Corrections, 198
National Organization for Women
(NOW), 5, 85, 90–91, 96; Madison
and Wisconsin chapters, 194
National Women's Political Caucus, 5,
96; Wisconsin chapter, 194
New Right. *See* antifeminist backlash
No More Assaults Month, 131
nonelitist relationships, as feminist
principle, 58–59, 63
NOW. *See* National Organization for
Women

Older Women's League, 8–9
Organization of Pan Asian American
Women, 96

Padgett, Deborah, 25
patriarchal systems, 19, 53, 66, 69, 79,
97, 98, 144, 186
personal is political, feminist principle
of the, 7, 16–17, 52, 56, 89, 184

Planned Parenthood, 11
Playboy Foundation, 32
power, concerns over, 146

racism, 38, 56, 87, 89, 96, 98–99,
100–102. *See also* women of color
radical feminism, 51, 69, 74, 89, 186, 187
radical feminists, early, 4–5, 18, 85, 89,
144, 172, 183, 186, 192; history of,
7–8, 9, 91, 97. *See also* women's
liberation branch/movement
Radicalesbians, 91
Rape Crisis Center: founding of, 27–28,
29–32; funding, 30, 31–32, 47, 108,
109, 110–11, 115; men, roles of, 82,
184; mission statement, 31;
organizational structure, 64, 145,
153, 155–56, 158–59, 161–63,
173–76, 177–79; overview of
organization, 3–4, 47, 54–55,
199–200; services, 59–60, 120–21,
126; social change efforts, 128,
132–33, 135–37
Reagan, Ronald, 12, 193
Reinelt, Claire, 192
Republicans for Choice, Wisconsin
chapter, 194
reverse discrimination, accusations of,
195
Rich, Adrienne, 91
Riger, Stephanie, 189, 192
Roe v. Wade, 11

Sagaris, 97
Schechter, Susan, 10, 58
self-help, feminist principle of, 49, 57,
58, 117, 118, 119, 120, 185
separatism, 14, 81, 85, 91
sexism: in mainstream services, 11–12,
38, 70; woman abuse and, 38, 54, 80,
168. *See also* gender inequality; male
domination
Sexual Assault Awareness Month, 196,
200
Shulman, Alix Kates, 201

sisterhood, feminist principle of, 17, 27, 48, 49, 57, 62–63, 117, 185

Snitow, Ann, 201, 202

State Division of Corrections, 2, 40, 47, 111, 112, 124, 191

State of Wisconsin Bureau of Alcohol and Other Drug Abuse, 47, 112, 113, 130, 191

State of Wisconsin Bureau of Substance Abuse Services, 200

study, the: focus of, 20–21; methodology of, 1, 21–25

substance-abusing women. *See* chemically dependent women, women's issues and

"Take Back the Night" rally and march, 79, 170–71, 200

Thelen, Rose, 203

Title VII of the 1964 Civil Rights Act, 6

Title IX of the 1972 Education Amendments Act, 6

Title XX funding, 110

traditional female socialization, 31, 53, 61, 72, 76, 78, 85

traditional male socialization, 31, 78

United Way, 36, 37, 47, 139, 165, 167, 191

University Methodist Church, 36

University of Wisconsin-Madison, as source of funding, 33–35, 45, 47, 50, 109, 191, 195

Urban League, 101

van Wormer, Katherine, 204

victim blaming, 10, 28, 29, 31, 56, 100, 108, 203; helping consumers reject, 30, 57–58, 59, 185

VISTA. *See* Volunteers in Service to America

Volunteer Resource Development Project, 43

Volunteers in Service to America (VISTA), 12, 31

WAAODA. *See* Wisconsin Association on Alcohol and Other Drug Abuse

Washington Feminist FaxNet, 194

white privilege, 97, 101

white women, traditional, 88–89, 97

Will, George, 194–95

Wisconsin Association on Alcohol and Other Drug Abuse (WAAODA), 2, 42, 113–14, 145

Wisconsin Coalition Against Woman Abuse, 36, 128

Wisconsin Council on Criminal Justice, 31–32, 40, 45, 111, 163

Wisconsin Women's Alliance on Alcohol and Other Drug Abuse, 42, 130

Wisconsin Women's Network, 128–29, 194; Task Force on Women in the Criminal Justice System, 130; Women and Substance Abuse Task Force, 130

Wisconsin Women's Summit, 194

woman-identified women/organization, 51–52, 83, 94

Women for Sobriety, 12, 123

women helping women, feminist principle of, 49, 50–52, 68, 87, 103, 179, 195, 201; benefits for consumers and members, 76–80, 184; debates over, 80–85

women of color: critiques of feminism, 97–98; members' efforts to include, 98–102, 191; participation in the women's movement, 96–97; writings on racism and sexism, 97. *See also* racism

Women Reaching Women: founding of, 28, 42–44; funding, 43, 47, 113–15; men, roles of, 43, 51, 184; organizational structure, 64, 145, 178; overview of organization, 4, 48, 55, 71–73; services, 61, 122–24, 127; social change efforts, 128, 130–31, 133, 140–41; status as of 1996, 200–201

Women's Candidate Development
  Coalition, 193
Women's Center, 33
women's centers, 9–10
Women's Coalition on Rape Prevention,
  28–29, 35
Women's Equity Action League, 5
women's health centers, 10
women's health movement, 10, 11
women's liberation branch/movement,
  6–8, 13, 27. *See also* radical
  feminism; radical feminists, early
women's rights branch/organizations,
  5–6, 68, 194. *See also* liberal
  feminism
women's studies courses/programs, 9

Women's Transit Authority: founding
  of, 27–28, 29, 32–35; funding, 33,
  34–35, 47, 107–8, 109, 110, 195;
  men, roles of, 33, 51, 81, 184, 196;
  mission statement, 34;
  organizational structure, 63, 145,
  153, 155, 159, 164–65, 169–73,
  177, 178; overview of organization,
  4, 47, 55, 195–96; services, 59,
  81–82, 107–8; social change efforts,
  131, 133, 137
Working Women: A National
  Association of Office Workers, 9

YMCA, 34
YWCA, 30

About the Author

Diane Kravetz is a professor of social work and a member of the women's studies program at the University of Wisconsin-Madison. Since the mid-1970s, her publications have focused on women's issues in social work practice and on women and mental health. Her research projects have included studies of women's consciousness-raising groups, feminist therapy, and feminist service organizations. She has taught courses on women and mental health and on feminist social work practice. She was the chairperson of the women's studies program from 1976 to 1979 and associate chairperson from 1982 to 1986. She was the director of the School of Social Work from 1985 to 1990, where she is currently the associate director as well as director of the undergraduate program.